*"We loved to work cattle so much we'd just be sittin' around cryin'
for daylight to come. . ."*

Will King
1902–1985

To the memory of Louis Power
Teacher, hero, and legendary cowman
1875-1946

To the memory of my grandmother
Kate S. O'Connor
Who taught me to love and value
historical preservation

CRYIN' FOR DAYLIGHT

Duke Ranch cow crowd, 1930's.
L-R front, Simon Reyes, Arthur Stone, Alvin Power, Norvell Brown, Willie Jones; L-R standing, Hennon Collins, Pablino Cantu,
Joe De Los Santos, Pete Ybarbo, Gilberto Perez, Louis Power, Jesse Jones, Sam Jones, Autery Brown, Florencio Hernandez, "Jose."
Photo by Dennis O'Connor [II].

CRYIN' FOR DAYLIGHT

A Ranching Culture In The
Texas Coastal Bend

Louise S. O'Connor

WEXFORD PUBLISHING
Austin, Texas

CRYIN' FOR DAYLIGHT
First Edition

WEXFORD PUBLISHING
Austin, Texas

Manufactured in the United States of America

ISBN 0-9624821-0-2
Library of Congress Catalog Number: 89-51738

CONTENTS

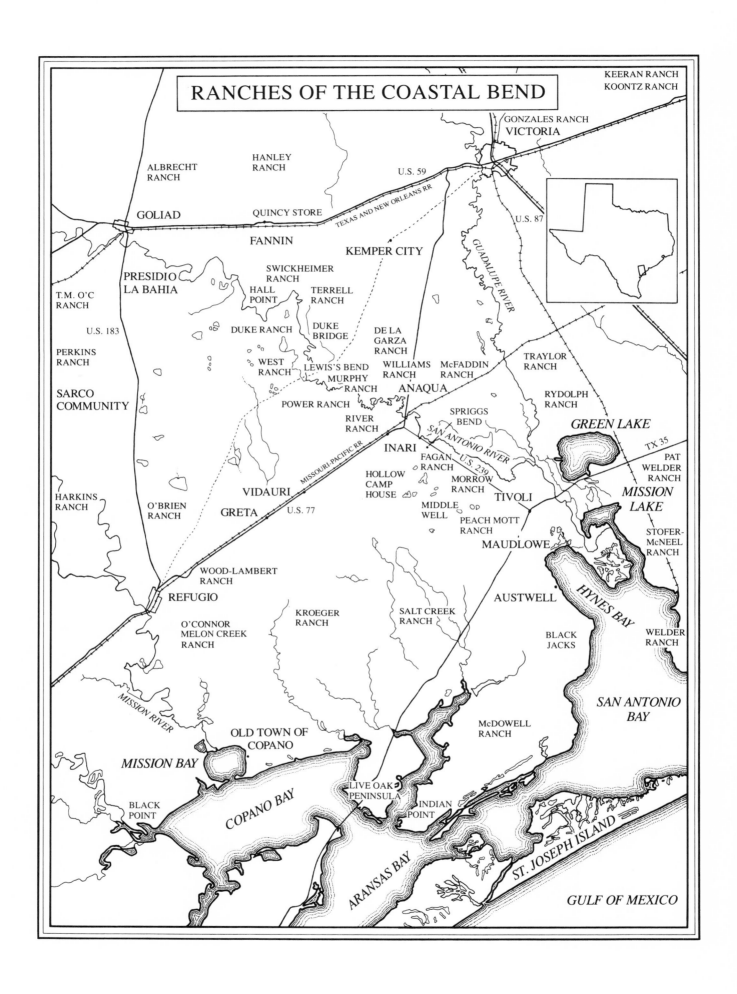

RANCHES OF THE COASTAL BEND

Foreword

"This whole project is based on sounds — they're echoes from the past callin' to us to be remembered. We're movin' too fast to hear them now; we'll have to go into the past to recover them, to recover a way of life that is gone, a better way of life. There was a lot wrong back then, but there was a lot more right. The good keeps on comin' back, tryin' to be heard. These people are the instruments of those righteous echoes."

Nathaniel Youngblood
Tophand
Welder Ranch
Vidauri

Since 1980, it has been my pleasure to serve as an observer and sometime adviser to Louise O'Connor as she has used photography and oral history to document the passing of "the old ways" of labor, management, and play associated with the great ranches of South Texas, the crucible of the American cattle industry. Hers is a major contribution to our understanding of ranch life in the twentieth century and to the history of one of the earliest settled regions of Texas. Using an approach similar to the recollections of life on the cattle trails preserved in J. Marvin Hunter's *The Trail Drivers of Texas*, she has let those who did it and knew it tell the story: some with nostalgia, others with ambivalence, all with an innate sense of self-worth. *Cryin' for Daylight* contains the memories of people deeply involved in a ranching culture transformed by technology, urbanization, mechanization, and other economic and political interventions of modern life. These are real people speaking: men and women, bosses and workers, black and white, Catholic and Protestant, cooks and helicopter pilots — diverse individuals tied together by the land and their labor on it. Given the special conditions defining her time and place, Louise O'Connor has opened windows on a world that few have seen and fewer still could have opened for us. It is a world that has played a fundamental role in shaping the peculiar ethos that we call Texan.

Louise O'Connor's contribution to scholarship and to the preservation of our documentary heritage continues beyond this valuable and entertaining book. Her effort to preserve the extensive archive of sight and sound that she created over the several years of her project, of which *Cryin' for Daylight* is but a small sample, means that these materials will serve the needs of social science and humanities research in years to come. This archive, like her book, is destined to become a most fitting legacy to a woman who has so effectively illuminated one aspect of Texas' recent past.

Don E. Carleton, Ph.D.
Director
Eugene C. Barker Texas History Center
University of Texas at Austin

"All I can give you is the echoes of all this. The rest you gotta work out for yourself."

Richard Harris
Foreman
Murphy Ranches
1891-1988

Preface

In the early 1970s, I began photographing people and cow-working around the O'Connor ranches. My work went through several stages, including a five-year period during which I had no idea what form my efforts should take or what their real purpose or direction should be. Then, one morning in 1982, I began talking to some of the older ranch hands about members of my family. About fifteen minutes into the first interview, I suddenly realized that I had found the direction I was seeking. The vivid recollections of these old-timers, plus those of many more, steered me toward documenting a culture that I knew would soon be extinct. The desire to know what these people did and why they did it, and how they responded to those experiences, provided me with a completely new and unique perspective to what otherwise might have been just another family history.

Neither the language, appearance, nor experiences of these men and women are particularly unique in the world of cattle ranching. My interest and motivation came from the realization that, to my knowledge, no one had ever before let a group of ranch people tell their story—in their own words.

These people responded to me in a way that seemed as if they had been waiting for someone to tell their story, and apparently I fit that description for them. I had grown up in a ranching family, but because of women's limited role in ranch life of the past, I evidently posed no threat to them. I was never viewed as an authority figure, as a man would have been, and consequently they trusted me to tell their story just as they wanted it told.

The men and women I interviewed loved their working days and wanted to share their experiences with others. Possibly because tale-telling was one of their major forms of entertainment, they were extremely articulate in expressing the texture of their lives. Thus I have not tampered with the pure form of their expression and thoughts, which represent the realities of their lives as they remember them. Their eloquent answers to my questions needed no revision other than an occasional word or two for clarification. A glossary at the end of the book contains explanations of Spanish words, special ranching terms, unusual regionalisms, and various place names in the tri-county area.

The people in this book wrote their own story. They are masters at condensing their experiences into a sentence or phrase that pretty much says it all. They love to talk about their work because few people ever knew what they did or how well they did it. In many respects, they were artists— geniuses at their job.

These interviews capture the heart, soul, and fiber of these people, portraying a side of them that we never realized existed—their sensitivity to and awareness of the world around themselves, each other, and the animals they worked with and cared for. Their vivid memories are extraordinary and constantly amazed me. I finally asked several of the cowhands how they could remember the minutest details from fifty years ago. Their immediate reply: "You can read and write a hundred miles an hour. Most of us can't do neither, so we have to rely on our memories to get by. Our minds weren't cluttered with much else than our jobs. That's how we remember so well."

Many of those interviewed articulate best the day-to-day routines of cowboying, while others have saved for us the essence of the romance and fun. I never encountered anyone who related an experience in a boring fashion. They were not the laconic, casual, and close-mouthed cow people who are generally portrayed in books and movies. They were good at their work and they knew it, and loved to talk among themselves and to others about their experiences.

There are many ways to present history, and converting oral history into a written record is often difficult. I have tried to present this material in such a way as to leave the reader with the same impressions I received while interviewing. At the same time, I have attempted to provide insight into the lives of these ranchers and cowhands in a unique manner.

People are strongly influenced by the way they think life is or have been told that it is or was. Therefore, it is important to know these influences and to observe how they have affected an entire culture. All of my text has been derived from primary research. None of this material has come from other published works. I wrote the historical section from memory. I absorbed it from years of conversations with my grandmother, Kate S. O'Connor. On summer afternoons we would sit in her library at the Melon Creek Ranch as she passed her extensive historical knowledge on to me. I have a mental picture of her in her rocking chair in front of an entire wall of books on Texas history. The collection included everything from *The Narratives of Cabeza de Vaca* to Larry McMurtry's works, as well as her

J. D. Mitchell and
Tom O'Connor [II],
ca. 1914.

own book, *Presidio La Bahia*. It seemed that everything ever written about Texas was in that library, and I felt as if she knew it all. Her view of history, along with those many volumes, could be considered indirect source material for the historical section of this book.

I have treated this ranch culture as a microcosm and have remained within it for all information and conclusions. There may be occasional inaccuracies, but this is how these people remember their experiences or believe them to have taken place. This look at their lives and their work, therefore, proceeds from these premises.

I have often been asked whether I thought these people might lie to me on occasion or, at the very least, exaggerate the truth. I must reply that this project has been approached from the standpoint of the preservation of a collective memory. This is not a chronology of factual information—I leave that endeavor to someone else. What I am presenting here is a feeling about a particular time—and of a certain group of people. I wanted to capture the essence of an era, which has its own validity.

Almost all of the information here was obtained in audiotaped interviews. In a few instances I have used material from written articles, interviews, and oral histories in other people's files. Most of these were done many years ago by persons now deceased. I interviewed almost everyone connected with this particular ranching culture in the three-county Coastal Bend area. Ranchers, cowhands, foremen, cooks, and midwives spent countless hours wired to my microphones. Where a recollection could be documented, it has invariably proven to be true. Material derived from the interviews is attributed to the speaker. Occasionally I have combined people's comments on a particular subject and these are followed by a listing of those persons whose words are included in the synthesis. Unattributed portions of the text, primarily the first chapter and introductions to succeeding chapters, are my contribution to this archival project.

This book was planned to introduce some of the men and women who played key roles in the settlement, development, and continued growth of the Coastal Bend. *Cryin' for Daylight* tells who these individuals are and how they define themselves. After talking to them for thousands of hours, recording their movingly expressive comments on tape, making thousands of photographs of them in countless situations and sifting through hundreds of old photographs from personal collections, I developed a strong conviction that anyone who hasn't been a part of ranch life has missed something. The innate strength, knowledge, and experience of these people comes through in the clarity of their voices, which must be heard firsthand to be truly appreciated.

This volume would not have been possible without the wholehearted cooperation and deep interest of hundreds of men and women who allowed me to interview and photograph them.

These people, who have shared with me both the good and the bad, are aware that their way of life is rapidly vanishing and were eager to help me document and preserve it as they lived it. Thus I wish to offer my heartfelt appreciation and thanks to all the interviewees for making every day on the project a joy.

The success of this effort must also be shared with a small group of dedicated individuals who helped me draw together this mountain of oral and visual information and convert it into a cohesive presentation. To all of the following individuals, I am deeply grateful: all the ranch owners and foremen, for their patience and assistance at all times—even when we were disrupting their sanity and their ranches; Steve Wiener, chief executive officer, for keeping the world off my back and for perceiving what I wanted to say, at times better than I could; Leah Bianchi, my secretary, for her invaluable speed, efficiency, and organizational skills; Paul Bardagjy, project director and photographic assistant, for his loyalty, honesty, patience, good humor, enthusiasm, and guidance; Mark Coffey, Vince McGarry, and Ed Guinn, sound engineers, for hearing, recording, and preserving all the words and sounds just as I heard them; Nancy O'Connor, for her friendship and unique perspective; Tommy Tijerina, for expediting and scheduling this entire project; Willie ("Cotton") Brown, deputy sheriff of Refugio County, for always being there with a smile when I needed him; Terry Wayland, photographic archivist, for being very quiet and very talented; John Fox, research assistant, for just being "Artly"; Dick Reeves, book designer, for handling my work with respect and understanding; Pam Kohler and Pam Winsier for their long hours of production and type-setting; Danny Garrett, illustrator, for his skill at converting words into pictures; John Wilson, illustrator extraordinaire; Andrew Bardagjy, editorial consultant, for making sense out of a mess; Alison Tartt, copy editor, for a fine eye for detail; Don Carleton, director of the Eugene C. Barker Texas History Center, for his constant encouragement and belief in the value of this project; and to Debbie Howe, my good friend, for proofreading my proofreading. Finally, I am indebted to J. Frank Dobie, J. D. Mitchell, Roger Fleming, Dennis M. O'Connor [II], Vincent Fritz, Kate S. O'Connor, and E. C. Ketler, who preserved for us the images of people and events from 1900 to 1970.

Louise S. O'Connor
Gaffney Ranch, 1987

L. V. Terrell throwing a calf, late 1930's.
Photo by Dennis O'Connor [II].

CHAPTER ONE

COWBOYING AND RANCHING
IN THE COASTAL BEND

Dennis Williams
Photo by Louise S. O'Connor.

COWBOYING AND RANCHING IN THE COASTAL BEND

The Coastal Bend of Texas is a region with unique characteristics. It has been called bastard country—lying halfway between the Deep South and the West and married, from its inception, to Mexico.

The area was formed by the elevation of the Coastal Plain during the Cenozoic era, the most recent period of time in the geological history of the North American continent. The plain stretches approximately 150 miles along the Gulf of Mexico and encompasses a prairie extending inland 30 to 50 miles.

It is a highly productive, fertile region sloping gently toward the Gulf. The three counties examined in this book are located here—Refugio, Victoria, and Goliad. They are different from the rest of the Texas coast. Located in a geological pocket along the Gulf of Mexico coastline, their particular location creates a unique environment for ranching. It includes areas of prairie, fertile river bottoms, and brush country.

The climate, the soil, and the grasses are different. The amount of annual rainfall is greater than in areas south and west of the region. There is more rainfall to the north; however, the higher acid content of the soil, in addition to its more rugged terrain, proves less suitable for cattle production. Much of the Coastal Bend is blessed with rich, black land high in potassium and this, combined with the ample rainfall, creates an environment for natural grasses which are extremely high in nutrients. The soil to

Coastline on Copano Bay, site of the old town of Copano.
Photo by Louise S. O'Connor.

the south and west is much loamier, and therefore, less conducive to raising nutritious grass.

The natural elements in this region seemed to work with man, not against him, as long as he maintained a certain respect for that land and for nature.

The area could be called gentle country, especially when compared with the more rugged rangeland to the north and west.

There was little to tame here, since water and food were in abundance for humans and animals, and the short winters were relatively mild compared with those endured by cattle people further north.

This is livestock country, with pastures of vast proportions, where the raising of beef cattle has been a source of wealth for many generations.

This land is valuable, profitable, and productive, despite a few drawbacks such as parasites and extreme heat. This is also noisy country. The region is an animal, bird, and insect paradise. The sounds of nature are everywhere.

According to some historians, society was fairly tranquil from pioneering times. The European immigrants in Texas, as well as the Mexican settlers in the early 1800s, were not in mortal conflict in any organized sense with the Indian tribes in the area. The free, open range disappeared very early. The Coastal Bend was divided into ranches, and the perimeters of most of the ranches were fenced by the mid-nineteenth century.

The communities of the pioneering days were essentially the same as they are today, with the towns of Refugio, Goliad, and Victoria being the hubs of the developing Coastal Bend area. Smaller communities such as Port O'Connor, Indianola, and Fulton grew up on the coast as major shipping areas for the hide and tallow industries, as well as ports for receiving much-needed goods for the early settlers. As roads improved and the railroads were brought in, these areas either died out or dwindled into the small, stagnant communities they are today.

Ranching in the Texas Coastal Bend dates back to the early 1720s when the Catholic church brought Spanish soldiers and cattle to Presidio La

Presidio La Bahia before restoration.

Bahia, near the present-day town of Goliad, to support its mission system. As the missions declined and the herds of cattle grew larger, the soldiers seemingly made a transition to cow-working, thus becoming *vaqueros*. The general area also began to be settled by Mexican citizens fleeing from the political turmoil in their own country and by soldiers who had originally come to the region as members of military expeditions.

By the 1820s, despite these earlier immigrations, Mexico desperately needed colonists to ensure possession of its vast holdings to the north. Mexico, being a Catholic country, insisted that the colonists be of the same religion. A group of Irishmen, living in Mexico as citizens, quickly put the pieces of this puzzle together and went to the Mexican officials with a plan for bringing groups of Catholic colonists from Ireland to settle Mexico's northern territory. The Catholics in Ireland at this time were unable to own property, hold office, or exercise much personal freedom because of the oppressive English Penal Codes. Because of these and other conditions, the Emerald Isle had a large pool of potential emigrants. The Mexican government accepted the plan and gave huge land grants in the Coastal Bend to these *empresarios*.

One of these *empresarios* was James Power, a native of County Wexford, Ireland, who had many relatives still residing back in his home county. He invited several of these relations and other Wexford residents to a meeting at his sister Isabella's house in Ballygarrett in 1834. Power persuaded many of them to emigrate to his colony in the New World. The very young Isabella and her husband, Thomas O'Brien, agreed to go with the group. Unfortunately, O'Brien died of cholera on the sea journey. Thomas O'Connor, Power's teenage nephew, was also among the group to migrate to Texas.

James Hewetson, Power's partner, left the colonists entirely in his partner's care and eventually moved back to Mexico. Thus, Power was the only person in the group to have any knowledge of their new home. When the settlers first arrived, they feared that the Indians might be a problem, so they formed small towns to serve as protection. Although there was never a major Indian problem in this part of Texas, Indian raids did occur sporadically until the mid to late nineteenth century.

The settlers were kept in a constant state of confusion over controversial political issues and disputes over land ownership. These people are to be greatly admired because they managed to survive and flourish amidst all the confusion and change. What is even more remarkable is that they built empires in this turbulent political and legal climate and did so at a very early age.

Within a span of twelve years, they had lived under three governmental entities — Mexico, the Republic of Texas, and finally the United States.

Though living in a more temperate environment than settlers of other regions during the era of westward expansion, these colonists still had to deal with problems such as floods and droughts. Disease took its toll on the population. Many died from cholera and other epidemics that frequently swept through the region. The Irish, however, with their almost primordial attachment to the land and their rural traditions, were tough, intelligent, committed people, and they had nowhere else to go. They could not go back to Ireland, as they had sold everything to come to Texas. This was a great incentive to stay and succeed.

The Irish colonists who did survive soon dominated the area and began building the land empires that have lasted to the present day. Predominantly tenant farmers in the old country, they sought personal freedom and came here to acquire land, not necessarily to raise cattle. This land-poor group of Irishmen inherently knew that land equaled wealth and security. They were not as concerned with what to do with their property as with simply acquiring it.

Their timing was perfect, as large tracts of land were soon vacated by Mexican loyalists who had colonized the area decades earlier, but who returned to Mexico during and following the Texas Revolution.

De la Garza, Tijerina, Rodriguez, and Perez—these names continue to live in the ranching culture of this area like echoes from the past. The families had lived here under Spanish and Mexican rule long before the Anglos arrived. They had large landholdings along the San Antonio River, and there were many Spanish and Mexican settlers in this three-county area.

For example, the Carlos Ranch was known throughout Mexico as a place that gave refuge to anyone seeking to escape the sometimes violent political controversies that frequently broke out in the provinces south of the Rio Grande. In spite of this, Don Carlos de la Garza and his brothers were known to be sympathetic to Mexico's claims to Texas. After the Texas Revolution, they were ordered off their land by General Rusk, commander of the Texas Army in Victoria in 1836. Because of the high esteem in which he was held by his neighbors, however, Don Carlos de la Garza was allowed to remain on his land until his death in 1882. Most of the Carlos Ranch was purchased from his widow by area ranchers when he died.

Many people of Spanish and Mexican descent living along the San Antonio River today own small plots of land from Don Carlos's original Spanish land grant. Most of the other Mexican families in the area say that their families fled Mexico during the numerous uprisings that began after Mexico won independence from Spain in 1821. Proud and able people, as well as superb cowhands, their names still linger in the folklore of the area.

The ranching activity of all of the area's settlers remained at a subsistence level until after the Civil War, when the beef markets in the North and East greatly expanded demand. This forever changed the complexion of ranching operations in the Texas Coastal Bend.

Some of the white colonists had brought slaves with them, but not until after the Civil War did blacks begin to join the work force as cowhands. They settled in several Coastal Bend communities. Few people are aware of the existence of large numbers of black cowhands in America and of their significant contributions to the development of Texas and the United States west of the Mississippi River. Generally, they are portrayed in the cowboy myth as rodeo performers and outlaws. At one time, however, there appeared to be as many black cowhands in the Coastal Bend area as Anglos and Mexicans. They settled mostly along the San Antonio River after emancipation and formed small settlements such as Lewis's Bend, the Black Jacks, and Spriggs' Bend.

These newly freed people knew how to farm, and they raised their food on a subsistence level. Their land was either bought from their former owners or, in many cases, given to them by their owners. As the ranches grew larger and the demand for more workers grew, they signed on with the cow crowds and became some of the finest cowhands that ever lived.

This ethnic and racial combination of cow people in such relatively equal numbers is just another peculiarity of the Coastal Bend ranching culture.

The inhabitants of this tricultural region today speak a language born of black dialect, Spanish idiom, and white Southern regionalisms.

With the men away fighting in the Civil War, the herds of cattle eventually grew to such vast numbers that something had to be done with them. At the same time this surplus of cattle appeared in Texas, the demand for beef in the East began to grow. Because of the severe lack of rail facilities in Texas, ranchers organized trail drives to move the animals to railheads in Kansas for shipment to northern and eastern markets.

Fortunes were made from the sale of cattle raised on Coastal Bend pastures. With the establishment of cattle-raising operations throughout the West and Midwest, however, and the decline of the Eastern markets due to a glut of beef, the Texas cattle industry collapsed in the late 1800s.

The cowhand appeared to be in danger of extinction. Then the discovery of vast reserves of oil in the Coastal Bend in the 1920s and 1930s enabled the larger ranches, and even some of the smaller ones, to achieve economic stability and to maintain a semblance of ranch and cowboy life as it once existed.

The similarity today to the industry as it once existed, however, is small. The old-timers who are still around miss the old ways, their work, and their friends.

That life and these people will soon be a thing of the past.

Branding cattle on the Albrecht Ranch, ca. early 1900's.

CHAPTER TWO

SOUTH TEXAS EMPIRES: THE RANCHES

Georgia Lee Swickheimer
Photo by Louise S. O'Connor.

SOUTH TEXAS EMPIRES: THE RANCHES

Most of these Coastal Bend ranches are far from being the largest in Texas, but they are among the most fertile and productive ranches in the world. On the average, they are capable of pasturing one cow to ten acres, and in a good year their carrying capacity can go even higher. This is much greater than the capabilities of ranches to the north, west, and south.

Not all of the ranches located in this three-county area are included here, since I am not attempting to do a comprehensive ranch history of the region. This historical background covers only the ranches mentioned by the people I interviewed.

Most of these ranches have been in the same families since the Texas Revolution, and in the case of the area Hispanics, the land came into their families as Spanish land grants as early as the 1700s. The Spanish land grant system was a system whereby the Spanish government would deed property in one of their unsettled colonies to a capable individual, called an *empresario*, for the purpose of settling a large area of land.

Cattle ranching began in Texas on this land, while it was still a largely unsettled Spanish colony, ruled by Mexico to the south. Most of these ranches sprang from several large Spanish and Mexican land grants. The Power-Hewetson colony was dominant in the Refugio area, and the Martin De Leon grant was preeminent in the Victoria area. Goliad, however, did not fall under the grant system. In 1829, Texas and Mexico declared La Bahia Presidio a town and named it Goliad, after Father Hidalgo.

Throughout this book, you will see many more ranch names than the twenty-two this book documents. Under these primary ranch names are secondary names denoting divisions within the main ranches.

Few of these ranches have ever been sold; but, if they have been, it has almost always been to a neighboring rancher. Seldom has this land been sold to a genuine outsider. Frequently, the new owner will retain the original name of the ranch, as the purchase becomes a division of the ranch to which it is newly attached.

Among the larger ranches, at one time or another, a division has occurred between members of one family, usually for economic reasons or for ease of management. Each of the divisions would then be given a (new) proper name. This name was often the pasture name that the area carried as a part of the whole ranch.

It did not take long to build these small empires, but it did take hard work on the part of the founders of these ranches. The necessity for hard work continues to the present day. Obtaining, building, and holding on to this land was, and is, no small task.

In a ranching culture, a brand carries the same importance as a family crest. Brands are passed down from generation to generation, and frequently later generations add embellishments or modifications to the original design to distinguish it as theirs. In Spain and Mexico these flourishes were called *tahuitas*. Because branding gave legal protection to livestock owners, brands were government-registered. Any unauthorized use

"Look as poor as you can when buying cattle and as rich as you can when selling them."

Armel Keeran Baker
Rancher
1901–1967

of a registered brand was a criminal offense, punishable at one time by hanging. With the disappearance of the open range, brands are less important in identifying ownership than in keeping track of breeding lines or age. But they are still a source of family pride and a valued tradition.

This is beautiful, fertile, productive land. It has been cherished and cared for by the men and women of these families for many generations. They have been loyal to it in good times and bad. We have them to thank for its preservation as ranch land to the present time.

Family names are faithfully preserved in this culture. The same Christian names are passed down from one generation to the next. It is sometimes difficult to know which person is being discussed, because often the suffixes (Sr., Jr., etc.) do not follow the natural generational order. To prevent confusion, I have given to each member of the same family having the same name a suffix in brackets designating his birth order. They may or may not necessarily have used these suffixes during their lifetimes. Their purpose is for clarification only.

The families take great pride in their ranches and in their family histories as well. In almost every generation of each of these families, there has been one person who kept the history of the family and the ranch intact for future generations. On the following pages, descendants of each family tell the story of their ancestors and their ranches.

The Keeran Ranches

The Keerans came from Scotland to the Shenandoah Valley of Virginia, and then raised beautiful horses in Kentucky. During the Gold Rush era, Captain John N. Keeran went to California to establish a horse farm there.

Keeran Ranch House

No one knows why he left California, but he and his family sailed around the Horn and landed at old Indianola. That was back in the days when land was ten cents an acre, but nobody had ten cents. The captain had brought some gold from California, and he bought part of the ranch with it in 1867. He named it the California Ranch. It had previously belonged to the De Leon family and was a Spanish land grant.

Captain Keeran and his close friend, A. H. "Shanghai" Pierce, were instrumental in bringing five Brahman cattle from India to this area in 1878. Pierce got the bull and Keeran got the cows, one of which was named

Claude Andrew Keeran
Rancher
1862–1931

Lalarook. The two men had found a pest-resistant breed that could endure the heat of South Texas, and a new chapter in the cattle industry began.

My father, Claude Keeran, was born in California and was five years old when he came to Texas with his parents. The Keerans have always been cattle ranchers. My grandfather started out raising Longhorns, and when my father inherited the ranch, he crossbred the Longhorns with Brahmans and Herefords.

After my sister, Armel, and I started ranching, she got interested in Brahman cattle and started breeding and raising them. This was to become her lifelong occupation. Her intensive and intelligent breeding programs produced the largest herd of Brahmans in the country at that time. She felt that the same pasture needed to raise an ordinary animal could just as well be used to raise one of much higher quality. And from the day she started, she never sold a female animal. She was the first woman to raise Brahman cattle in the United States and the second woman ever to sit on the board of a major cattle registry association.

My country and my brother's ranch are now leased, and until his death, my nephew, Henry Clay Koontz [IV], was one of the most prominent Brahman breeders in the world.

Emily Keeran Campbell

Captain John N. Keeran
Rancher
1825–1904

John Newbanks Keeran
Rancher
1905–1983

The Koontz Ranch

Henry Clay Koontz [I] came from Switzerland to New Jersey around 1828. Later he moved to Alabama and then to Texas, where he obtained a headright that is now the town of New Braunfels. A short time later, he married Dorothy Ulrich. The couple moved to Indianola, where they had a daughter and two sons. Both parents and the daughter died during a yellow fever epidemic, and of the remaining two sons, only Henry Clay Koontz, Jr. [II], survived.

Henry Clay Koontz, Sr. [II]
Rancher
1847–1908

Henry Clay Koontz, Jr. [III]
Rancher
1888–1954

Henry [II] was raised in Arenosa. Brother Mason, a member of a local religious order, was his guardian, as well as a Judge Varnell of Victoria. The judge was dishonest and sold Henry's inheritance of jewels and land. The young man never saw the proceeds from the sale and was left destitute.

Although he received only a sixth-grade education, Henry was exceptional at math. He acquired land around Arenosa and Inez. He rode the range and branded cattle for Varnell until a Judge Jordan advised him to design his own brand and keep the mavericks for himself. He took this advice and created the C-H-E brand. Henry was also a postmaster and horseback mail carrier, and owned a lumberyard, mercantile store, cotton gin, and hotel in Inez. He acquired land around Arenosa and Inez, but in 1930 lost a lot of his land due to the Depression.

Henry Clay, now Sr. [II], married Mary Ann Finnegan, and they had ten children, one of whom was Henry Clay, Jr. [III]. Young Henry worked in the cattle industry and his father's cotton gins, and spent four years with the Missouri-Pacific Railroad in Louisiana. He later returned to Inez and became the town's postmaster. There was a member of the family serving as postmaster in Inez until 1966.

Henry, Jr. [III], took over the ranch and began raising Brahman cattle and crossbred and graded cattle as well. He married Armel Keeran, daughter of neighboring rancher Claude Keeran. They had four children—Henry Clay [IV], Carolyn Ann, Diana Keeran, and Gertrude Emily. Henry, Jr. [III], was killed by a Missouri-Pacific train in 1954.

The ranch was inherited by Diana Keeran Koontz Massey and is still being managed by the Masseys and their six children—Sherrice, Diana, Carolyn, Mary Ann, Robert Lee II, and Clay Koontz Massey.

The Koontz ranches have established a worldwide reputation as breeders of high-quality Brahman cattle.

Diana Keeran Koontz Massey

Human buzzards on the fence, Koontz Ranch, early 1900's.

"Buy land and never sell. Land can't die and it can't run away."

Tom O'Connor [I]
Rancher
1818–1887

Dennis Martin O'Connor [I]
Rancher
1839–1900

The O'Connor Ranches

The building of the O'Connor ranches started in 1836, the year Texas declared its independence from Mexico. Every soldier who fought with Sam Houston for the Texas cause was awarded a land grant of 650 acres. In Houston's army was a young Irishman, only eighteen years old. He had been cited for meritorious service and given the acreage he was entitled to before he was sent home. That land was the beginning of Tom O'Connor's vast landholdings in the Texas Coastal Bend.

Young O'Connor came to this country in 1834 with his uncle, the noted *empresario* James Power, and became a saddletree maker to earn his living. At this time, the Texas countryside was free range, and anyone could use it without holding title.

During this time, land scrip was often used as legal tender. Whenever O'Connor received this scrip as payment for services or for one of his saddletrees, he would register it in his name at the land office instead of using it as money. Any money he was able to save from the sale of his saddletrees he would also invest in land. It has been said that O'Connor walked or rode over every acre of land that he ever owned. If this story is true, then by 1876 he had walked or ridden over each of the 500,000 acres that he had accumulated up to that time. He built his empire at a very young age, as did most of the immigrants who settled this country.

Tom was considered a bit eccentric, if not downright crazy, for buying land when there was so much of it available that was free. Vast fortunes were then being made in the cattle industry, and no one could understand why he was putting all of his earnings into the purchase of land and not cattle. Inexplicably, the young Irishman could foresee the day when this

O'Connor cow crowd, 1912, Refugio, Texas. Louis Polka, Foreman, far right.

land would be fenced and used only by the people who owned it. He was heard to say, "My people will be riding when others are walking." He never lost faith in his belief that the free range would end, and continued to add to his landholdings until his death in 1887. He was proven right when the Texas cattle industry collapsed in the late 1800s and those who held the land were the ones who survived economically.

After O'Connor's death, ownership of the ranch passed to his two sons, Dennis Martin [I] and Thomas Marion [I]. They divided the ranch, but continued in business together for many years. The second division of the

SOUTH TEXAS EMPIRES: THE RANCHES

Thomas Marion O'Connor [I]
Rancher
1857–1910

Joseph O'Connor
Rancher
1880–1932

Will O'Connor
Business Manager
T. M. O'Connor Ranches
1884–1950

Mary Ellen O'Connor
Rancher
1891–1967

ranches took place after the death of Dennis Martin O'Connor [I], and the ranches have remained unchanged since. Cattle ranching is the only business that has ever been conducted on this land, and it is hoped that it will continue to be used for this purpose for many more generations.

The O'Connor ranches have been passed down from one generation to the next, and the sixth generation is now serving their apprenticeship before taking their places among the numerous descendants of an Irish orphan who came to this country looking for freedom and land.

Kate S. O'Connor
1883–1979

Jim O'Connor
Rancher
1888–1956

Martin O'Connor
Rancher
1875–1949

"Keep an old cow's body comfortable and she'll make you money."

Tom O'Connor [II]
Rancher
1882–1946

"Damn the market! Sell the cattle when they are ready."

"I have been all over the world looking at ranchland, and the area from the Guadalupe River to the Nueces River and forty or fifty miles up from the coast is the finest native cow country I have ever seen."

**Al McFaddin
Rancher
1863–1930**

The McFaddin Ranches

The McFaddins are of Scottish descent, and the first one, James A. McFaddin, arrived in Beaumont, Texas, around 1817 when there was nothing there but Indians and alligators. He soon went to Louisiana, but returned to Jefferson County in 1821. His son, William, was a veteran of San Jacinto, and William's son, James A., born in 1840, migrated to Refugio and became the town banker. He had the only safe in town in his store, and freighted cotton from Refugio to Brownsville during the Civil War.

At that time, there was no land available around Refugio County because the O'Connors and the O'Briens had already bought up most of it. So James began buying property in Victoria County, just across the San Antonio River. The earliest records show he bought land in the area from Joseph Toups, Tobe Wood, and Dennis M. O'Connor [I], as well as land patents from the state. Later, around 1900, he bought the Garcitas Ranch north of Victoria. Basically, the McFaddin ranches were put together between 1877 and 1900, but there were additions as late as the 1940s by my father, Claude McCan, Sr.

Branding cattle at McFaddin Ranch, Mariana, Texas, early 1900's.

James raised and sold mules and thoroughbred horses. He also cleared land along the river and raised cotton, and built an extensive system of dams and levees to control the water and keep it away from the cotton. James's son, Al, was a big cowman; he bought and sold steers and wintered cattle on the salt grass in Brazoria County. From there, he would send them to Kansas and Oklahoma. The McFaddin ranches were among the first to import Brahman cattle; allegedly, they were bought from P. T. Barnum's circus menagerie. James took part in the trail drives, but by Al's time, the railroad had come into Mariana, as the town of McFaddin was then called.

Al McFaddin
Rancher
1863–1930

Claude K. McCan, Sr.
Rancher
1899–1974

Patrick Lambert
Rancher
1851–1909

The town had a cotton gin, mercantile, post office, school, machine shop, and a Catholic church.

When Claude McCan, Sr., nephew of Al McFaddin, took over, he formed the Welder-McCan partnership with Jim Welder on the Roche Ranch in Refugio County. That land was originally Driscoll property, but it has been leased since 1900. Welder-McCan has leased this land for more than fifty years. My father liked steers, but he also bred quarter horses and moved the ranch from tenant farming into irrigated pastures so he could winter-feed the cattle on oats. These ranches have always engaged in activities other than cattle raising. Cotton gins, grain elevators, cotton, and feed grains have been income-producing businesses over the years. At present, my son, Bobby, is successfully raising a string of polo ponies. These same horses are also used in the ranch *remudas*.

Claude K. McCan, Jr.

James McFaddin, Rancher, 1840–1918 with prize Brahman bull he purchased at the World's Fair, ca. 1880.

The Lambert-Wood Ranches

The Lambert side of the family came from Ireland and the Woods were from Holland by way of Hyde Park, New York.

Walter Lambert of County Wexford was the first to come over here. He saw action at the Battle of San Jacinto and voted for the Constitution of the Republic of Texas as well as the annexation of Texas to the United States. He was a merchant in Copano and was sheriff of Refugio County. He married a daughter of the *empresario* James Power. They raised five children, and he was also a chief justice of Texas. He was an illustrious citizen of Texas and urged his older brother to join him there.

Martin Lambert arrived at Copano with his wife, Catherine, a son, Nicholas, and a daughter, Margaret. It is likely that he worked with his brother in a mercantile and freight-forwarding business at Copano. After their arrival, another son, Walter, was born; a third son, Patrick, was born in 1851. Their last child, Mary, was born in 1853.

Carrie Genevieve Lambert Wood
Rancher
1887-1983

The lack of water, the menace of Indian attacks, the prevalence of disease, and the scarcity of provisions created many hardships for the citizens of Copano.

Hardships were compounded by the death of Martin in 1859. Shortly after his father's death, Nicholas, with the help of his Uncle Walter, purchased some farm lots near Refugio.

During his youth, the younger Patrick also often looked to his Uncle Walter for guidance. He was now the oldest boy at home and head of the family. During this time, he probably worked at the packeries that were located between Copano and Refugio on the Mission River.

At fourteen, Pat rode the mail from St. Mary's to Beeville. It was a day's trip in each direction, and no small feat for a boy that age.

Widowed Catherine Lambert lived with her children and died in 1891. Nicholas married Bessie McGuill in 1879, and they had eight children. He lived in Goliad County, not far from the Refugio County line, until his death in 1920. Mary married Bessie McGuill's brother William and had seven children. Walter never married and died in 1902.

Major John H. Wood and family.

It would be conjecture to speculate at what moment young Patrick developed his love of the land. It was probably a combination of the spirit of the new frontier and the legendary Irish love of the land. It was also most surely connected with a lifelong relationship to his mentor and friend, Tom O'Connor [I].

Pat went to work for Tom O'Connor around 1870 as a cowhand. He worked diligently and became respected, if not loved, by his fellow cowhands. He excelled in the eyes of his boss and was probably considered a de facto son of O'Connor. By the 1880s he was head foreman for the O'Connor ranches.

John Howland Wood
Rancher
1816-1904

Nancy Clark Wood
Rancher
1820-1891

Richard Henry Wood
Rancher
1886-1963

As early as 1872, Patrick was the owner of two acres of land and fifty head of cattle. In 1884, Pat acquired the River Ranch from his former boss. O'Connors never sold land, and the fact that Tom O'Connor would sell to Lambert was a tribute to the young man.

About this time, Patrick married Mary Frances Low. A daughter, Carrie Genevieve, was born to them in 1887. A son, James Walter, was born in 1888, but died as a small boy.

At age forty, Patrick had succeeded. He had a prospering ranch, a family, and community respect. He was elected county commissioner in 1901 and contributed his salary to churches—yes, plural—he played all bases. He also supported the building of the railroad through the country. Pat was quite a pragmatic man, known to cuss a blue streak. He was devoted to his church, his family, and his land. He worked hard for what he had. Patrick was a man of strong opinions and a steel will. He had convictions and he cared. The death of their only son Jimmy at the age of five was a tragic loss for Patrick and Mary Frances, but he continued to acquire land. In two purchases in 1896 and 1898, he acquired from the O'Connors—Dennis and Tom—what was to become the home ranch.

In 1904, 1905, and 1906 he made his last land purchases, adding to his ranches by effort and determination.

Patrick died in 1909, and Carrie and his wife inherited his properties. His surviving child Carrie was the joy of his life, and he had always intended the Sarco Ranch to be a wedding present for her. Following his death, Mary Frances agreed on the separation of the properties, giving the Sarco Ranch and the so-called River Ranch to Carrie, and retaining what is known as the Lambert Ranch.

Carrie subsequently married Richard Henry Wood, son of Tobias De Cantillion Wood, a soldier of fortune who fought with the New York Regiment of the Texas Army. He landed in Texas in 1836 and fought at the Battle of San Jacinto. He also assisted in the burial of the bodies of Fannin's men at Goliad. He remained in the army and was a quartermaster in Victoria. He accepted cattle and livestock as part pay and embarked on the ranching business in Jackson County and then Refugio County. His brand was JW, and later he added N and NC.

John Howland Wood married Nancy Clark, who had come to Texas with her mother in 1839. From this marriage were born twelve children, including T. D. Wood, and a grandson, R. H. Wood.

Major Wood received a series of inheritances and turned these into land and cattle and real estate in Texas. In 1849, Major Wood moved his family from San Patricio to Black Point and began his famous Bonnie View Ranch. Major Wood continued to add to his landholdings.

The marriage of Richard Wood and Carrie Lambert consolidated their landholdings.

These ranches have always been cattle ranches. There were attempts to raise sheep and goats, which the coyotes loved, and horses; and the farming of cotton, corn, wheat, grains, and grass seed has been a ranch enterprise. Oil came along in the 1930s.

All of us have been enamored with land forever. Everyone here believes in real estate. We all find new and unique things to do with this land in each generation. We haven't begun to find all the ways this land can be used. We old guys retard the progress of the young ones by our attachment to it. We cling to the old ways rather than being practical. This land is the basis of everything we have accomplished.

James Lawrence Wood
Richard Lambert Wood
1925–1988

Mary Fox Kroeger
Rancher
1875–1967

The Kroeger Ranch

Henry Ludwig Kroeger, who was born in 1820 in northeastern France, arrived in the United States at the township of Lamar, Texas, around 1850. He married Eve Thomas, a native of Switzerland, and they had three children: Henry William, born in 1853, died in 1873 of typhoid fever; Mary Ellen, born in 1855, died in 1887; and John Henry, born in 1866, died in 1950.

Henry accumulated numerous plats of land around the Salt Creek area, most likely through land grants. According to legend, he acquired a number of separate parcels of land that were not contiguous and were scattered throughout the O'Connor Ranch. Mr. Dennis O'Connor approached Henry (so the story goes) and asked him if he would accept the present-day ranch at Salt Creek in exchange for these scattered tracts. The deal was concluded and it proved advantageous to both men. Mr. O'Connor was able to consolidated all of the small parcels into his larger ranch, and Henry now owned one large contiguous piece of property. Henry died in 1908, his wife in 1884.

L-R, John H. Kroeger, Sr., Mae Delisle Kroeger, John H. Kroeger, Jr., Mrs. John H. Kroeger, Sr., Reginald J. Kroeger.

John Henry Kroeger married Mary Fox of Victoria, and they had three children: Mae Delisle, who died in 1962; R. J. Kroeger, who died in 1977; and John Henry, Jr., my father, who married Beret Hagen, who is now living in San Diego. My father died in 1944 in Africa during World War II.

Presently I hold sole ownership to the ranch. It is a working ranch with about 50 percent devoted to farming and 50 percent to cattle.

John Kroeger

The McDowell Ranch

The McDowells came from England and Scotland in the 1700s and settled in Pennsylvania. My mother, Waldine, was a Rathbone from Cuero. Her family was originally from Tennessee, and some of her people landed in Indianola around 1845.

My family had no agricultural background. They were merchants. My grandfather, Jesse Clark McDowell, was in the oil business in Pennsylvania with the Rockefellers. He came to Texas with Spindletop and started the Gulf Oil Refinery in Beaumont. My father, Horace McDowell, was in college in Pennsylvania and came down one summer on a tanker to see his father. He said that when he first set foot on Texas soil, he decided that he never wanted to leave. They had a hard time getting him to go back and finish college.

When grandfather came in to help organize the Gulf Oil Company, they decided they needed a local attorney to do their legal work. I don't know exactly how they met, but he chose Mr. Fred Proctor, who was in Houston. Fred's brother, Venable, lived in Victoria, so it was through them that Dad got down to Victoria, where he met Mr. Al McFaddin and other local ranchers and businessmen.

My grandfather was an adventurous and curious man who wanted to invest in land in Texas. He went to see Preston Austin, and they formed the Refugio Land and Irrigation Company. The town of Austwell was named after them. After several years, the company was dissolved and my father was given his father's share of the land. He took the portion of land along

L-R, Vida Finney, Horace McDowell, Waldine McDowell, Catherine McDowell, and Jack McDowell on San Antonio Bay, ca. 1916.

the water and started farming and raising Hereford cattle. All of this area was originally a Spanish land grant that belonged, successively, to the Hynes, DuBois, Lucas, and Dunman families before my family purchased it.

My father's sole business was that ranch; he loved it. He owned the land from around 1905 until 1938, when poor health forced him to sell it. My brother, Jesse Clark ("Jack") McDowell, was not interested in ranching. He liked the oil business. I loved the ranch and begged my father to let me have it, but he was determined to make me a lady and wouldn't let me ranch the land.

When I was a girl, there were large white birds with red heads that came to our ranch every October. The whooping cranes were not famous back then, just large white birds that made lots of noise. The area was a natural wildlife preserve before my family owned it and during my childhood. Birds of all kinds, deer, coyotes, rabbits, raccoons, and squirrels were everywhere. When my father decided to sell the ranch, the government bought it for the Aransas Wildlife Refuge. It is one of the most beautiful pieces of property imaginable.

Catherine McDowell

Jesse Clark McDowell
Rancher
1852–1927

Horace H. McDowell
Rancher
1885–1950

Preston Rose Austin
Rancher
1872–1929

The Stofer-McNeel Ranch

The Austin family moved to Victoria County around 1875 when Preston Rose Austin was three years old. He was raised in and around the Victoria area. Educated in Virginia, he returned to Texas and married the daughter of W. B. Traylor. From the late 1890s he began leasing and acquiring ranchland. His principal holdings were in Refugio and Calhoun counties, but he also leased land in West Texas and Kansas for running cattle.

Austin was instrumental in the formation of the towns of Tivoli and Austwell, and was in a land partnership for many years with Horace McDowell, another local rancher. At various times, he owned the Powderhorn Ranch, the La Salle Ranch, and the Thomas Ranch, and he also leased ranchland from the Traylor family.

Preston Austin was a renowned raiser and seller of steers. That was his only interest in the cattle business. He was never involved in a cow-calf operation, as many of the local ranchers were. The only thing he liked a cow for was to produce a steer. Austin's Long Mott Ranch, which remains in the family, came from both the Austin and Traylor sides of the family. It is still being operated as a cattle ranch by his grandson, Preston Austin Stofer.

Terry Stofer Hewitt
Preston A. Stofer

James Power, Jr.
Rancher
1833–1886

Philip Power
Rancher
1848–1934

The Power Ranches

The *empresario* James Power was born in Wexford, Ireland, in 1789. He apparently left Ireland, as many others did, to escape overpopulation, the English Penal Codes, and the practice of primogeniture. Power arrived in Philadelphia in 1812, and sometime during the next eight years, moved to New Orleans. By 1820 he was a merchant in that city. While living there, he met James Hewetson, and they began discussing the possibility of colonizing Texas. By 1828, they had formed a partnership for this purpose and received land grants from the Mexican government. Power was granted three and one-half leagues of land—about 15,000 acres—in the Refugio District. Hewetson eventually went back to Mexico and lived there until his death.

When he died in 1852, Power left all of his property to his children. James, Jr., and his brother-in-law, John Welder, husband of Power's sister, Dolores, seem to have managed the property until it was inherited by the next generation. Philip Power then administered and managed the estate containing the original land grant, and added to the property around 1915. Much of this land was either willed back to Philip by members of the family or was bought back by him. He had consolidated much of the original ranch by the time of his death in 1934.

Joseph Daniel Shay married Philip's daughter, Mary Agnes, and managed the ranch until it was passed along to their children Wallace, Lawrence, and Phil. The Power Ranch has always been cattle country and is still being managed by descendants of the *empresario*.

Wallace Shay

The West Ranch

A history of the West Ranch is unavailable. Part of this property was purchased by the J. F. Welder heirs in 1933 and the remainder in 1935. It is now a part of the Welder Vidauri Ranch.—**L. O'C.**

Chris West
Rancher
1877–1947

Peter Fagan
"Curly Pete"
Rancher
1843–1929

The Fagan Ranches

Nicholas Fagan, a blacksmith from County Meath, Ireland, sailed out of Cork and landed in New York in 1817. At this time he was married to Kate Connaly, and they had two children: Annie, who married Peter Teal, and Mary, who married Tom O'Connor [I]. A son, John, born later in St. Louis, married Helena ("Ellen") Fox; they were parents of the Peter Fagan known as "Curly Pete," who married Texana Clark.

Fagan apparently migrated from New York to Philadelphia, then to Cincinnati, and finally to St. Louis, where his first wife died. Sometime after that, he moved to New Orleans, where he must have had contact with James Power. They seemed to have reached some agreement about Fagan acquiring land in Power's prospective colony in Texas. While in New Orleans, Fagan married Catherine Hanselman Balsch, a widow, and they came to Copano on the same boat with Power in 1829.

By 1830, Nicholas had his land staked out along the San Antonio River, and he received his grant in 1834. He fought in the Texas Revolution. Although captured by the Mexicans, his life was spared because his blacksmithing skills were very useful to his captors.

Fagan died around 1850, and Catherine was named administrator of his estate in 1852. She died in 1856 before the estate was settled, leaving her son, William Nicholas Fagan, as administrator. The original land grant

Oscar G. Fagan at the Fagan Ranch House.

ranch was still intact until 1861, when there was an application for partition of the property of Catherine and her sons, William Nicholas and James Christopher.

The division was completed by 1863 and the land divided among the heirs, which left the ranch in three parts. Catherine Sidick, Frances ("Fanny") Elizabeth Warburton, and Peter Henry Fagan each received a share of the ranch, which has all been passed down to heirs through several generations. Frederick William Fagan, the son of Peter Henry, and his wife, Zilpah, had nine children; after his death in 1954, his wife divided their land among their children and a daughter-in-law in 1962.

This division stands today, and the Fagan ranches are still owned and run by the direct descendants of Nicholas Fagan of County Meath, Ireland. The Fagan ranches have been cattle country for over 150 years and have never been sold or leased outside the family.

Hallie Fagan Snider

Frederick William Fagan
Rancher
1874–1954

Armour Fagan
Rancher
1901–1967

The Williams Ranches

David F. Williams was born in Kentucky in 1818 and lived there until he moved to Vicksburg, Mississippi, in 1845. There he owned an interest in a tavern and married Julia Devine in 1852. They came to Victoria County by way of Saluria and Indian Point.

Williams purchased his first half-league of land on the east side of the San Antonio River from Antonio and Tomasa de la Garza in 1854. His I-P brand was registered there the next year, and his address was the Carlos Ranch. More land was purchased from Henry Devine in 1858, and additional land along the San Antonio River was acquired in 1860.

After the death of his first wife, David married Amanda Jane Kemper. They had three children: Samuel John, Mary Catherine, and Robert Sydney. Amanda Jane and David joined their properties after they married, but eventually they sold the Kemper's Bluff property that belonged to Amanda and acquired additional land in the de la Garza and Santiago Serna leagues.

David died in 1881, and hard times followed. Cattle prices dropped and there were floods and droughts. After Amanda died in 1903, the ranches were inherited by their three children. Mary Catherine married W. A. Simmons of Florence, Alabama. He worked cattle for the Terrells and had gone up the Chisholm Trail. They built a home on the Santiago Serna league, and Mr. Simmons speculated in land. Samuel John married Zilpah Stoner, and they had three children: David, Mary Claire, and Kemper. After Zilpah's

Residence of Robert S. Williams, Anaqua, Texas. Photo by Parks.

death, Samuel married Mary Ella May of Yoakum, and they had four children: Amanda, Mildred Evelyn, Syble Elaine, and John Robert.

Samuel and his family later moved to Kerrville, seeking a healthier climate. The family holdings were run thereafter by Robert Sydney Williams. He traded horses in Mexico and the United States. His I-P brand was registered in 1886. Until his death in 1958, he lived on his division of the ranch, the de la Garza survey.

The descendants of David F. Williams still live in the area and ranch parts of the land that he and his wife put together.

Elaine Williams Wagner
Kemper Williams, Sr.

David F. Williams
Rancher
1818–1881

Samuel John Williams
Rancher
1872–1958

Robert Sydney Williams, Sr.
Rancher
1874–1936

Gonzales Ranch House, Nursery, Texas

The Gonzales Ranch

My family came from Saltillo, Mexico. The first one here was my grandfather, Jose Maria Gonzales, who was born in Monterrey in 1842. He came to Texas as a young boy and later married Magdalena Lopez, a local girl who was born in Reynosa.

It is not known whether Jose Maria bought his property north of Victoria in the Nursery area or whether it was a land grant; but it was here that Jose Maria and his wife raised five children: Mauro, Manuel, Librado, Jesus, and Tony. They lived in a three-room house that contained a bedroom, a commissary, and a kitchen. A big porch ran from one end of the house to the other.

The early business on the ranch included raising cattle as well as corn, cotton, horses, and farm animals. After Jose Maria's death, all five children inherited the ranch from their father. Mauro eventually bought Jesus's and Tony's shares and part of Librado's. Mauro and Manuel continued to manage the ranch—each running his own part. My daddy, Mauro, was in the horse business, too, and drove horses to Kansas.

My father and mother, Rosa Gutierrez Gonzales, raised seven children on the ranch: Mary, Mauro, Jr., Henry, Frances, Sophie, Nellie, and myself,

Felice. After our father's death in 1941, the ranch was inherited by the three surviving daughters, Frances de la Garza, Felice Gonzales, and Sophie Brown, and by my brother Mauro's daughter, Bertha Zamora.

At this time, the running of the ranch fell to me, and I have managed it for my two sisters from 1941 until the present. For twenty-two years, I was helped by my foreman, Marion Ohrt. Now his son David has taken over that job. I raised cattle, cotton, and maize and shipped corn to support the ranch. My niece, Bertha Zamora, is running her ranch.

The Fortran Ranch was purchased from the Galveston-Indianola Railroad in 1902 by my father and added to the family holdings. The Gonzales land is still owned and ranched by the remaining female heirs of Jose Maria Gonzales.

Felice Gonzales

**Jose Maria Gonzales
Rancher and Farmer
1842–1899**

**Mauro Gonzales
Rancher
1862–1941**

**Manuel Gonzales
Rancher
1874–1956**

Richard Harris and Agnes Murphy, on the Murphy Ranch.

The Murphy Ranches

The Murphy ranches trace back to Nicholas Fagan, the early Texas patriot and Irish immigrant. After his arrival in Texas at the old town of Copano in 1829, Fagan searched the area for a place to settle. He finally decided to locate on the South Bend of the San Antonio River. After Power and Hewetson settled their colonists in the area, Nicholas Fagan joined them and became part of their colony. Because of this, he was entitled to a league and a *labore* of land, which added to his already substantial holdings. After Power's Irish colony was settled, a small community was formed in the area with the Sidick, Teal, McDonough, and Fagan families living as neighbors.

Nicholas Fagan's daughter, Annie, who was born in Ireland, married Peter Teal in 1833, and they had two children. They lived on Teal's ranch near the Don Carlos de la Garza Ranch. Julia Victoria Teal was their only surviving daughter. Julia inherited land in the Teal survey through her mother, who had inherited from her father, Nicholas Fagan.

Michael Murphy arrived in this country from Ireland in 1855. He located in Victoria County in 1871, where he ranched and became a merchant and ferryman. He had property near Carlos Lake.

When Julia Teal and Michael Murphy married at La Bahia, their properties were joined to become the Murphy ranches. At Michael's death, his son, James Joseph ("Jim"), took over management of the Murphy ranches for his mother.

Julia died in 1923, leaving five heirs: Rose Murphy Morris, Grace Murphy Gaffney, William Murphy, Agnes Murphy, and Jim Murphy. The ranch was divided among them. Some of this land is still run as cattle ranches by the heirs of Julia Teal Murphy and Michael Murphy.

Marye Murphy Greer

Michael Murphy
Rancher
1838–1895

James Joseph Murphy
"Jim"
Rancher
1872–1952

Agnes Murphy
"Miss Aggie"
Rancher
1891–1980

Julia Victoria Teal Murphy
Rancher
1852–1923

Grace Murphy Gaffney
Rancher
1886–1957

James Joseph Murphy, Jr.
Rancher
1907–1980

The Rydolph Ranch

Pete Rydolph, born in 1888 to Fred and Rosie Bass Rydolph in Bloomington, Texas, was one of eight children. His family came to Texas from Botetourt, Virginia, and he grew up on the 200 acres his parents owned near the McFaddin Ranch in Victoria County.

As a child, Pete learned to be a skilled hunter and was trained by his father in farming and ranching. As a young man, he became a successful

Old Rydolph homestead near McFaddin, Texas, 1913.

trapper and fur buyer because the area then abounded in fur-bearing animals. He shipped pelts to the F. C. Taylor Fur Company in St. Louis, Missouri, and was the first person to ship via the B&M Railroad from Mariana, now known as McFaddin.

He was a very frugal man, always wisely investing the money he earned. He purchased land near Bloomington, which proved to be excellent cow and oil country. The Rydolph Ranch raised cattle, swine, horses, sheep, goats, and crops of corn, cotton, hay, and other grains. The cattle were shipped to the Houston Packing Company or sold to local meat markets. The success of the Rydolph Ranch can be attributed to the owner's frugality, his hard work, and his ability to trade close.

From the archives of local historian Henry Hauschild.

**Pete Rydolph
Rancher
1888–1980**

**Gertrude Rydolph
Rancher
1886–1981**

The Swickheimer Ranch

The story of the Swickheimer Ranch begins in Germany, where the family originated. John Swickheimer arrived in this country in 1850 and settled with his wife, Anna, on an Ohio farm where they raised two sons, Dave and George. By the late 1800s, both brothers had settled in Texas, where they contributed greatly to the building of Goliad County, but only George remained there permanently.

George Swickheimer in front of Swickheimer Ranch House, Fannin, Texas, early 1900's.

George Julius
Rancher
1860–1928

Lula Goff Swickheimer
Rancher
1872–1960

W. D. Swickheimer
(seated)

Lee Swickheimer
Rancher
1899–1963

George Glover Swickheimer
Rancher
1911–1981
(standing)

George Julius Swickheimer and his wife, Lula M. Goff, purchased a large piece of the Payne-Briscoe property on the San Antonio River in 1901. This was the beginning of the Swickheimer Ranch, which still remains in the family today. It has been run successively by George Julius, the founder, and by his two sons, George Glover and Lee. After their deaths, the ranch was inherited by George's children, Georgia Lee and David, who manage the operation through the ML Cattle Company. This company, established in 1890, has always managed the family's land and cattle holdings down through the years.

Georgia Lee Swickheimer

The O'Brien Ranches

**John Morgan O'Brien
Rancher
1866–1941**

The history of the O'Brien ranches begins in much the same way as the history of other ranches in the area. The family had been induced to come to Texas from Ireland by *empresario* James Power. Thomas O'Brien, his wife Isabella (Elizabeth), who was Power's sister, and their two sons, John and Morgan, sailed for America aboard the *Heroine* from Ballygarrett, Wexford, Ireland. Unfortunately, O'Brien died during the voyage. His widow and two sons landed at New Orleans and shortly thereafter continued on to Texas. They arrived at Copano and settled in Refugio in August 1834.

The Isabella O'Brien grant was located just north of Refugio, and Isabella and her sons established the original O'Brien Ranch on this property. They raised cattle to support themselves, probably Longhorns and then Brahmans and Herefords.

Morgan O'Brien remained a bachelor, and John O'Brien married Johanna Whelan. They had four children, to whom they left the ranches when they died. Their only son, John Morgan, carried on the tradition of ranching for the family. From 1927 to 1934, he added property at Greta and Quincy to the family holdings. After his death, the property was inherited by his son, John James, born in 1898, who added to the family holdings by purchasing the Greta Farm and the Sarco Ranch. He also added some small parcels of land to the Sarco as they came up for sale.

John J. O'Brien married Fern Dolores Ohler in 1924. Two of their children, John Morgan O'Brien and Janie O'Brien Harkins, are ranching the

**John James O'Brien
Rancher
1898–1975**

family holdings today and have added land to the ranches in Goliad County.

Cattle ranching has always been the family business, to which oil and gas were added after their discovery in the Refugio area in the 1930s. The original Isabella O'Brien grant is still in the family and is currently being ranched by Janie O'Brien Harkins.

The O'Brien ranches still try new types of cattle, crossbreeding to improve their stock as did their forefathers. O'Brien heirs today run the land acquired by the family in the colonial days of Texas.

**Dudley Skeen
Business Manager, O'Brien Ranches**

Patrick Hughes Welder, Sr.
Rancher
1830–1902

The Welder Ranches

The Welder ranches on the coastal plains of South Texas trace their origin to the family's three immigrant ancestors — Portilla, Power, and Welder — and to the intermarriages of their children. Portilla and Power were recipients of Mexican land grants, and the Welders, who came to Texas as permanent residents in 1836, were entitled to and received headrights. These ancestral lands are still held by some of their descendants into the sixth and seventh generations.

Felipe Roque de la Portilla, born in Santander, Spain, came to Mexico about 1786. He was married to a Spanish maiden, a native of Mier, on November 12, 1799, by Father Nicholas Balli. Church records show that the ceremony took place in the Balli Chapel at the old settlement known as La Feria. Portilla is recognized by historians for his attempted colonization of Villa San Marcos de Neve, an area near the present town of San Marcos. This settlement of Mexican citizens proved to be an unsuccessful venture; floods and constant harassment by the Indians doomed it to failure. Portilla, his wife, Maria Ignacio de la Garza, their children, and the colonists returned to Mexico.

A few years later, the family came to the coastal area of Texas, where Portilla and his sons were granted several leagues of land on the Aransas River by Jose Jesus Vidaurri of the Power-Hewetson Colony. The daughters, Maria Dolores and Maria Tomasa, figure importantly here, for both of them married James Power — first one and then the other.

Pen work at Welder Vidauri Ranch, Refugio County.
Photo by Roger Fleming. Courtesy of Institute of Texan Cultures.

James Power of County Wexford, Ireland, came to America and was in and out of Texas and Mexico for the first quarter of the nineteenth century. As an *empresario*, he was given permission by the Mexican authorities to bring colonists into this area, where he co-founded the Power-Hewetson Colony. At one time, Power was in possession of many leagues of land. Unfortunately, due to a technicality in the law, he lost many leagues when the courts repudiated his claims and ruled in favor of his adversary. A tract of land on Chiltipin Creek adjoining the Portilla grants was given to Power by the Mexican land commissioner and is a part of the Welder ranches today.

John James Welder
"Jay"
Rancher
1854–1923

James Power married Maria Dolores Portilla in 1832 in old San Patricio, and they had two children, James and Dolores Power. Dolores married John Welder, and they were the parents of ten children. After the tragic death of Maria Dolores at her brother's ranch, Las Rucias, Power married her sister, Maria Tomasa Portilla, by whom he had five children. Tomasa raised Dolores's children as well as her own.

It should be noted that Colonel Power put his funds, and indeed his very life, in jeopardy more than once in the cause of the Texian colonists and was a signer of the Texas Declaration of Independence. He is also recognized by many historians for his contributions to the freedom and welfare of the citizens during the Texas Revolution, the days of the Republic, and after Texas became a state. It would seem that there was no justice for him, for I believe he died a defeated man.

The third ancestor, Franz Welder, his wife, Anna Maria Hannes, and their children, all natives of Bavaria, came to the eastern shores of America in 1830, making their home in New York. They heard about Dr. John Charles Beales, who was soon to leave New York for Texas to establish the Rio Grande Colony and a villa called Dolores, and the Welders went to Texas. The colony did not prosper and the colonists dispersed, with the Welders going to San Fernando, Mexico. They remained there for only a short time, later moving downriver to Matamoros. When Anna Welder died there, Franz and the children decided to return to the Copano Bay area, their first Texas port of entry in 1833. They landed at Black Point sometime in May 1836.

The Welder family settled on Live Oak Peninsula, near James Power, and

James Francis Welder, Sr.
Rancher
1863–1931

John James Welder II
Rancher
1889–1936

Robert "Rob" Hughes Welder
Rancher
1891–1953

a few years later applied for headrights. Franz Welder and two of his sons, John and Thomas, went into the cattle business, the father alone and the brothers together. The first land owned by the brothers was a one-hundred-acre tract at Shell Reef on the Aransas River, which they bought from Philip Dimmitt. They built a home there and established a small ranch. Being good businessmen, and with a bit of luck, they soon acquired large

Roger Fleming
Naturalist and Photographer
Rancher

Foreman
Welder Ranches
Vidauri
1901–1971

herds and tracts of land in Refugio, San Patricio, and Bee counties. Franz retired from active business, dividing his herd and land between John and Thomas. He died in old St. Mary's in 1883.

Thomas ("Tom") made his home near St. Mary's, where his children were born. After he died in 1865, his widow, Louisa Hennenberg Welder, moved to Bee County, where their descendants still hold the same ranches founded by him. John and his wife, Dolores Power Welder, lived for a time on the Aransas River close to the northern boundary of the Portilla grant. They also lived on Live Oak Peninsula and eventually built a home in Refugio. All of their ten children were born in what is now San Patricio County.

In May 1877, John Welder and a companion were both murdered on the road between Refugio and St. Mary's. The companion was shot to conceal the motive for the crime. Welder had been involved with a neighbor over a serious land dispute, and the court had ruled in favor of Welder. This enraged the neighbor, and he saw to it that Welder would not live to enjoy his legal victory. After the loss of her husband, the widow Dolores and their youngest children moved to Victoria, about 1887, where some of the older children were already living.

After the death of John Welder, and before and after the death of Dolores Welder in 1898, their holdings were bought, traded, and exchanged among their ten heirs. Their son, John James, and his wife, Eliza Hughes Welder, made their headquarters in San Patricio County, a few miles north of Sinton. In addition to their original holdings in Refugio, San Patricio, Nueces, and Bee counties, they acquired large pastures in Victoria and Calhoun counties. Portions of the Calhoun land had been passed down to

James F. "Jim" Welder, Jr.
Rancher
1896–1941

Patrick Hughes Welder, Jr.
Rancher
1902–1946

W. D. "Billy" Welder
Rancher
1924–1972

Eliza Welder by her father, Patrick Hughes, and her grandparents, Winn and Martha Ann M. Chapman Traylor. The ranches of John and Eliza H. Welder have been divided several times and are now in the possession of grandchildren, heirs of their sons John James ("Jay") Welder, Robert ("Rob") Hughes Welder, and Patrick Hughes Welder.

Through his will, Rob Welder established the Welder Wildlife Refuge, a private foundation with more than 7,000 acres, which provides a haven for the study of wild species of all kinds and functions as a cattle ranch as well. The heirs of Jay Welder operate ranches on some of the Victoria and Calhoun county pastures. An heir of Patrick Welder holds land in Victoria, Calhoun, San Patricio, and other South Texas counties.

James Francis Welder, Sr., son of John and Dolores Welder, and his wife, Katie Owens, established their headquarters at Vidauri on land granted to James Power. The family acquired large adjoining tracts and land in other South Texas counties. These ranches are still intact, have never been partitioned, and are owned by the J. F. Welder heirs under the management of his grandson, Leo J. Welder of Victoria. The ranches of John and Dolores Welder's daughters—Lina Welder, Lizzie Welder, and Agnes Welder Fleming—are now owned by Agnes Fleming's heirs.

For well over a century, the Welder families have passed on their holdings to succeeding generations, descendants of those three Europeans, Portilla, Power, and Welder. These men of diverse backgrounds shared one common objective—to seek a better life for themselves and a future for their children. They came to what they thought would be "the promised land." What they encountered, however, was a wilderness, beautiful but desolate, filled with danger, uncertainty, and change. Somehow they endured, as many others did in that era. They managed to survive the hardships that plagued their daily lives and built the foundations of the ranches as they are today.

Lela Welder Cliburn

L-R, Clyde Bauer, Tom Traylor, Bull Harvey, Bud Harvey.

The Traylor Ranches

The Traylor family originated in France. Winn Traylor, who was born in Georgia, was a brickmaker in Alabama before moving to Texas in 1839. He received his land grant in 1840 and lived on it until his death in 1883. He lived in Texas during the pioneer days when settlers were still fighting the Indians, and would often tell tales of these adventures to his friends.

Upon his death, his ranch was inherited by his son, William B. Traylor, who continued to run cattle on this land near Victoria. William's son, Thomas P. ("Tom") Traylor, was the next heir to this ranch. He was a man much beloved by his cowhands, his friends, and his associates. His son, Billy, died at the age of seventeen, so his daughter Maddeline's husband, Clyde Bauer, ran the ranch after Tom's death in 1952. Clyde and Maddeline had three children—Thomas, Barbara Bauer Briggs, and Frances Bauer Wedemeier. The ranch was bought from the Traylor family in 1985 by my husband, Robert W. Briggs, Jr., who continues to run this 1840 land grant as a cattle ranch.

Barbara Bauer Briggs

Winn Traylor
Rancher
1807–1883

William B. Traylor
Rancher
1835–1913

Thomas P. "Tom" Traylor
Rancher
1871–1952

Clyde Bauer
Rancher
1907–1976

Billy Traylor
Rancher
1906–1925

Thomas Traylor Bauer
Rancher
1944–1976

Edgar Albrecht at old Albrecht Ranch House, built 1890.

The Albrecht Ranch

William F. Albrecht I, son of one of seven brothers, came to this country from Germany in 1855 or 1856. He was about eight years old at the time and arrived with his parents, Christoph and Johanna Albrecht. Christoph and his brother, Andrew, were the last members of their family to emigrate because the German government disapproved of people leaving the country.

Another brother, Frederick, had arrived in Texas around 1848 and purchased his own ranch. His land was passed along to his son, Frederick, Jr., who eventually willed it to his son, Edgar, who manages the ranch today.

When Christoph and Johanna arrived at Indianola, they thought about settling somewhere in the Meyersville area. By a stroke of luck, they happened upon yet another Albrecht brother, August, who was hunting at the time in the area near Victoria. He had arrived in this country about a year earlier. So that is where the newcomers settled.

Christoph Albrecht
Rancher
1820–1897

Johanna Albrecht
Rancher
1823–1892

While Christoph was away fighting in the Civil War from 1861 to 1865, William cared for his mother. He began buying land at a very early age, earning the money by skinning dead cattle that froze during the bad winters. He also earned money by roping and branding unmarked cattle.

William purchased his first parcel of land from his parents in 1874 for four dollars an acre. It was a 172-acre tract on Little Coleto Creek, also known as Eighteen Mile Creek. Over the years he purchased or traded for many parcels of land, and his holdings eventually totaled more than 100,000 acres.

William had a large family, and upon his death his property was divided among his ten living children. The original part of the ranch is still held by the W. D. ("Billy") Albrecht family.

W. D. Albrecht

Frederick Albrecht, Sr.
Rancher
1824–1894

William F. Albrecht I
Rancher
1848–1909

William F. Albrecht II
Rancher
1897–1971

Frederick C. Albrecht, Jr.
Rancher
1866–1959

Caroline Albrecht
Rancher
1869–1947

John H. Elkins
Rancher
1855–1928

The Perkins-Elkins Ranch

This ranch came from the Elkins side of my husband's family. Samuel Elkins, his wife, Susie Turner, and their son, John H., took two years to get here by covered wagon from Arkansas and Louisiana. They decided to come to Texas because Mrs. Elkins' two brothers, Jack and Boswell Turner, had already settled here. Jack ran the ferry on the San Antonio River and Boswell farmed in the area.

Samuel, Susie, and John Elkins arrived around Christmas, 1865, and settled a short way from the present ranch house, probably on a land grant or land purchased from the government. They made their living raising cattle and farming, and added additional land to the ranch whenever they could.

After settling here, the Elkins family grew. Another son, Charlie W., was born, and then two daughers, Nettie, who remained unmarried (as did her brother John), and Georgia, who married Emmet Perkins.

Eventually, the Boswell Turner property was added to the ranch. No one knows whether it was inherited or purchased, but it is now part of the Perkins-Elkins Ranch.

The Perkins family came from Missouri and, like the Elkins family, were not really ranchers until they arrived here. Emmet, who married Georgia Elkins, was born on the O'Connor Ranch near the Motts. Their son, Willis W., who was to become my husband, was born in the Sarco community on the ranch in 1901 and lived in Goliad as a child. Willis and I were married in 1933, and we moved to Corpus Christi with Humble Oil and Refining in 1942.

Nettie Elkins
Rancher
1877–1963

Georgia Elkins Perkins
Rancher
1874–1959

Emmet Perkins
Rancher
1876–1953

Around this time we began to realize that Aunt Nettie Elkins, who lived in the old home place at Sarco, badly needed help. We began commuting on weekends and holidays and added some more land to the ranch and began building fences and pens. When we first came back to the ranch around 1948, we had no power, no telephone, and the roads were impossible in bad weather.

But Willis was a determined and ambitious man who usually got what he went after. Before long, by the late 1950s, we had windmills, electricity, and a paved road that is now Farm Road 2441. It is one of the original roads in

Willis W. Perkins
Rancher
1901–1982

Texas, and was traveled by Santa Anna and his men. And finally, after ten years, we got a telephone.

The Perkins-Elkins Ranch has always been known for its tradition of extending hospitality to one and all. Willis always enjoyed opening the ranch to hunters, but insisted that the rules of the state and the rules of sportsmanship must always be observed. After my husband died in 1982, I continued to run the ranch. We have been neighbors of the O'Connors since the early 1900s and have never had problems over fences or cattle. Although there have been some hard times over the years, this has always been a friendly place to ranch.

Jeanette Johnstone Perkins

The Hanley Ranch

My mother and father, Katherine and Robert Stroebel, were born in Germany. I don't really know the exact years that they arrived in this country, but it was way back in the 1800s.

Bud and Ada Hanley at old Hanley Ranch House, 1906.

My mother had a sister who was already in this country. Her sister was so homesick that mother came to visit her, and never went back to Germany. She and my father met over here. They were both working for the same family in Illinois. Mother worked in the house, and my father did outside work. They eventually married, and the whole family moved to Texas for Mother's health. They settled on the Fleming Prairie in Victoria County.

In my mind's eye, I can still see my mother looking out the window during a thunderstorm. She never said a word, she just stared at the lightning. I often wondered what she was thinking about. Home, I guess.

C. C. Hanley
"Bud"
Rancher
1866–1941

C. C. Hanley
"Dick"
Rancher
1901–1981

C. C. ("Bud") Hanley, my father-in-law, worked for Jake Castle, a cattle buyer. The Hanleys originally came from Virginia, and his wife was a Goff from this area. Bud eventually became a cattle buyer himself. He first bought fifteen acres. Then after he and his wife, Ada Douglas, who grew up on Manahuila Creek, were married, they built the original ranch house. Each of their four children, Maude Hanley Scott, Lanier Hanley, Nott Houston Hanley, and my husband, C. C. ("Dick") Hanley, were born there in the old "fireplace room."

Bud eventually accumulated 2,400 acres by buying little pieces of land around the original 15 acres. I don't know exactly when he began full-time ranching, but he would keep a few head of cattle when he was buying and selling. Dick never called the place a ranch. He felt that it was silly to call any piece of land under 10,000 acres a ranch.

It was on the Fleming Prairie that Dick and I met and married. We had one son, Charles Scott Hanley. Dick and I lived on the ranch and raised cattle. My husband was the only child interested in ranching.

Bud Hanley died in 1941 without a will, so all the children got together and gave the ranch to his wife. Dick was the executor of the will and ran the ranch for his mother. After her death, it was left to all the children, who eventually divided it.

Dick and I continued to ranch our part of the land. During the screwworm days, we had our hands full. I helped him every day. It made me very nervous when I had to drive the truck and he roped cattle out of the back.

We worked side by side until shortly before he died. The last two years of his life, he really couldn't do anything, and I took over the ranch. But he was still there to talk about it.

After Dick's death, I took over, and Willie Reyes has been my foreman all these years.

This ranch will go to my grandchildren. Several of them are interested in running the place, but nowadays you have to have another job to survive. Ranching a place this size just isn't economical any more.

I don't know what will happen to this ranch—I kind of hope the children will keep it together.

I've lived here since I was married at eighteen, and I'm eighty-four now. Naturally, I love the place. I keep the cattle going even though it is hard work. Selling the cattle would be like selling part of Dick.

Mabel Stroebel Hanley

THE CODE OF THE RANCHES

- *Never talk about how many head of cattle you have and how much land you own, and never ask another man about his holdings.*

- *Don't say something bad about a man's cow or horse; say nothing if you can't say something good.*

- *Try to brag on another man's mount or animal.*

- *Don't pry into a man's ranch operation; don't ask specific questions.*

- *Never use another man's horses or equipment.*

- *Never wear spurs in the house.*

- *Never ask a man about his wife unless he mentions her first; but it's okay to ask how his family is.*

- *Never reprimand a cowhand in front of the other men.*

- *Be honest with people.*

- *Don't steal.*

- *Be someone who can be trusted to help a man if he is in trouble.*

- *Don't run a horse unless you have to.*

- *Don't be rough with a horse or any animal unnecessarily.*

- *Stay out of trouble.*

- *Speak up for each other.*

- *No fighting.*

- *The rules are different on each ranch; check them.*

- *Don't talk about the boss.*

- *Don't talk about each other off the ranch.*

- *Don't tattle on each other.*

- *A man's word is his bond.*

CHAPTER THREE

STEWARDS OF THE LAND: THE RANCHERS

Tom O'Connor, Jr. [III]
Photo by Louise S. O'Connor.

STEWARDS OF THE LAND: THE RANCHERS

The multigenerational ranchers of this area feel a strong bond with the land, a responsibility to those who came before them and to those who follow.

Most began working at a young age, learning from the older cowhands. They can be tough, almost ruthless if necessary, to protect their land. However, beneath this rugged exterior can be found souls more sensitive than you might expect. There are strong, artistic sensibilities among most ranchers. It is not a business that attracts those with mathematical or mechanical minds.

The land is very demanding. These Coastal Bend ranchers do not spend a lot of time away from home. Few travel extensively, and when they do, they are eager to get back home. Most do not like mountains. They understand and prefer their flat land.

Time builds attachment to the land, and these men and women are fourth-, fifth-, and even sixth-generation ranchers. There is a feeling of tradition, obligation, and heritage; and today's ranchers do not want to be the ones who lose it. Weekend ranchers are not very highly thought of here.

Their recreation and entertainment is often ranch-related. Rodeos, hunting, horse racing and even polo, as well as just riding around looking at the

Ranch scene, Refugio County, Texas, early 1900's.

land and animals, fill as much of their free time as any other activities. The owners' individual personalities strongly affect the personalities of their ranches. Every rancher I interviewed displayed a great sense of humor, as if dealing with God's reality gives them a healthy attitude about everything.

The ranchers help each other and share information among themselves. There is little reason for competition among them, as they have a great respect for each other's individual abilities and rights of ownership and private property. There are virtually no social or economic distinctions among them. Ranch and herd size does not matter. Above all, they have a boundless respect for their cattle, acknowledging that it was this animal that made the raw land valuable. Breeding cattle is fun to them. It is a creative endeavor.

Ranchers have a code of ethics and behavior among themselves, as do the cowhands. Each ranch has its own set of social rules and etiquette. These people and this culture do not accept those who do not understand this way of life. If strangers are rejected, however, it is not merely because they are strangers but because they refuse to understand ranch life as it is or because they attempt to ridicule or disrupt its natural order.

There is a strong bond of friendship between the owners and the cowhands, reinforced by family ties, mutual respect, and time spent together through many generations. The cowhands were worked hard, but the men who bossed them were right by their side, working every bit as hard. The relationship between the ranchers and their cowhands is also the result of the *patron* system, which has links with feudalism, Latin American peonage, and Southern slavery. It was a system in which a large landowner would maintain a permanent labor force on his land. These workers were paid subsistence wages, but their needs—and those of their families—were taken care of from the crib to the grave. The owner provided for their housing,

Ranch recreation, bull riding.

food, medical care, transportation, place of worship, and their children's education. Thus the ranches became self-contained communities, with generation after generation living and working together in the same place. I tried for six years, almost on a daily basis, to get someone who had experienced the *patron* system to criticize it. I was never successful, even though the interviewees were free to say whatever they chose.

The land here owns the people, not the other way around. It forms their opinions and actions. Everything that they do in some way goes back to the land. All of the people I spoke with would sacrifice themselves and their

L-R, Newman, Thomas O'Connor [II], Joseph O'Connor, ranch gardener.

comfort to protect and save it. To many observers, ranchers were the first environmentalists. Their whole mission in life was to protect the land. They feel they damage themselves if they damage their land. This love of the land comes from a deep respect for the space that they control, a realization that the land is an irreplaceable resource. Their attachment to the land is about the earth itself, not about what the land can do for them. Ranchers and cowhands alike are acutely aware of their environment and are fascinated by the sights, sounds, and smells around them.

Land is the ranchers' biggest asset, and they entertain no thoughts of selling it. They will continue to try to protect and keep it. Just as the owners need their land, the land needs the owners—people who are willing to cherish it and safeguard it from those who see land only as a source of economic profit. Oil has played a prominent role in the entire ranching culture here, either by its presence or absence. Everyone appreciates the benefits resulting from the oil income and realizes that many ranches exist today because of these revenues. Yet, because they feel that oil production tampers with the precious land, an undercurrent of resentment is discernible when talking to most ranchers.

Sunday afternoon horse races. Junior Groll on Blackout, 1947.

The women who ranch this area, by fate or by choice, work in a profession usually reserved for males. Much like the Coastal Bend itself, they are a cross between Southern gentlewomen and the women of the Western frontier. These women had role models, too. Often it was a mother or grandmother who ranched, although just as many were trained by a father, a husband, or grandfather. Even if these role models were not actually engaged in some phase of ranching, they were all strong, gutsy people who had a deep, abiding interest in nature.

Female attributes are very useful in certain aspects of the ranching

"I do not feel that I am holding the land for the benefit of anyone other than my heirs. We owe the land everything. We sprang from it. In our family, we are fortunate to know that we are going back into that land when we die."

Tom O'Connor, Jr. [III]
Rancher

business. The lady ranchers I interviewed believe that they are more attentive to detail, are better observers, and are more meticulous. They approach things more logically and tend to rely more on organization than physical strength as a means of resolving difficulties. The women do not feel any alienation from society because of their work, and the men do not resent a woman who ranches out of necessity or who occupies a managerial position. If there is any resentment, it is directed toward those women who merely play at cowboying just to have something to do. The ranch women agree that the men are very helpful to them, seeming to understand that, as girls, they were not trained from childhood as the boys were.

Most of the women on the ranches study and regularly attend seminars and training programs about the cattle business, and they get together and help each other more often than the men. They practice the Western custom of neighboring and seem to have a stronger understanding of and respect for the feelings of humans and animals alike. In their own quiet way, these ladies demand and get equal treatment in the ranching world.

The owners and their cowhands alike have worked on this land side by side for as many as five or six generations, sharing the work and the play,

Joe Keefe and Kai Buckert at the polo grounds, McFaddin Ranch.

the tears and the laughter, the good times and the bad. Often it is difficult to tell one group from another.

THE LAND: A Powerful Mistress

"There is a stewardship and ownership. You must leave it better than you found it. It's only mine to use."

Thomas Marion O'Connor [II]
Rancher

It all goes back to a love of the land. It's worldwide, a part of human nature. Owning cattle is often just a good excuse to own land.

If any of us had to give up anything, that land would be the last. It is the biggest asset we have, and we have a lot of respect for it. You can't abuse it. The land is too strong, it won't allow it. We damage ourselves if we damage the land. It is tangible — the ultimate asset. It cannot be produced again. We own it and we have to look down the line. We take care of it for future generations. Animals and land go hand in hand, but our love of the land is the stronger feeling.

Once you accept the fact that you will probably not make money in the cattle business, then your main job becomes the stewardship of the land. Protecting the land is our job. Most of us do this for the land's sake because we love it, not just to pass it along to our children. We are taught this respect for land from an early age. We must give a lot of consideration to conservation. To do this job, you have to have a fondness for the land. It has to be important to you. Progress threatens these ranches. Seeing the loss of property is sad, because very few people have that feeling for anything any more. When someone loses something they feel very strongly about, it is a tragedy.

Things have changed rapidly in our lifetime. Maybe it will begin to slow down soon. People are drifting into an easier way of life that includes less caring for nature. Ranching means being a slave to the land, but isn't that better than being a slave to some of the things people are attached to today? We have been on this land so damned long, we want it to stay in the family if possible. The attachment to the land among ranchers is most definitely an emotional and spiritual one — certainly much more than an economic attachment.

"The main job of a ranch owner is to protect what's there. Our forefathers were true Southern gentlemen. They wanted the land for their heirs. They were slaves to their ranches. You don't do this for yourself. You do it for family."

Roger Welder
Rancher

We will all fight to keep this open country. It would be devastating to lose it. It would be a sad thing for everyone, even if you don't own it. The tradition is the freedom and the space around us. Unless you have had this experience, it is hard to explain. Some people have the need for space and for solitude. This seems to be the strongest need in us ranchers. Even when the land belongs to many people, we each seem to feel that it is ours. We have put a lot of work into this land, but many of the absentee owners have these same strong feelings about the land. There must be something genetic about it.

Ranchers were the first environmentalists. Their whole "put together" is to protect the land.

It seems that if you grow up in the country, you either stay with the land or you head for the bright lights. Many eventually return to the country. Freedom, space, and nature are powerful mistresses.

The clan structure is important to landholding. The corporate structure doesn't work the land well.

Our concept of the land here is going to change. It is better that we choose how that change is going to occur.

The younger generation seems to be thinking about this in a constructive way. They will have a tough job hanging on to it.

Buster Bickford, T. Michael O'Connor, Freddy Fagan, Wallace Shay, Claude K. McCan, Jr., Bill Welder, Thomas Marion O'Connor [II], Lawrence Wood

Thoughts on the Bovine Aristocracy

This ranch has been in my family for one hundred and twenty years. Keerans have always been landowners and agriculturists, but I can do a much better pedigree on any one of my cows than I can on myself.

I grew up here on the HK Ranch. There were no roads in or out. Nobody wanted them because they thought they might hurt the horses' feet. Since there weren't any roads, we couldn't get into town to go to school. From the first grade until I was a sophomore in high school, Mama had tutors for my sister, Gertrude Emily, and me out at the ranch. I really didn't get a decent education. There was no competition, and I read English history while I was floating in the pool. Mama didn't let me do a whole lot of reading anyway. My eyes were weak, and she was afraid I would ruin them, and wouldn't be able see the cattle well enough to run the ranch.

In ten years we had forty tutors. Life out here was pretty rough on some of them. To give you an example, one time Mama went off to buy some calves. She always went in her old car so the sellers wouldn't raise their price when they saw her coming. After she got those calves home, one of them got sick and she had it moved into the living room so she could watch it. The only way old Mr. Hall, the tutor, could get to the bathroom was to go through the room where the bull calf was. After several weeks of this, Mr. Hall went to Mama's room one morning and said, "Either the bull goes, or I go." Mama asked him what was wrong. He said he had to stay in the bathroom all night, because every time he tried to get back to his room the bull snorted. Mama fired him right then and there. She said she didn't want the likes of him teaching her children if he was scared of a little calf like that. "Hit the road, you sissified son of a bitch," she shouted, and that was the end of another tutor. Something like that happened to nearly every one of the poor things, and that was pretty much the story of my early education. Every time we managed to run a tutor off, we got a month's vacation until Mama found another.

We never associated much with other children except some who lived out here with the oil-field workers. Working cattle, riding horses, and getting rid of schoolteachers was about all we knew. When I was a sophomore, the

Henry Clay Koontz [IV].
Photo by DiAnne Malouf.

recruiter from Texas Military Institute came to the ranch and Mama decided that was a good place to send me. When I got there, I didn't know how to use a dial phone, or what it meant when the class bell rang. At home the tutors waited until I was through before we ended a class, or stopped everything and explained something to me if I didn't understand it. I stayed on at TMI, but it was sheer hell. I'd dream I was at the ranch, and when I woke up in the morning, I'd look out my window, see reality, and say, "My God!" I had never seen a football game and didn't even know how to put on a uniform. The first game we played was against the team from a school for the deaf. I couldn't see too good without my glasses, but I was big, and they told me just to charge ahead. One time I caught a pass and didn't know what to do with the ball, so I stood up and took a bow. It was a complete cultural shock, going from this ranch to TMI, but I got through it.

Some people ask me where I got my accent. I don't really know. Probably a composite of all my tutors. When I went off to TMI, they sent me to an elocution teacher to change my accent. But, after a month, the teacher quit because she was picking up my accent instead of changing it. We were pretty bad as kids. We terrorized the help, tried to drown the Shetland pony, and got rid of tutors. It kept us pretty busy.

Ranch people are eccentric. We won't turn loose of a fight for hell. We live in so much peace and quiet that we need something to stir up our juices occasionally. City people are looking for peace and quiet after a day at work. I never minded a fuss—it's exciting. I never step aside, I just go ahead on into them. We may not be considered normal in other cultures, but others sure as hell aren't normal when they come into ours. Out on these ranches, we have more opportunity to be individuals. We can do exactly as we want and it nurtures and feeds our unusual behavior. Our children are not as eccentric as we are. They have more contact with the outside world. For instance, I do exactly as I want to do, see who I want to see, and talk to whom I want to talk to. I want to be with interesting people and if I'm alone, I don't mind being alone. We are self-satisfied. We have a lot to do—there is always something to do on the ranch.

My children love the ranch, but they are all pursuing other careers. You have to be interested in this job to do it right. My ranch always makes a profit because I have always been terribly interested in cattle. I think that's why I'm successful. I know my business and I love being tops at it. I first got interested in cattle when I was a child and was given a dogie calf to raise. People learn ranching in different ways. Mechanically minded people are not good ranchers. Ranching and breeding cattle is an art—you either have it or you don't.

A rancher's medium is the cow and the bull. You use them to create better forms of both. You can call out an animal's name and a picture of him comes to me. I have a photographic memory for cattle. I can't remember people's faces nearly as well. In cattle breeding, the eye is the most important thing. Some people are using computers now. They can destroy entire herds of cattle this way. You need the instinct and the eye. That is what sums it all up.

I never felt out of kilter here. I can fit in with any group, except maybe the young executives who play golf and go to the country club. Although I had an unusual upbringing, my grandmother devoted a lot of time to teaching us etiquette. People have preconceived notions about ranchers, anyway. Sometimes I give them what they think they want to see, and sometimes I give them what I really am. Most people from other countries or even from other cities expect what they see on TV. Ranching is a prestigious business; farming is not. This is because the public sees it that way. It has been played up that way throughout history, and ranchers have been given a certain image. I think all of us ranchers use that image when it is to our advantage. I can act like a real bumpkin if necessary. You know, some people think we still shoot Indians before breakfast.

One of the things that I have to do that irritates me most is to sell my very finest cattle to people with money who have no earthly idea what they are doing. There is no security in the cattle business, even when you raise registered cattle. Things were kind of a mess when I took over these ranches during a big drought. I was left with a herd of very wild Brahmans. I didn't have a reputation as a breeder when I took over. The only identity I had was from my ancestors. I began by selling hay off the ranch until my herd became well known. The cattle's genes were good, but I needed a few years to hone their temperaments. I made my own reputation, and I am very proud of this fact.

As hard as I have worked on these cattle and as much as I love them, I still love the land better. You can always replace the animals. Our land has always been taken good care of. I think an owner should leave the land in as good shape as he found it or better. Land reform destroys the land. No one can make a decent living off a small place. It is nonproductive. Being able to maintain these large ranches here has done much to preserve the quality of the land.

Ranching to me is a hobby, a business, and a way of life. It's what I do for a living and for fun. It's what I am. A perfect day for me is when I can make some kind of cattle deal. I love the intrigue. It's fun, like playing cards. My definition of a fair trade is where both parties feel like they have screwed the other person just a little bit. Commercial cattle raisers like me are different from the old-time cowmen. I have to deal with the public, but this doesn't bother me. I don't feel like I have to put up with their B.S.— they have to put up with mine. Buyers are captive audiences for my afternoon's entertainment. It's where I rear back and show off me, my, and so forth, which we all love to do. Believe me, I give out more than I put up with. But I'm always in control, which is 100 percent important. You have to be in control. I'm used to that. This is only on the ranch. I don't mind not being in control when I'm off the ranch. Some people have to control everything, I don't. I just want total control on this ranch.

A woman's role on the ranch is very important. Mary Sue keeps the place comfortable and helps me cover ground. She organizes the social life of the ranch. We work together, we are a partnership. We'd better be with this much isolation. We have respect for and great pride in each other's roles.

Gertrude Emily and Henry Clay Koontz [IV]

I grew up around women running ranches. There is nothing threatening or foreign to me about having a woman involved in this work.

A lot of people want to get back to the land now. I can understand that. I love it out here. I couldn't live in town. I need the room. I'm used to everything I see being mine. You can have money in the bank, but you don't have the same feeling of possession that you do with land and cattle. It's a different feeling of ownership—any other kind is so intangible, not enjoyable. This is mine. I can see it, I enjoy it, I can feel it.

Our ranchers' code in the Coastal Bend is very strong. Never ask how many acres or how many cattle a man owns. Our word and reputation are important. We do what we say we are going to do. Even though these old traditions are carried on, we must change with the times. Changing can be fun if you are alive and moving. Every day is different, that's what I enjoy. You have to continually streamline.

Ranching is not a hard life, but sometimes I get tired of it. The bills keep coming in every month, but you do what you have to do. You can make it hard or easy on yourself. I hate living on a ranch in January and February. The pens are muddy, the cattle are thin, not breeding, not calving. It's a horrible time of year. But I love spring, summer, and fall. I love the sound of rain at the end of a drought, the sight of fat cattle, and the smell of springtime when the winter feed bills stop. I even love to go around the ranch tasting water out of all the wells; each one tastes different. Our area is unique in a way. We have all been here so long, and very little land is for sale. We have all known each other and lived adjacent to each other for so many years. We are set in our ways and there is a great deal of stability here.

I don't dream about cow-working, but I often stay up half the night plotting—that's a lot of the fun. I like to get involved in projects other than just the cattle—and I certainly enjoy my phone calls. Cowmen are more understanding than most businessmen. They have a broader comprehension of the real things in life. Men in other professions can turn off their work at the end of the day, but here, your work is never completed. The fences are never totally done, the water troughs are never all clean, the yard always needs work. It's never done. Still, I can't ever divorce myself from this place. It's like a child, it's a living thing. I would die without this ranch. I love it. The expanse, the space around me, the land, the freedom. I love it.

Henry Clay Koontz [IV]
Rancher
1934–1985

This interview with Henry Clay Koontz [IV] was never completed. He was killed by a drunk driver in an accident in 1985. He was coming home from looking at cattle. I miss him to this day; we should not have lost him. He was a precious and original jewel, and the world is much less bright without him.
—**L. O'C.**

Names from the Past

Sometimes the naming of pastures, wells, and other areas of the ranch made sense or had a history, and sometimes it didn't.

I never knew about the Red Well or the Middle Well. The Red Well has nothing around it that is red, and the Middle Well isn't in the middle of anything as far as I can see. Twin Mott Lake was named after a double mott of oak trees on the road down there, but all but one of those trees have long since died. Only the naming of that lake is left to remind us of something that is now gone.

Many pastures are named after old ranch hands who were with the ranches all their lives, or those that were particular favorites of the owners. For example, the Quedino pasture on the River Ranch was named after Tranquilino "Quedino" Rodriguez. The names of these pastures, lakes, and wells are names from the past, and are examples of the continuity and tradition that has existed on ranches until the present time.

Tom O'Connor, Jr. [III]
Rancher

Pasture Naming: How It Was in the Old Days

Back in the old days, or since my mother quit living in the Little House at the Melon Creek Ranch, no woman has been allowed in there. It was the bachelor quarters. I spent a many a day sittin' around there, listenin' to the old-timers talk about how pastures and wells got their names.

No one seems to know how the Alameda pasture got its name, but the Melon got its name from the creek. Paul Rainey was an Englishman, a pal of Mr. Tom's. He gave the ranch a bunch of mares, and the pasture they were kept in became the Rainey pasture. Often times, water wells were named after drillers, too. The original Old Man O'Connor married for the second time, late in life, to a woman named Helen Shelly. Shelly Field was named after her or her family, I guess. The old-timers around here said that the Saddle Blanket Pasture got its name because it was so wet one time that a saddle blanket would bog down if you threw it on the ground.

A bunch of Mexicans were camped out in the middle of the ranch many years ago cutting fence posts, and to this day the area is called the Mexican Water Hole. Twenty-Four Farms was an area that was cut up into twenty-four tenant farms—the venture failed, but the area has kept that name.

The old hands, and some that are still alive today, always refer to the Lake Pasture area of the River Ranch and the northern end of the Melon Creek Ranch as the Big Prairie and the Worldly Pasture. That was back before the ranches were divided, and to the cowhands that area was as big as the whole world. The fence that divided that area from the south end of the ranch was built in 1910, because of the tick-fever dippin' laws that came in around that time, and was always called the 1910 Fence.

I would love to have lived back in those days. It was a different world back then.

E. D. "Rusty" Coward
Foreman
O'Connor Melon Creek Ranch

The Cowaholics

"We're 'cowaholics.' That's why we keep it going. Wouldn't matter if we starved to death, we'd still have a cow out there to worry about."

Wallace Shay
Rancher

"That's all I know. It's a family tradition. The land came down to us through the family and that's important to me. I like it; that's why I keep on doing it. The family tradition is strong. The land is part of me."

John Morgan O'Brien
Rancher

"Why do I ranch? It's a tradition in my family. I don't know anything else and never really gave another profession much thought. I'm my own boss, and I love being outside. I have a lot of pride in the ranch."

Leo Welder
Rancher

"A cow and a plow was all I ever knew."

Herbert B. Bickford
"Buster"
Rancher

"Cowboyin' was a way to make a dollar. I didn't like the farm. There just wasn't nothin' in farming—never was and never will be."

Henry Morrow
Rancher

"I grew up on a ranch, following in my father's footsteps. The cowboy life, that's what I've always wanted."

Freddy Fagan
Rancher

"My grandfather Stoner tied me on a saddle when I was two. As soon as I was big enough, I went with the cow crowd. That was play to me. I always wanted to ranch; I was raised here. Even though I was prepared for a career in chemistry, it never occurred to me to be anything but a rancher. I do it because I love to work cattle, not because it is my responsibility."

Dennis M. O'Connor [II]
Rancher

"I didn't play cowboy; I worked cattle. My father taught me how to ranch. I don't know anything else. The cattle are what I love about it. I also love the land and being outside. What else is there?"

John J. Welder IV
Rancher
1913–1987

"I always wanted to ranch. I don't even know why. I guess it's because I own the land. It must be in my blood. I certainly don't do it for the profit. I love it in the spring when the calves hit the ground. I'll probably always run a few cows somewhere. It's a way of life."

Preston Austin Stofer
Rancher

"I can remember riding behind Hamp Terrell at two or three years old. I was always around ranching, and I'm happy in it. I admire the people, and I have a certain degree of freedom, even working for someone else. I like that. Who wouldn't? I'll keep my land if at all possible. It fed me, clothed me, and gave me good memories. It's part of me."

Leroy Tibiletti
Rancher, Foreman
Patrick Welder Ranch
Freer, Texas

"I wanted to be a cowboy ever since I can remember. Started working goats when I was six. I've just done it all my life. I love it."

Wesley Vivian
Rancher

"We're gonna keep it afloat. We're gonna keep it goin' even if it takes a different approach."

Patrick Hughes Welder, Jr.
"Pat"
Rancher

"I'm a flatlander; I understand flat country. It's an awesome feeling out on that prairie. You see a lot of sky."

Claude Kerry McCan, Jr.
Rancher

The *Patron* System: A Symbiosis

The *patron* system, the way it was explained to me, is this: An owner or an individual is in charge, and everyone owes him their allegiance. He, in turn, takes care of their needs and wants, and this arrangement is passed down from generation to generation on both sides. There was allegiance to the boss man or *caporal*, but the landowner got the primary loyalty. I can't think of another business where this exists—where the families know each other on a day-to-day basis.

There was a tremendous amount of loyalty on both sides, with the families growing up on the same piece of land and the children coming along behind them. They had the feeling it was partially theirs, even though it was not—a feeling for the land as if it had been their own.

I have the same feeling. I don't want to misuse it, because I have grown up on these ranches. I feel I am a part of it and it's a part of me. I'm sure that most people down here have the same feeling.

The *patron* system is more about the individual than the land, but they are so closely tied together that is is hard to say what is really going on. There are many instances of people leaving the land when it is sold to someone else. That indicates a loyalty to a person rather than a piece of land. Today, the *patron* system is frowned upon by certain labor unions, churches, etc., because they don't want people to feel obligated to work, period. That is the way the world is today. Observe our own government welfare systems, for instance.

A lot of people got upset when the ranch employees were put on a retirement plan. They liked it better the old way. I believe that they felt it was a more personal way of taking care of those who have taken care of you.

The employees' part of the *patron* system was to be loyal and work. They would be compensated for their work, but they were expected to work more diligently and be more committed to their job than someone who was hired

off the street. They were to be loyal and conscientious even when it was too cold or too hot or too wet. In return, the worker always had the security of knowing that his job was there and that his family would be taken care of as long as he did his job right and behaved in a civilized manner.

In the old days, the ranches provided the employees with homes, paid their utility, medical, and funeral bills, and educated their children on the ranches or at a nearby rural school. Today, we still provide the homes, utilities, and religious services. We help them with funerals and have a payback system for their medical bills. The ranches also pay for school lunches. Even though the income on these ranches is not high for the employees, those dollars are spendable income.

What happened to the *patron* system? I think one of the main reasons it went downhill was not that the ownership changed, but that the involvement of owners in other activities caused them to spend less and less time on the ranches. A close sense of community and constant involvement with the people is essential for the *patron* system to work. The younger generations in many of these families did not grow up with each other on the land, and this is not a close-knit society any more. People travel around too much now to maintain this kind of community. Everybody used to stay here and live here; now everyone is going somewhere else all the time. Much of this is related to the current speed and ease of transportation.

The main thing that broke up the *patron* system was this breakup of community. The schools are consolidated now, and parents are no longer closely involved with their children's education or with each other through the schools.

I think the government directly or indirectly had a major and adverse effect on ranching and, consequently, the *patron* system, with the enactment of the minimum wage law. This cut down on the return to the owner, and in turn he had to reduce the perks he could give to his employees. Once they were given a higher wage and told they had to take care of themselves, the strong bond that had existed between employer and employee was broken.

After World War II, many men did not come back to these ranches. They were trained and given skills that opened the world up to them and gave them the opportunity to get other jobs. However, many did come back to work right where their fathers, grandfathers, and even great-grandfathers had worked before them.

Can we ever go back to the old system? There are many families out here who feel that we have never left the system. They feel their obligation, and they are aware of our obligation when they have a need. But this is usually

only among the older families that have been around for many generations.

Most people who are severely critical of the system understand it as it was practiced in Mexico and South America with the peon system. Under that system, the *patron* owned everything and the peon had nothing. They were not rewarded in any way for their work, or if they were, it was only a minute amount compared with what they received under our system. I am sure there were exceptions to this rule as there are in any situation.

Our system here, even though it is an outcropping of the peon system, has a number of differences. Here the people are free to walk off or quit if they choose. Under the other system, if they tried to leave, drastic measures could be taken to stop them.

"It seemed like the bosses were our parents, too."

**Clayton Isaiah
L. V. Terrell
Tophands
O'Connor Ranches**

I think that our *patron* system is probably even more closely related to the slavery system than to the peon system of Latin America. In this part of the country, anyway, there was a certain amount of loyalty between the owner and the slaves and vice versa. The better a ranch or farm did economically, the better everyone lived, and this created a mutuality between the two groups. Again, there are exceptions to everything, but most people did not abuse their slaves. In fact, many owners continued to care for their people even after emancipation and at great cost to themselves. I think this occurred mainly out of the mutuality and loyalty I mentioned earlier.

On most of these ranches, the symbiotic relationship continues today to some degree, no matter what the government tries to legislate. I guess things have to change. Years ago, when someone wore out, you took care of him. People didn't live so long back then. Life expectancy is so high now, nobody could afford to support everyone who has had to retire.

**Dennis Williams
Foreman
O'Connor Brothers Ranches
Rancher**

Debts of Gratitude

Owners and workers were close in those days. Most of the cowhands were born and raised on our places; they were part of our family. The bosses became really involved with their ranch hands and were proud of their abilities—much more so than today.

But even today, there is a closeness that doesn't exist in other jobs. Everyone knows everyone else well. We all get great loyalty from our cowhands. They give a certain part of themselves to us. We feel a debt of gratitude to them, and we in turn try to make them feel important and take pride in their work.

John Cliburn, Henry Clay Koontz [IV], Bill Welder, Dennis Williams

"Most of the cowhands I worked didn't know what politics was— they were only concerned about who was sheriff, and they wanted that to be Ira Heard. They had no more idea than a goose how he got to be sheriff nor gave a damn. He was just the high sheriff, and he took care of them."

**Tom O'Connor, Jr. [III]
Rancher**

Poll Taxes and Free BBQs

Politics? We didn't bother with that. Bosses would tell you who they were votin' for. We voted for who they said. We figured they knew the best side. We figured what was good for them was good for us. We never knew about votin'. All we paid attention to was who was sheriff. We all voted for Ira Heard because he gave free barbecues and treated us local cowhands right when we got in Saturday-night scrapes. Back in those days, the black man didn't vote 'cept for sheriff. Owners wanted the cowhands to vote for their choices. We asked their advice and they would pay the poll tax and we usually voted as they did. No one put any strain on us ever; we just took their suggestion.

Clayton Isaiah, Horace Joshlin, L. V. Terrell, Will Weathers, McKinley Williams

"Owners and workers were close in those days."

Rev. Mack Williams
Tophand
O'Connor Peach Mott Ranch

Hog killing time at Salt Creek Ranch, 1930's. Photo by Vincent Fritz.

Pullin' Together

Our families work together while we're alive, and we bury each other when we die. That's how the system works. We've all been together through the centuries and we love each other. We're family—black, Anglo, and Mexican. Our fathers and grandfathers and even great-grandfathers felt the same way about each other.

We've always been workin' the land together in this part of the world. Pullin' together, carin' about the land, we are all one. We love these ranches, they are our homes. There is closeness and love and respect for one another. There are no better people in the world than the ones raised in Refugio and on the banks of the Santone River.

Alex de la Garza, Tony Lott, Victor Rodriguez, Julian Tijerina

No Sweat

Ranch work wasn't payin' as much as other jobs, but everyone was happy. You didn't have to worry about the bills and you could kill food on the ranch for free. In town, it cost money. You didn't have a lot of money in those days, but you always had somethin' to eat. That's a lot more than anyone can say for the government's way of doin' things.

No matter what, you could go back to the ranches. You had a place to stay, steady work, and food. We were happy. These ranches were our strength, too. We never worried about food, shelter, or doctor bills then. And there are fools goin' around sayin' times are better now.

We don't know nothin' about any kind of system we lived under, but if it was a system, then there wasn't nothin' to complain about. It was a good way to live. You didn't have no sweat.

Jesse Jones, Rufus Moore, Suey Richardson, Elvin Scott, L. V. Terrell, Nathaniel Youngblood

"The patron system is like a commune with a dictator. You didn't pay much, but you took care of them. This system is like feudalism, and it works best where there is isolation. That's why it doesn't work too well any more.

"It's not the best of all systems, but it worked well here for both sides. People aren't as loyal as they used to be, but were they ever really that loyal?"

C. K. McCan, Jr.
"Kerry"
Rancher

It Went Both Ways

We growed up to be men at the O'Briens'. To this day we still miss him. We loved him like a daddy. He was like our father. Mr. O'Brien and Daddy taught us to have respect and courtesy; without those two things, you ain't nobody. You have to respect ladies, older people, animals, and the land.

He took care of us, too. There was a form of equality. We were well protected. Anyone says we didn't really like this system is wrong. We were never abused. The owners depended on us, too. It was a thing that went both ways.

E. J. Garza · Nick Rivas
Tophands
O'Brien Ranches

THE LADY RANCHERS They Just Want the Work Done

Some of these women were tough as any boot you ever saw, and some were gentle as lambs. There aren't many women ranchers to begin with, and some were really tough to work for. Things were done their way or you heard about it in fairly strong language. On the other side, many of them would ask us what they should do. We had experience, and they knew it.

Working for women is kind of uncomfortable sometimes. You're always in danger of saying something unbecoming around them.

Women get the work done. Maybe not the way we think it should, but they get it done. Many work cattle the way their husbands or fathers taught them to. The men laid the pattern and the women see no reason to change.

Women are more sensitive to people than men are. They realize you are tired and will give you a rest. That man, he keeps you going, rain or shine.

The women listen to us. Maybe not right away, but they usually do it the way we suggest. Men get set in their ways and won't change. A man will push you to the limit, always in a hurry to get through. Womenfolks remember there's another day.

The men are hard-core stuff—always testing you. They want to see what you're made of. Women aren't interested in that, they just want the work done.

We took care of the ladies. We respected them. That's the way it goes.

John Brown, E. J. Garza, Jesse Jones, Rufus Moore, David Ohrt, K. J. Oliver

Bicycles Were Too Dangerous

"I'm from a ranching family in South Dakota. But I grew up in Houston. My father wouldn't buy me a bicycle—he thought they were too dangerous—so he gave me a horse. I had dolls and all those girl things, but my horse was my true love. I've always loved ranch life and now I have my own herd of registered Longhorns.
"This is it—the best place in the world. I'm part of it, it's part of me. We're gonna stick it out together."

Jeanne Houghton Marks
Rancher

Housekeeping vs. Freedom

"Mother and Daddy would die if they knew I was ranching. I was raised to be a lady, but in school I was always a tomboy. I don't like housekeeping and I don't care for town. I like being outside. I was raised out there with freedom, the animals, and the quiet.
"I am stubborn, and when Daddy died, I took over the ranch. I loved it, seeing the calves grow. The banks gave me a chance and I prayed a lot, and I'm still in it. I couldn't see it being leased to someone else—that was not right. I love the land, it's just in me. That feeling, you can't get it out of you. I'm there every time we work cattle—I'm one of them.
"We have lived here attached to the land. It's not economics. We want to hold on to it. Something draws us to it."

Felice Gonzales
Rancher

"My Grandmother Murphy took me out to the ranch all the time. I grew up with it. I love the land, the beauty of it, and what it can produce. What you learn from the land no one can ever take away from you. I need that land. I can't imagine ever selling it. It keeps me busy."

Marye Murphy Greer
Rancher

Marye Murphy, Duchess of Victoria.

"When I first married, I didn't ride or know anything about cattle, but I learned. Now I love them, I call them my babies. I just do what my husband taught me to do. I do it just the way he did it."

Mabel Stroebel Hanley
Rancher

"Land goes so far back in the family, I have a real thing about it. There was something about the country that felt good to me. I can't even imagine parting with that land. I was going to learn to ranch, somehow, some way."

Mary Jo Fagan Smith
Rancher

After My Debut. . .

"I grew up in San Antonio, but I always spent my summers on the ranch. After I made my debut, I traveled a lot and didn't spend much time down here until after my father died. There was no one else to run this ranch, so I did it. I had to learn from scratch, but I had good cowhands to teach me. I wasn't thrilled about it, but I did it: branding, vaccinating, gathering, dipping, and selling. I did it all. The selling was my favorite part. Any man who wouldn't take orders from a woman couldn't work for me."

"I love this land. It has been in my family for over a hundred years. The land is first, economics second. I'd never sell this ranch. It's my strength."

Emily Keeran Campbell
Rancher

Hard Times and Good Times

"Why do I ranch? My husband loved this place. I'd like to carry it on as long as possible. That would have pleased him. I could lease or sell, but I learned to love the cattle. We've been here a long time; I'd like to see it stay that way.

"My husband taught me what I know about ranching. I never threw calves, but I rode horses, handled the branding irons, penned horseback, sterilized vaccinating needles, and pitched many a bale of hay. We've had hard times and good times out here, but I've enjoyed it."

Jeanette Johnstone Perkins
Rancher

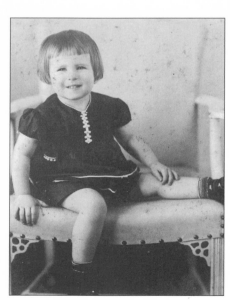

Mary Jo Hogan Fagan, 1937.

Mabel Stroebel, age 15.

Georgia Lee Swickheimer, 1947.

CHAPTER FOUR

FOOLS ON GOOD HORSES: THE COWHANDS

Alejandro de la Garza
Photo by Louise S. O'Connor.

FOOLS ON GOOD HORSES: THE COWHANDS

"I started workin' cattle when I was fourteen. I been on horseback that many years. I love the work—don't care how hot, how cold. I love it."

Alejandro de la Garza
"Alex"
Tophand
O'Connor Ranches

Most cowhands are portrayed as drifters and loners, as rough and somewhat uncivilized. The men who care for cattle in the Coastal Bend are neither. For the most part, they are family men deeply rooted in the fertile soil of the area. As a rule, they are gentle, creative people who live in harmony with nature.

The Coastal Bend cowhands are sedentary, and for generations they have lived on and worked the same land that their ancestors inhabited.

Many are still working here one hundred years after the great cattle drives, and some of their families have been ranching the area for over one hundred and fifty years. Most cowhands have their own family cattle brands. If they are Hispanic, their brands can usually be traced back to ancestors who ranched during the land-grant era. When freed blacks moved into the cow crowd, they created their own brands—frequently from their initials. These brands were seldom registered because they were not used except as ornamentation—on the cowhand's saddle or perhaps his pet dogie. Yet these brands were important to the cowhands because it gave them a sense of belonging.

Milam Thompson, 1920's.

These cowhands did not live an unfettered life of romantic activity with no one telling them what to do or restricting their movements. Independence was apparently not the great attraction for them, nor did others look at a Coastal Bend cowhand as the ultimate free spirit. They were not independent loners or so-called "sentinels of freedom," as cowboys are almost always depicted in novels and movies and on television. They were generally poor, hard-working family men who did what they were told to do—when and where they were told to do it. If not, they didn't have a job, their families didn't eat, and they might wind up looking at life—and the rear end of a

A typical Coastal Bend cowboy outfit, 1930's.
Photo by Dennis O'Connor [II].

mule—from behind the dreaded plow. This was a way of life they had at least partially escaped by becoming cowhands.

Cowhands in this region differ in yet another way. In other ranching cultures, cowboy boots, ten-gallon hats, and sheepskin leggins were standard apparel. Here in the Coastal Bend the cowhands and ranchers didn't dress "cowboy." Any old clothing that could be salvaged and worn was used. To this day, many of the cowhands wear items of clothing, some frayed beyond repair, that they have used for years. The first men who appeared in so-called Western dress were ridiculed as sissies. Khakis are now the traditional dress of the ranch owners and foremen. Blue jeans didn't appear down here until after World War II.

Few cowhands were educated beyond the elementary grades, and others only "walked past the schoolhouse." Yet many of them have acquired an education in life often unsurpassed by those more thoroughly and formally educated. Most of the men wanted to be cowhands since childhood, although, in reality, there was little else they could do in the area. Many came from farming families, and that seemed to give them the incentive for learning to ride a horse. With few exceptions, they say they would do it again, given the chance. The ranchers will tell you much the same. No other way of life ever occurred to them, or they were born to it and stuck with it.

The cowhands, and even some of the women, played cowboy as children, copying what the real cowhands did. Roping their mothers' turkeys and chickens was one of their favorite pastimes. Miniature cattle and horses were made from mud, and stick horses were made from "seeney bean" branches. They rode hogs and tree limbs and harnessed horned toads to their matchbox wagons. They created toys out of their environment and games out of their imaginations. They enjoyed their play, but the greatest day of their lives came when they were allowed to join the cow crowd as full-time cowhands. "Watching them old heads" was how most of them learned their profession. Some had concerned fathers who took the time to teach them, while others had the knowledge pounded into them by stern taskmasters such as Uncle Louis Power, foreman of the O'Connor Duke Ranch.

Becoming a working cowhand meant becoming a man. The youngsters were put through a number of initiation rites before they became full-fledged cowhands. This was necessary for everyone's safety. An inexperienced hand who did not know his business could endanger the lives of everyone.

The cowhands were not, as one might think, constantly working cattle. That occurred seasonally. The rest of the time, they were involved in the never ending maintenance work on the ranches. They were adept at many jobs. Often they were also carpenters, amateur veterinarians, and pretty good windmill men. Many were itinerant cowhands in the sense that they moved from one ranch to another in the immediate area. They or their fathers farmed on "halfsies," on small plots of land given to them by the ranch owners. When cow-working time rolled around, they were called to join the cow crowd. This tenant-farming system gave the cowhands a steady living and provided the ranchers with a readily available work force.

Tasso drying in cow camp, Duke Ranch, 1930's. Photo by Dennis O'Connor [II].

The happiest time of the cowhands' lives came when the call went out for the cow crowd. This meant money in their pockets, a good horse under them, and as much as a month of camaraderie in camp. There was little leisure time. Their work had to incorporate their play.

Nap time in the camp house, Duke Ranch, 1930's. Photo by Dennis O'Connor [II].

Cowhands enjoyed their work as few other people do. The love for their work was constantly in their conversation. No matter how hot, tired, dusty, or cold they were, they could find something to enjoy in every day's activities. Pride in their work was evident in every sentence they spoke, even though these men were a long, long way from being the folk heroes cowhands are today. They did not then and do not now fit into the commonplace myth of the cowboy. It was just among themselves that being a good cowhand mattered. They were ordinary working people, although a bit poorer than most. Despite this, they are quick to remind you that they always had plenty to eat and that life was better back then.

Pen work, 1930's.
Photo by Dennis O'Connor [II].

Cowhands observed a hierarchy that kept the ranch running smoothly. The foreman was considered the boss (although "boss" is sometimes used to refer to the owner). He was in charge of personnel and the day-to-day operations of the ranch, serving as a liaison between the owner and the cowhands. The foreman's assistant was the straw boss. Among the cowhands, those who were better than average at cowboying and perhaps superior in certain skills were the tophands.

Cowhands have always admired each other's abilities and will be the first to acknowledge who was the best at a certain job—even if that person happened to be himself. These men were superb athletes. It obviously added to their joy in their work and their ability to do it so well. Were they young men now, some of them no doubt would be stars in the world of professional sports, as a number of their children have become. A cowhand's superior skill was not resented by the others because that very skill might some day save a life. It also made everyone else's job easier. There was little jealousy among the cowhands; they trusted one another and could depend on each other's help. Conflicts were rare among the cow crowd. They knew each other well and respected one another's territory.

Cow-working is a dangerous business. It is hard, sometimes isolated work. These factors and the constant contact with nature have created some very sensitive and aware human beings.

Cowhands eating dinner at Welder Ranch, 1950's. Photo by Roger Fleming. Courtesy Institute of Texan Cultures.

The mystique of the mounted man runs strongly in the ranching culture. One characteristic is prevalent—their horses were their true loves. They respected them as intelligent, precision tools, as well as a means of making a hard day's work easier. From the day they first got up on a horse, their lives changed. At times, they confess to loving these animals more than their women, a fact seemingly understood and overlooked by those women. The quality of a ranch is judged by its horses, because even today the horse is irreplaceable in some situations. Often the source of fun and enjoyment, a good horse could help make up for low pay and hard work. The day the

Jesse Jones mugging a steer, 1930's.
Photo by Dennis O'Connor [II].

good life ended for most of these men was the day they had to get off that horse for the last time.

Cow people talk about cattle as most people do their children—as creatures who need constant care and attention. They hate to see them helpless or in pain. They have a great affection for the cows and talk to them differently than they do to bulls or steers—almost as they would to a woman. Cows are often called Honey, Sweetheart, Mama, Sugar, or Baby. Bulls or steers will be roundly cursed and called unprintable names at the slightest provocation; but even this is tinged with affection.

Many of the cowhands seem to have a greater love for these animals than they do for the land. To them, the land is the primary responsibility of the owners whereas the animals were in their care. It was a job they took seriously.

Their hearts were always in their jobs. They regarded the land and animals in a way that only comes after being in the same place and doing the same job for generations.

While cowhands generally had an abundance of pride in each other, their work, the ranches, the horses, and the cattle, their greatest source of pride came from being with one ranch family throughout their lifetime. The ranches were their homes, their security, and their strength. They protected the land and the animals, cared for the equipment as if it was their own,

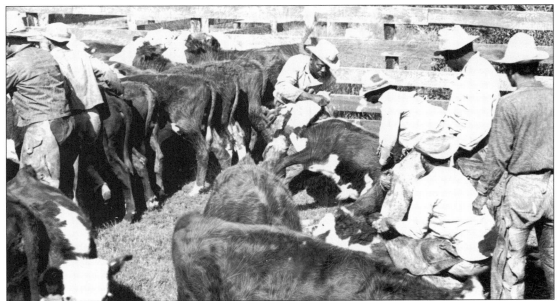

Clayton Isaiah and L. V.
Terrell pen work, 1930's.
Photo by Dennis O'Connor [II].

and had a deep love for the ranches where they worked. The owners, in turn, took great pride in their cowhands and often proudly displayed their talents to other ranchers.

Most of the old cowhands are deeply religious, or have come to be in their later years. They now cling to their congregations as they once were bound to their cow crowd and their work. They are disdainful of the new cowhands, yet hasten to defend them by saying that the newcomers don't really have a chance to learn. To most of the old-timers, mechanization and modern technology have forever changed the old ways that produced first-

"Hook Him!"
Open herd work, 1930's.
Photo by Dennis O'Connor [II].

class cowhands. Though they don't complain about mechanization or even resent it, they recognize it as the ruination of the real cowhand. Most of the older ones I interviewed told me that they weren't as good as their forefathers. They describe themselves as the descendants of the "real" cowhands, preferring the way life used to be while acknowledging the genuine advantages of recent improvements.

Many of the cowhands left the ranches at one time or another, hoping to provide their children with an opportunity for a better education and better-paying jobs. They soon discovered that they had not achieved what they

Going down the rope, 1930's.
Photo by Dennis O'Connor [II].

were searching for. With few exceptions, they do not approve of their children's newly found attitudes or behavior.

The hard work of ranch life was a bond among the cowhands. Moreover, their imaginations served them in their work, so they were never bored. They frequently made their work into play. The cowhands loved and respected one another and genuinely enjoyed each other's company. When asked how such hard work could be so much fun, one old cowhand replied that he never really understood why it was so much fun either, but that it was, and concluded: "That's why they called us crazy."

It's All a Dream. . .

Lately, I been seein' my old friends and talkin' to them. We was all raised up here together. In my dreams we get together, then all at once they're gone—dead and buried. Sometimes I get to thinkin' back and it feels like I'm rememberin' further back than that. I dream I was back there every once in a while.

I was born in 1892 or thereabouts—don't really know how old I am. Born on the river and grew up here on the Murphy Ranch. I stayed with Mrs. Murphy until she died, then I was with Mrs. Grace Gaffney for three years, and with Miss Aggie till she died. Then, I went to town. I been cowboyin' all my life, ever since I got big enough. I was always lookin' at the cowhands and didn't never go to no school. I sign my name with an "X". Mrs. Murphy kept me goin' all day, so I didn't want to bother with books at night, but she learnt me lots anyway. I went to where them cowhands was. That's where I got more enjoyment. I didn't think I'd live this long, didn't think I'd need an education.

Richard Harris, age 16, on the Murphy Ranch.

I was a foreman for the Murphys and learnt by goin' along with Mr. Murphy. Nobody was over me. I just watched Mr. Jim cuttin' and classin' cattle. I watched the old hands, then I went on and did it just like they did. I been that way all my life. I just kept on goin' until I got shortness of breath and had to give it up. I didn't have a whole lot of other things to think about—just cattle.

The weather is different now. It's warmer. I used to freeze. In them days, it was rough out in the cold. Mr. Murphy took us out facin' the north wind for six miles. We was so cold we couldn't turn our horses. I skinned cattle while standin' on the ice for days at a time. Stayed all day in the cold; my fingernails and my forehead was cooked from the cold. We didn't know when those big freezes was comin' in the old days. We didn't have no radios or telephones.

I can tell you everythin' I went through in a day — just ordinary. Did a little bit of everythin' — house, yard, barn, cattle. A cow-workin' day began at three or four in the mornin'. Sometimes we had to work all night, just lay down a little bit to rest. We rode horseback everywhere. Young cowhands now don't know nothin' about cattle compared to what we did. They just don't care and they don't want to learn — except their way.

There wasn't many I could depend on back in the earlier days, either. Rafael de la Garza was one. He was with me, workin' even at night. As old as Rafael and me is, we never went on the trail drives. I can name the nights I let sundown catch me out of Victoria County. I didn't think I was that old until people got to dyin' all around me. The Murphys all died, I lost children, mother, and father. I guess I'm goin' to die soon, too.

Better for me now? No, it ain't better for me now. Now I works cattle through dreamin' — workin' them yet. That's all I do now, go to bed and go to dreamin'. When I wake up, I been workin' cattle, me and Rafael doin' the work. I'm sweatin' till I get over my dreams. I was enjoyin' it, but when I wake up, it was all a dream.

You know, sometimes I think it all went in the wind. I dream so much. A nightmare gets over me as I go over different country, dreamin'. I just goes and meets the old-timers. All the people I associated with are dead — just dead. All the old ranchers done gone — Fagan, Terrells, Old Man Jim Welder, Frank West, Phil Power. All of them was friends to me. These are the people I dream about. But it don't change, it just goes on.

When Miss Aggie got ready to die, she called me. She felt like I ought to been there. I was wore out. I give the Murphys my life. I represented the Murphys all my life — wherever I was or whatever I was goin' through, I held them up. That was my life. Miss Aggie died, my horse died, and possums were in the well, so I had to sit down.

I never played cowboy much. I guess I was workin' when I was playin'. We rode stickhorses and played like we was ropin' cattle. All the time, I was watchin' and I kept it in my head. Then I got big enough to do it. I been in dreams and fights and one thing and another, but when I woke up, I was on the good side all the time.

This ranch belonged to the Murphys. Everythin' I did was in their interest. I never really grew to feel like it was mine, but I think I cared about it as much as the Murphys did. I didn't have nothin', only what they gave me. Money ain't the whole thing. I could have worked somewhere else and made more money. But I wasn't no town man. I never did work in no town. I didn't call it work out there. Ranch workers just didn't make lots of money — never have. Why did I do it? Just to get things right. This was my home, and till yet I feel like it is home.

I didn't know I was good until you told me. Every old cowman knew how to do the work just like his cowhands did. They done the work then.

It's all in books now. I didn't call myself no cowman—I was just workin'
cattle. A cowman works with his brains; a cowhand works with his hands. I
done a little bit of both.

Farmin' and ranchin' is the best business for young men to grow up into.
You can look at everythin' grow up, plants and cattle developin'. It's not
really no hard life. Work don't hurt nobody. I just did too much of it,
worked too steady too long. I rode in a west wind with a light jacket and
caught a cold and never got rid of it.

I must be considered an old cowhand because I ain't one of these new
ones. Some of these new ones do nothin', and some just run their mouths.
I've seen some changes in my time; some things are gone in the wind and
some things are holdin' on. The world's movin' too fast. It's comin' down—
everythin's comin' down. People are offendin' God and nature now. I'm no
church member, but I follow Jesus through the world. I go through things
I don't like, but if Jesus is with me, I'll get through. All I ever been around
is Catholic and Baptist. The only difference I see is Catholics are quiet and
Baptists you can hear all over the river bottom. To my way of thinkin'
they're the same, just different.

It was real unusual for a black man to be foreman back in my days. Just
me and Louis Power was real foremen. The black man didn't get credit
back in them days unless you was with the O'Connors or the Murphys. Miss
Aggie appreciated me like you O'Connors appreciated Louis Power. Blacks
and whites got along back in them days. People are all the same. Blacks,
whites, Mexicans will all try to run over you when you're bossin'—if you let
'em. I just done what there was to be done.

I dream of workin' cattle now; then I get tired and rest a while. I can't do
nothin' now. I used to work hard to get the job done. I wish I could get up
now and go on brandin', cuttin' cattle, drivin' them, doin' one thing and
then another. I'll be doin' it the way I used to do it until I wake up.
I dream in all kinds of colors. Then it all passes away and I wake up and
repeat: "It's all a dream."

Back when I was ridin' I always talked to the cattle. When I couldn't talk
to cattle no more, I give up and went to town and sat down. I guess I liked
my horses better than people. I'd be with my horses all the time, talk to
them, call their names. Some horses are pretty smart. You can say most
anythin' to them—like they was a person. One time, Old Gruilla stepped in
a gopher hole and I fell off and hurt my back. She came up and asked me
if I was hurt. I never was lonesome around my cattle and horses, but I get
a little lonesome now 'cause I'm settin' down and can't do nothin'. I sang to
my cattle until I lost my breath. That's when I had to get off my horse,
too, and stop ridin'.

I loved my work. I'd be there now if I could do anythin'. The life I'm
livin' now is real but I don't know much about it. All the rest is past. I miss
the whole thing, the life that's all I knew. Now, everythin' aggravates me.
I miss the ranch life and my horses. I was a boy, then I became a man.
I lived the life of a man. I went through everythin'. I guess I had brains
enough to know when it comes to the showdown, there's credit in the

distance. I guess that's what you're doin' writin' my story.

Bein' old means settin' down. I hate it 'cause I can't do what I want to do. Louis Power and Will Upton—they died at the ranch. I would like to have done that, but there's no more Murphys to look back on. I felt like nobody ever got old, they just passed away. Then, I was old myself. Old age will hold you back, but when I got through, I didn't owe nobody a dime. I ain't got no more to say, nothin' to worry about. I'm goin' to heaven.

Richard Harris
Foreman
Murphy Ranches
1891–1988

Mucho Diferencio. . .

I was born on the old Williams place on the Santone River Road in 1888. That was close to Anaqua, a small place where I went to school with Miss Kate Stoner, Miss Mary Gertrude "Birdie" Amery, and Cornelius Simms. The post office was in the Amery house. Mr. Amery was a judge; he married people all the time. Anaqua ain't there no more, and back then McFaddin wasn't much neither before they built the railroad in 1905. I tried

Class from Anaqua School.

workin' on the railroad for a few days, but I didn't like it.

I liked to ride from the time I was little, playin' cowboy. I jumped rope with one of Tom Ball's boys. We made our own toys. We made stickhorses and little cattle and horses out of mud and corn cobs; we would heat a wire in the fireplace and brand the cobs. There was no stoves in those days, just fireplaces. We played with tin cans and thread spools; that's all we ever had to play with. We lit the lamp for a little while in the evening—we couldn't afford to burn too much oil. Later on, Daddy got a radio; it was battery-operated.

St. Anthony's Chapel, O'Connor Brothers River Ranch, 1938.

I always wanted to be a cowhand; I was born that way. Maybe it was because of my ancestors, who came from Spain. They lost everythin' in the Mexican Revolution, but my family always stayed near the land. My grandpa, who worked for the original Old Man Tom O'Connor, was Lupe Hernandez. He went up the trail to Kansas. He told me he was on the drive where some man who said his name was O'Connor killed the foreman, but the man was a liar. My grandpa never told me much about the drives except they only took steers. He said some of the animals got sore feet and they would leave them behind. Sometimes those same cattle would follow the trail and catch up with the herd later.

I'm so old I can remember when Highway 77 was just a dirt road. There wasn't no church here when I was a boy. A preacher would come by once in a while. I was six or seven before I was baptized at the Carlos Ranch. Everyone used to come from Goliad to be baptized. After they built St. Anthony's at the ranch, we would go over there. That was the first church I was ever in.

People used to come up from Mexico to pick cotton. They come across country. There was no fences back then. They come afoot and on *carretas*. The women would wash their clothes on boards in the river. I was a little fella when all this was happenin'.

I started workin' in 1899 durin' the big freeze. It come up on a Saturday and by night everythin' was frozen. Mr. Louis Sitterle had given me a new saddle and an old dun horse. When I got that saddle, I put it in the house with me so I could get up at night and touch it to be sure it was still there. The next day, I put on my heaviest clothes and my grandpa put me up on that horse and tied me to the saddle to help him moss the cattle during the blizzard. From that time in 1899 to 1905 I worked with Tom [II] and Joe but I never got no pay until 1904. Then I started gettin' fifty cents a day. In the spring, we were movin' cattle to the Duke Ranch. Mr. Sitterle was boss; he was ridin' Carta Blanca, a proud walkin' horse.

I began workin' so long ago, our ropes were made of hair and rawhide. I even remember Mr. Dennis O'Connor [I]. He and my daddy was *compadres*. One time, in 1905, we was bringin' cattle from the Duke Ranch. We worked all day shapin' them up and we branded them the next mornin'. The temperature started droppin' and by the time we finished, the water buckets had ice in them. Must have been 30 degrees; we had frost in our hair. Never really knew how cold it was because we didn't have no thermometers then. When I was young, I'd go around barefooted, workin' in the cold. My feet would crack. Now they put shoes on the kids when they're born.

I learned to work cattle on the Big Prairie with Louis Power and Mr. Sitterle and the old guys. Mr. Sitterle, who was German, brought me up in the cow business. Sometimes I'd wake up at night from a dream shoutin', "Yessir, Mr. Sitterle." I was raised with him and I worked for him. He was a good man, but he didn't know a lot about cattle. He knew people real well, and he could read you just by lookin' at you, and the same with horses.

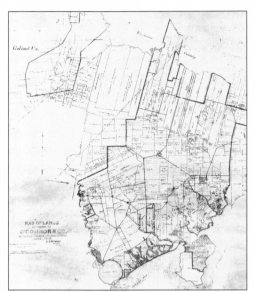

O'Connor Ranch Division Map, 1907.

I was also raised with Louis Power, who was at the Duke Ranch. He learned me how to work cattle. In 1917, he sent for me to come to the Duke to cut cattle. Mr. Louis knew everythin' about cattle there was to know. He showed me how to rope in a *remuda*, how to make a herd. He taught me about bein' quiet—those Spanish cattle were wild. You had to know what you were doin' back then. He say, "Be quiet all the time."

I worked the 1907 division. From the time we started, we never stopped. Mud, water in the pens, we never stopped. Some people quit, the work was so long and hard. Louis worked as hard as his men did and more. We were camped at Cavasso Creek workin' at the dead part of the night for a dollar a day. We worked from the day's start to the finish and never quit. Louis did the brandin' and the cuttin'. We used to brand with a runnin' iron and a wood fire. We used lime and water for sop on the new brands. Durin' the division there was three cow crowds. We was brandin', and the others was drivin' cattle through the pastures. Louis was gatherin' the cattle while we branded. Charlie Cantu, Juan Garcia, and Louis Power were runnin' the cow crowds.

I can remember when each ranch was just a pasture of the whole big ranch. Everythin' was open then; you could see the whole world. Now everythin' is brush. There wasn't many windmills, either—mostly artesian wells, and no fences anywhere. They fenced when they divided in 1907. When I started workin' we could go from Tivoli plumb to the Melon Creek

Commerce on the Guadalupe River.
Photo by Parks Photo.

and from the Guadalupe River to Copano Bay. Before these ranches was fenced, we worked cattle out in the open and lived in camps. We didn't have no horse traps, and had to hobble the horses to keep them from runnin' off. We worked big herds of four to five hundred head. Used to work cattle all day and not finish, the herds were so big. The cattle were thick around the water holes.

Everythin' has changed from then to now. We went everywhere, no fences. There wasn't so much brush as there is now, so we went barefoot. Now you have to wear shoes. We just cut across the pastures to get from

FOOLS ON GOOD HORSES: THE COWHANDS

town to town. We rode wagons or horses or just walked. Women used to wash clothes in the river; it would take them two days. Now they do it in an hour and a half—*mucho diferencio*. We used lots of plants and herbs as medicines when we got hurt. We never stopped workin' and never went to the doctor.

We used to go fishin' and didn't have to have no license. We hunted a lot back in those days for food and to get hides to sell. One New Year's Eve, I killed a big possum over by the Dunn pasture—oooh, he was big. I got ninety cents for him. For the others I got thirty cents. When one of my sons was born, I paid the bills with polecat hides.

They don't work cattle the same way now, either. They work a few days, no Saturdays or no Sundays. We were gone thirty to forty days with no holidays—only Christmas. We didn't get no birthdays off, either. We were asleep by nine at night and up by five in the morning. You know, we didn't mind it then—hot weather, cold weather, no matter. Now, it bothers me. We never went to a fire and got warm or we would have frozen to death when we went back out. We did all kinds of work on the ranches, just like now—buildin' fences and cuttin' wood. In them days, you had to use lots of wood. If you wasn't workin' on cattle, it was somethin' else, always. It didn't make no difference if the weather was hot or cold when I was a cowhand. We didn't have no fancy clothes then—yellow duckin' jackets and slickers was about all. You had to ride to cut cattle out in the open; them Spanish cattle would run a mile or two. You couldn't break them down. But we would break a horse down runnin' and rippin'. People were tougher then because we were always workin'; the harder you worked, the tougher you got. We used to come in from the pasture and would keep right on workin' if it wasn't dark.

The remuda. Cutting out horses for the morning mount, early 1900's.

I used to ship cattle at night. It was cold. Once, Dick Avery and I was white with frost. When he saw the frost, Dick said, "If I'd a-knowed it was this cold, I'd a-died." We would load three hundred calves and two carloads of cows. We couldn't see good with lanterns, but we worked half the night sometime. We just had supper, that was all, and breakfast the next mornin'—*carne, frijoles, arroz, papas*. We had fun all the time ridin' fast, ropin' and ridin' pitchin' horses. Now, when you work cattle, you can sleep around the outside of the herd.

A fella came by one time who was a farmer and said we had life easy

FOOLS ON GOOD HORSES: THE COWHANDS

because we only rode a horse. I asked him if he wanted to go work cattle with us. First day he worked with us, he got all bruised up. He said, "No more *caballito*." I say, "Uh-huh, you always say it's nothin' to *caballito*." People who don't work cattle say it's not hard work. Workin' cattle is hard, but we never thought it was. I liked it so much, I didn't care. We worked fourteen hours and more a day, never less than ten hours. When you ride one horse all day, you get tired. If you change horses like we used to, you feel good all over again.

When I was young I wanted to be a cowhand all the time. I didn't like no other work. It's a whole lot of difference now, a lot of things are a whole lot different. Cowhands never used to be still. I liked to run and rope but there's none of that no more. I wouldn't like to be a cowhand now. I don't like the way they work cattle today—ain't no fun. No runnin', ropin', ridin' on pitchin' horses. That was the fun of it, ridin' those pitchin' horses on a cold day, chasin' three or four loose cattle at the same time. Some people used to tail stray calves—Cornelius Lewis, Lupe Garcia, and Romero Rocha. The animals never got away from them. Nobody don't know nothin' about that no more.

We went out to work real early, sometimes so early we would have to keep the horses up all night. When we were workin' cattle, the *remuda* with five hundred saddle horses followed us around. We divided the *remuda* into groups of eighty horses; they were changed every two weeks. One time we

Cowhands at chuck wagon, Welder-McCan Lease, 1950's. Courtesy Institute of Texan Cultures.

was brandin' there on Copano Creek, me and Blue Gibson. We had lots of fun; he was always hoorawin' me—called me "Collins" after a man from Refugio who was so red he was ugly.

It never got too cold or too wet for us. Sometimes when we were workin' cattle, the horses' manes would freeze. We had no fires and we slept in tents. Fred Rivas said coyotes used to come around their camp. There was *lobos* and wildcats on the Big Prairie when I was young. The cook wagon was pulled by horses or mules; the mess box sat behind and the cover dropped down to make a table. Mostly we sat around the fire and helped

Rafael de la Garza, 1918.

ourselves. There was lots of devilment in camp, always playin' jokes. Camp food was good: stew, barbecue, beans, dried apples and prunes, and cowboy stew. Flies used to be all over. Now they say watch out for the germs. I've drunk water out of a hog wallow. Sick? I didn't know what that was. I'd drink water out of the lake along with the cattle.

Cowhands was tough then. You rode the horses they gave you or you went home. We had to furnish our own bridles, ropes, saddles, and spurs. They gave you only the horse. A rope cost four bits, spurs cost a dollar, a saddle was twenty-five to forty dollars, and boots were seven dollars.

I don't go to rodeos. I seen enough when I was young. Sometimes, on a cold mornin', when three or four horses were pitchin', that was a real rodeo. I broke horses at the ranches myself with no help. I had a few wrecks but I never got hurt bad; just lucky, I guess. Sometimes when you broke a horse yourself, you wouldn't let nobody else ride him.

I was sittin' around the house one time in 1922, broke; it was hard times. I had to do somethin' I was so broke. Tom Dinkey, the bootlegger, came by my house. He got me to make some home brew and he also paid me two dollars a pint to sell his whiskey. I sold out everythin' the first day, those cowboys was so thirsty.

You ask me about hard times. I guess people now would think it was back then, but we didn't think nothin' about it. We used to work in all kinds of weather. One time a man named Sam Upton froze to death at Twin Mott. We were skinnin' cattle that died from the cold and we found him. There was terrible cold spells and dry spells between 1899 and 1924. In 1917 there was a big drought; you could see a jackrabbit a mile away. Cattle would stand on their hind feet like dogs to eat moss out of the trees. Horses ate bark off the chinaberry trees. In 1938 there came a freeze on Thanksgivin' Day. We skinned dead cattle all day. You did what you had to do then—no matter if it was a holiday. We worked when mosquitoes was so bad you had to get on a windmill to get relief, or use broomweed to switch them away when you were on horseback. We lived through hurricanes and worked cattle when lightnin' was dancin' off the cattle's horns right by us.

What makes a good cowboy? You got to be born with it. What you got in your head when you are little is what you are. That's what you're gonna be. I ain't worked no cattle in forty-five years. Sometimes I dream about cow work and the old folks like Louis Power and Louis Sitterle. I dream all the time. The other night, my dream was about drivin' a bunch of cattle. I was left out alone with a herd; I didn't know which way to go.

I'm glad I cowboyed in the old days. I used to love my work. I wish I could do it again, because if I could, it would be like the old times and I wouldn't get so lonesome. Now I get lonesome just lyin' around the house. Sometimes I have hard days, but I'm glad I'm still livin'.

Rafael de la Garza
Tophand
O'Connor Ranches
1888–1988

Cowboyin' Was Deep in My Blood

"I wanted to be a sho'nuf cowboy, a wild rider. I felt free when I was workin', young and strong. I was a cowhand right off the bay, out there livin' like a wild dog, tryin' to make a livin'. We used to work two days out of one. When night come, you'd be ready for that Dudlow Joe. That's the life of a cowboy."

Monroe Shaw
"Bailey"
Itinerant Cowhand
and
Well Digger

I got some Upton, Shaw, and Riley blood in me. I come from old-timers who lived around the Black Jacks. One of my grandpas was an Irishman named Riley and the other one was a slave, Old Man Han Shaw.

I worked for Uncle Louis Power out there for nine months once at the Cottonwood Hollow. He was a fine man who tried to run a ranch right. He was a good foreman, and he had plenty of work for us to do. One time, Mr. Will O'Connor was out there drainin' off some animals after they came out of a dippin' vat. They was bad animals and one of 'em hit him in the face and knocked him in the vat. I was standin' there and I grabbed a calf hook and got him out. We had to pump water on him and wrap him in blankets. I took him up to the McNamara house and then to town. But he was OK—he hadn't swallowed no dip. Mr. Louis teased me a bunch about dippin' men instead of cows. Mr. Louis was a fine man, but he couldn't ride no horse. He said he just couldn't; he wasn't used to horses like all us boys were.

The only thing we had to do in this country was work cattle. That's all we done. I've worked all around. I know a bunch of cowboys like Ike Dunman and Joe Dunman and Old Man Fagan who rode a mule. I used to be a pretty good rider, but I got throwed when I was down there. I was ridin' a black horse called Caranto. He was a bad one; he throwed every

Tick dipping at Mexican Water Hole, ca. 1922.

rider ever rode him except Monroe Benson and Albert Duke. They was sho'nuf riders.

One time I told Monroe I didn't think no horse could throw me, so he went and got an outlaw horse named Booger Red. Now I figure if he got hair on him, I can ride him, but everyone thought I would get killed. You know, we just ran around—he didn't pitch. Uncle Tom Ball say, "He know he was gonna get chastised, and that's why he won't pitch." Uncle Tom finally broke him to a buggy and his wife used to drive that horse to church and other places. That was the style in them days—wasn't no cars. First car

Monroe "Bailey" Shaw.
Photo by Louise S. O'Connor.

I ever seen, Mr. Driscoll Rooke owned it. You cranked it from the side. Everybody around here used to say, "I wouldn't ride in that thing." That tickled me 'cause everybody rides in 'em now.

My daddy cooked for Mr. Tom O'Connor [II] for years. During 1917, in the drought, he was feedin' cattle at the Iron Gate for Mr. Ed Coward. I was down there with my grandpa feedin' 'em and burnin' prairie wood brush. He was tryin' to keep the cows alive. We stayed down there until after the drought and then I went to work helpin' Mr. Ed Coward. I also put up them silos down there for Mr. Tom O'Connor. All of them's tore down now but we used to have to fill 'em every year. They built 'em to use in case of another drought, but that didn't happen, so they just went to ruin.

I grew up around here and never did stray off nowhere. I been some places as a grown man, workin' on pipelines around Jackson, Mississippi. I guess I was about forty-five, though, before I ever went off these ranches. After I left O'Connor, I still worked in the area for a long time. Mr. Johnny Power had a ranch, and he was a cowman! Them Shay boys got that ranch now. Well, anyway, Johnny Power hired me. He was always after me to go out there with him. He used to buy cattle from Mr. Kroeger and we'd drive 'em from the bay to the Santone River. I worked for Mr. Jim Coward, Uncle Louis Power, and for Mr. Sitterle. Never did work for Mr. Louis Polka, one of the O'Connor foremen. Sometimes I worked for Mr. Fagan, but I was really only a handyboy there. They didn't pay much back then, but it was ours when we got it, not the government's. I worked for John J. O'Brien, too. I made a many a track out there with Valley Elliot and Love Shaw.

I've seen some riders in my time. Willie Jones was one. He broke a horse one day called Funny Paper. Them Dunmans was somethin' else, too. Ike, Joe, and Henry were all good riders and so was those Tillmans.

I didn't play cowboy as a little boy, I just went into the business when I was real young. You see, my people owned cattle and horses. Our brand was the S-U. That's where I learned how to handle cattle. I'll tell you, that's a pretty rough job. Some people works 'em wrong. Now, my way of work-in' 'em would be slow. You don't chause cattle, you'll knock the fat off 'em. Now, you take Mr. Jim Coward. He's about the best ranch man I ever worked for. He told you what to do. He didn't yell and he didn't expect you to know what he wanted without tellin' you. He didn't want you to run his cattle or holler at 'em.

I've worked for a lot of people who started runnin' them cattle when they hit the pasture. They rodeo 'em. That ain't no way to work cattle. You gotta work 'em slow. Dogs make 'em even wilder. I don't believe in runnin' cattle. I figure that ropin' and doggin' 'em don't do 'em no good. It just makes 'em mad. So if you start ropin' and doggin' 'em and if you got dogs, you gonna have a bunch of racehorses when you go to work 'em.

The young cowboys ain't nothin' like them old heads I used to work with. One day for Mr. Jim O'Connor up at the Clipp section of the ranch, we throwed a thousand and ninety-six head before the sun went down. Murray and Marion Keyes could tell you if they was alive. I was right there with 'em. Matt Jones was throwin' the calves. I seen a calf kick a ring off Matt's finger and we never did find it. He was a calf-thrower! J. B. Gipson was another one, so was Love Shaw, and I wasn't too bad myself. We sold five hundred before breakfast the next day. I tell you we were gettin' 'em down. Dippin' 'em and lettin' 'em go. Uncle Louis could dip more cattle than any man I ever seen. He worked night and day. Now, Mr. Jim wasn't like that; he would wait for daylight. You were up at three if you were workin' for Uncle Louis. You couldn't even see the cattle, you just knew they were there. I'll tell you, that's the way he worked. He had me shuckin' corn at three o'clock one mornin' and a snake crawled up my leg. He couldn't understand why I got nervous an' quit workin'. He just liked to work— that's all. We got six bits a day, and we appreciated it because we didn't have no other work to do.

There wasn't no boll weevils out here workin'. The work was too tough. A boll weevil don't know too much, but the boys that worked out here was pretty good. They had to be. Now you take them Terrells, Youngbloods, and them Lott boys—they was good riders. You would see a bunch of loose horses down here on a many a day. We had some bad horses. Dick Avery sometimes was the only person who could set 'em. He could even ride old Polecat.

Workin' down here in this brush was quite a job. I know a place there at Black Mott where you had to crawl for about a mile to get through. There wasn't no other way to get through.

Dehorning at Duke Ranch, 1935. Albert Perez, Butler Williams, and Jesse Jones kneeling.
Photo by Dennis O'Connor [II].

You know, the problems with these new cowboys is that some of 'em never was learnt good. They never did have nobody to chastise 'em. When we was coming up, we had to pay attention to what the boss man said—his orders was his orders. You couldn't talk back to people; you said "yes sir" and "no sir." A long time ago, you could talk to a cowboy and tell him what to do. Now you liable to send him out to do somethin' and you find him somewhere else. That don't seem right. We had to come out with it. I seen the day I'd be spittin' white foam. I been hurt a many a time. I've had cattle kick the wind outta me. If you workin' cattle in the pen, you don't know what's gonna happen. I don't know if they do as much hand work now as we used to. We'd throw 'em, mug 'em down. That's the way I like to see 'em do it, not using these flip tables. That ain't workin' cattle. Now Mr. Jim [O'Connor] used to have that knife blade in his mouth and he'd go into 'em. We'd each have a calf down—four or five men at a time—and we was workin'. We'd dip 'em, run 'em through, and holler for another pen full. Us colored boys was faster than them white boys, but we was all young and strong. We didn't care if an animal jumped in the middle of us. We had some good times out there. You could take a dollar and get somewhere. If you had four or five dollars, you'd be might near rich.

One time my grandpa told me to buy a few acres, but I didn't want none of that sand, even though it was goin' for two bits an acre. Now, don't you know they sold that land to some movie star and it's got oil wells all over it. I could might near kick myself. I had eighteen hundred dollars and I coulda owned the whole thing. My grandpa, he said, "Buy it, Son," but I didn't like that blowin' sand. I say, "Uh-uh. They ain't gonna trick me into buyin' that stuff."

They sure got some pretty homes in there now, all the way to Rockport. But this was back before there was a causeway. I'd have had to swim my cattle from the mouth of Copano Creek. If Grandpa was alive today, I'd take him to see those bridges 'cause he was right about buyin' that land. I just couldn't see it, though, havin' to swim those cattle every fourteen days to dip 'em. There was the dippin' law then to stop them fever ticks. This whole country was under quarantine. The government men came in and made sure we dipped every fourteen days. The dip was made of arsenic. That's why it was so dangerous to fall in the vats. Even when we got it on us, it didn't seem to hurt us.

My old man didn't have too much, just a little land and stuff. We'd make our own meal. We had to grind it—grits and stuff like that—out of corn we raised. What we lived off of was just what we got there at the farm, just a little old truck patch. We had a pasture for cattle, but we didn't have that much land like some people. We'd kill rabbits and javelinas, and we raised some hogs. We didn't go without meat. Flour, sugar, coffee, and tobacco—that's all we ever bought when we went to the store. I never got none of the tobacco. You had to be twenty-one before you could smoke.

At one time, cowboyin' was deep in my blood. If I wasn't workin' cattle, I wasn't satisfied. I could get other jobs and I wasn't pleased with 'em. I like to work cattle; I like to be on a ranch.

I've seen more mosquitoes than any man in this country. I seen the time you could be ridin' and you just had to put kerosene oil all on you to keep 'em from eatin' you up. I mean, they was really rough. We'd be working at Copano Creek, and we'd have to sponge those horses off with kerosene so they could rest at night. They would suck so much blood out of those animals that when I slapped one, my whole handprint on that horse would be nothin' but blood.

You know, I was sittin' here rememberin' old Valley Elliot. He could holler like nobody I ever heard. If Lester Roloff could preach like that man

"Mosquitos are bad"

could holler, the people all over the world would know we was sinnin'. Boy, we could hear that man all the way in the bottom. Not just in the church house, man, but all the way to New York. Lord, that man like to holler. He'd call it "tickling them a bit." He could crack a whip, too. You could hear it for miles and miles. Them cattle would move when he would holler or crack that whip.

There used to be lots of drinkin' and lots of bootleggin' around here—Tom Dinkey and Antonio Garza and a woman that was so old, all her hair busted off her head—can't think of her name. I quit drinkin' after Dr. Glover told me I would die. Soda water's about as high as I'm gonna get now. There used to be lots of drinkin' at Bob Bunton's. It was a cafe and a dance hall. He'd get a band from Santone and have one of those midnight rambles. People was scrubbin' and dancin'—sounded like a bunch of soldiers drillin'. I used to drink whiskey and get drunk. When I was cowboyin' I was crazy. I don't even drink beer now.

That freeze in 1924 was a bad one. The cattle was stacked up higher than our heads. They were driftin' and tryin' to warm each other and they froze stiff. We had to skin 'em to get the hides. Afterwards, we had to salt the hides so they could ship 'em away for leather. Now we don't hardly have no weather cold enough to freeze cattle. It used to be colder back then. I've seen it so cold a horse would want to turn that-a-way. We were young and crazy out there and we'd just keep on goin'. I got a thrill out of it when I was at it. I don't think there's nothing in the world to beat cowboyin'. We used to drive cattle. That was fun. Now they cut that out. They load 'em right where they put 'em in the pen. We used to catch the cattle down on the bay and drive 'em plumb to Greta. That's the only place we had to ship 'em. There weren't no trucks in those days, only trains.

Jose Serrata at Melon Creek Ranch, 1940. Photo by J. Frank Dobie.

You learned to eat all kinds of things out on these ranches. I ain't never bothered no skunk, and possum—I ain't too hot on him neither, but you get used to eatin' all kinds of things on a ranch. Them camp cooks was somethin' else, too. They could lay out that food. Tomatoes and sugar and bread was our dessert. I'll tell you about that tasso we used to have. They simmer it down low until it was real tender, and it would be fine.

I never thought these ranches belonged to me. All I did was know the stock. That's the life of a cowboy—knowin' the stock and livin' in camp, kangaroo court and playin' dominoes. We'd light that old lantern and enter-

Shipping cattle, Greta pens, 1930's.

tain each other that way. Kangaroo court was for somebody who done somethin' and doesn't want to own up to it. They got him in a trap, you know.

I don't dream about cowboyin' now because I give it up. It don't bother me no more, but when I worked on a ranch, I used to wake up lookin' for a horse and wantin' to be like them old heads—Serrata, Rocha, them Bensons and Averys. One of the best of them old heads was Will Elliot. He was good on the road, a good pasture rider. He knew the water and troughs and pastures like nobody else.

We lived by a code they taught us. They didn't believe in you doing things you had no business doin'. They didn't believe in you gettin' in trouble. You didn't find no thieves, neither. Nowadays, you can't trust nobody. You didn't have no job if you were a fighter. You might wind up in the rodeo. The rodeo business is a whole lot different than out here.

There are a whole lot of cowboys originated down in this part of the country when I come up around 1903 and a lot of 'em were black. That's mostly what you used to see around here.

When I started out, we used to cut stickhorses out of wood. We'd get on that horse and have him jumpin' and runnin'—but we was doin' the runnin' and puttin' the power on him. This was still wild country when I was pretty good size. There wasn't no houses out here, nothin' but bushes. All we had to ride was jacks, but I was goin' to be a cowboy. After I got to ride horses, that was in my blood, too. I'd help Old Man Toby Fox work cattle. That's the way I started. The first time I worked cattle I started out for fifty cents a day and then I went up to a dollar and a half with the O'Connors. That was great money in them days, but they had to pay good. That O'Connor brush was trouble. You could put someone out there who didn't know what he was doing, and lose him forever. You couldn't crawl through some of it.

There once was a woman out here named Aunt Rittie, I'm told. She could ride a horse as good as I could. They say she followed O'Connor's cow crowd, sleepin' on the ground and workin' cattle. She was little and bad, and had a herd of cattle here in town, but she was good at workin' 'em. That's why they allowed her to work with the men. She was a cowhand. She's the only one I ever heard of around here. She wore a long dress and threw it over the saddle when she rode. They say she throwed calves, too, and she didn't ride sideways. She kept a bunch of cattle out here on the common when I was a young boy. She made the best light bread you ever put in your mouth. She'd put a club on you if you didn't act good.

Cattle work really ain't no place for a woman to be. If I had daughters, I wouldn't want 'em workin' cattle. The best thing for a woman to do if she has cattle is get her a bucket and put out cake—feed 'em. Just call 'em so they'll come straight to the pen.

Now, you been listening to all this about how tough it was. Let me tell you—times are so tough now, I done took my gold piece off.

Monroe "Bailey" Shaw
Itinerant Cowhand
and
Well Digger

Dan Youngblood   Nathaniel Youngblood

Photo by Louise S. O'Connor.

Remembrances

"I love to talk about the day
My sinful burden will roll away;
I can't keep it to myself,
Myself alone.

"When I try to keep it in,
The tears of joy will then begin,
And that's why I can't
Keep it to myself.

"Now when the fire begins
   to burn
All in my bones —
All in my bones.

"When I try to keep it in,
The tears of joy will then begin,
And that's why I can't
Keep it to myself alone."

**Negro Spiritual
Sung by Dan Youngblood**

Dan Youngblood and Nathaniel Youngblood are cousins. They were raised together on the Welder Vidauri Ranch and worked together most of their lives. One day, after several hours of interviewing a group of old cowhands, I noticed Dan and Nathaniel sitting in the corner engaged in animated conversation long after their microphones had been removed. I listened to them for several minutes and realized that this spontaneous visit between two cousins, who were dear friends, was far more interesting and valuable than the material we had been working on earlier. Their microphones were put back on at my insistence, and "Remembrances" is the result of that conversation. — L. O'C.

Nat: *You know, it seems like yesterday, but a many a year has sneaked by. Back then, our lives revolved 'round that river. We even got our water down there.*

Dan: *We didn't go to town — we went to Lewis's Bend. We went to school down there in the twenties.*

Nat: *It was our livelihood and our fun.*

Dan: *I grew up down on that river and been here ever since — right here on this Welder Ranch since I was six years old and I was born in 1918. My people were farmers down on the Farley Ranch. I guess I made a record nobody else has. I been workin' for the same people all my life.*

Nat: *Me, too — been here all my life. I walked up that road there to school a many a day. When we was kids goin' to school down there, it was neighborly. If you hurt, I hurt. If you had a dime, I had a dime. Everyone's gotten away from that now. I don't know what happened, but a bolt come loose somewhere. There wasn't no phones down there in those days. People would have to ride horseback down there to carry any news. There was a strong feelin' of community down there.*

Dan: *Your mother used to tell how they would fight at those Saturday night suppers down in the Bends. Everybody had fun and then all hell would break loose. I don't know what would set them off — hoorawin', I guess, and someone would get mad.*

Nat: *It looks funny, but it seems like people had more fun back there than we do now. People was so much different than what they is now. There was some licks passed once in a while among us, but it was mostly in fun then — now it ain't in fun at all.*

Dan: *Everybody was related to each other down on the river.*

Nat: *Everybody down there was related to me, it seems.*

Dan: *Back in '34 and '35, shippin' on the railroad was the toughest. The Welders would buy calves from the O'Connors and bring them up to house.*

Nat: *That was lots of fun, turnin' them calves loose. I guess we got to crowdin' them calves too fast, and the calves scattered, and they were throwin' them guys fast as they grab 'em.*

Dan: *During wartime at Angelita we loaded the cattle with lights—trains were hard to come by then. They might say they were goin' to be there at noon and it wouldn't be till midnight.*

Then out came the lights. Loadin' a car a minute. The engineer would holler, "Come on, boys, put some Mr. Welder beans on those doors! Jump in them cattle, boys!" There was lots of hollerin' and laughin'—wild stuff—it was lots of kicks.

Nat: *Dust, yellin', hell raisin', and danger, but we'd do that all day long—no stoppin', no dinner—till we got 'em all loaded.*

Dan: *Everythin' worked like a clock. I've seen that brakeman not miss the chute by half an inch. They knew what they were doin', stoppin' those cars by hand without an engine.*

Nat: *We even had lots of fun with the railroad people—no disturbances, just fun—enjoyin' how good we were and how good the railroad guys were. Up at two in the mornin' and lay our slicker on the ground and wait for daylight so we could get to the pens to load. We couldn't see one another before that. Waitin' for daylight, we'd either sleep or shoot dice. Uncle Tom Ball loved to deal; we'd do some gamblin'.*

Dan: *That's when I was in my prime. I'd like to see it all again.*

Nat: *Yeah, we'd do it and leave the sun hangin'.*

Dan: *We baled two thousand bales of hay a day in our time.*

Nat: *They can't get nobody to match it now, and there was a many a one in our day couldn't take it, either.*

Dan: *Everythin' was clockwork—we learned how to do this from the old guys, them what knows.*

Nat: *You know, Dan, there ain't no more cowboys. We'd feed them cattle all winter and then have to go out there and mug them down.*

Dan: *Sometimes we'd have as many as sixteen hundred in a bunch in our day. Now we have Dairy Queen cowboys—nothin' but small herds that anybody can work. We had them bad steers and cows—had to ride in the brush to find them. You had to really be on your toes. They was bellerin' and we was yellin' "Let 'em out!"*

Nat: *Steers were draggin' two men on 'em.*

Dan: *On Saturdays, sometimes we'd have three or four hundred to throw—we get off when we got through. There would be five men throwing 'em—we'd finish by two or three. We could get down and move when we had to.*

Nat: *We'd eat breakfast here at Vidauri, dinner at Sarco, work the Terrell, and be back for supper.*

Dan: *We didn't know what a pickup was back then. We'd leave at two in the mornin'—make it fourteen or fifteen miles to Sarco by daylight. We'd dip and drench those steers—twenty-one hundred of 'em in three hours and fifteen minutes. Mr. Chris [West] was the best I ever seen callin' 'em out on the chute. We had a trainload once—every minute we would load a car.*

Nat: *They say we was the fastest up and down this line.*

Dan: *One day we moved the bull board too fast and a steer dropped down. Bill just dropped down and lifted him in that car while Boo was yellin', "Confound, let 'em come on!"*

Nat: *I don't care what you say—you never match it.*

Dan: *I don't know how we did it ourselves; these young ones couldn't do it.*

Nat: *No, they couldn't. Ain't got a horse now that can lope to the West Ranch.*

Dan: *I had the same horse fall with me five times in one day. Strange we never got banged up too much. I guess a lot of it was we knew how to do it—we understood how to do it.*

Nat: *One time we were swimmin' a cook wagon across the creek and the mess box floated off. We went through some stuff people today wouldn't believe. We'd be in a pen bogged down to our bellies and they never stopped yellin', "Bring 'em on, boys."*

Dan: *We had some bad days out there, too, when it wasn't fun—stampedes and thunderstorms. One day we got scared goin' from the Terrell Ranch to the McFaddin pens. There was a big hailstorm and we couldn't hold 'em. There were claps of thunder and lightnin' like big balls of smoke right over those steers. It busted over 'em and they almost stampeded. All we could do was stay ahead of 'em and hold 'em back.*

Nat: *The only stampede I can remember was down at Angelita—on a horse called Popeye. When they stampeded, that horse slipped and those steers was comin' over me like hotcakes. All I could do was yell "whoa"—and I never got a scratch.*

Dan: *The only way you can stop those boogers is to mill 'em. Circlin' 'em won't do it. Millin' and circlin' are two different things. When you mill 'em, you have to make 'em go back and hit their own selves. Circlin', they just keep on runnin'. You gotta know these things.*

The only time we're really scared was durin' a hailstorm. We usually got fun out of runnin'.

One year we was comin' out of Angelita to the pens with about fifteen hundred head of steers. The horses were just waitin' for 'em to break. Boo's [Fred Terrell] horse Pelau was really ready. He broke and there was steers goin' everywhere. We hit the brush and rounded 'em up and got 'em back to the pens—all in a day's work.

Nat: *Boy, we could count those cattle in those days.*

Dan: *Yeah, we had some good counters. Mr. McCan could count 'em fast; he counted thirteen hundred through a gate one time in an hour. He just didn't miss—he was good.*

Nat: *We was around Louis Power when they brought cattle over. He could count and he could pop that whip.*

Dan: *I like to see that cuttin' out of the herd.*

Nat: *Me, too. Catch the boss lookin' the other way so we could run. It was hard work, but it didn't seem like it. Hard workin'—didn't seem like we was doing nothin'—lotsa foolishness goin' on.*

Dan: *Yeah, we'd sit up till twelve or one—hoorawin' each other, even after all that hard work. That reminds me one time when we crossed sixteen hundred head of steers in a big rain. When we come to that creek, that water was boilin', just boilin'. That was one time I got scared. I sho' hated to cross that creek. Mr. Welder went to look at the Medio Creek and said we had to cross. I was really scared this time. Mr. Welder told us how to do it; he was right there with us. I didn't want to hit that water, but we had to. I hit it and my horse started sinkin' with me. I said, "Lord, this is it." I had pulled him too hard. Then I came to my senses and slacked him—that horse knowed what to do. When I slacked him, that's what he wanted. He just raised me up in that water. He had more sense than I did. We made it that day; we usually did. There were some drownin's out here, but my horses always got me through. We finally got 'em outta there—it was a rough day.*

Nat: *There used to be some wicked things happen down here, real dangerous stuff.*

Dan: *Yeah, there used to be big hailstorms durin' plantin' time in April. Back then, we was usin' horses and mules to plant. It come a big hailstorm one day before we could get to the end of the row. I couldn't hold them horses; the only way I could stop 'em was to whip 'em around into the wind and rain. I finally got my knife and got to cuttin' ropes and let 'em go. Everything they do now is push-button.*

Nat: *Yeah, we kept on workin'—we did what had to be done. I think it was healthy. It made you tough. It seems impossible the things we done. Doesn't seem like stuff such as that went on, but it did.*

When I look back on things like that I start shakin'. I wonder why in the world did I do such stuff.

Dan: *I guess the mosquitoes were the worst thing we had to go through. Them boogers was so big they could almost bite through a slicker. Me and a fella called Bully—me and him was big friends—they'd send us for cows, ridin' sometimes two days at a time and never see the backside of the pasture. We would go a long way in open country and not see no cattle. We covered a lot of territory in a mornin' and we'd wind up near the bay. We'd slip down to the bay and eat them oysters for dinner. That was on the Chocolate Bayou Ranch. Me and him was big friends; he always wanted me to ride with him.*

It wasn't just the cow ponies. We had some horses for pull that were as good as the cow ponies. I believe they could pull a mountain. We used them for a snatch team. It was a cold day—rainin' and sleetin'. I was gonna make 'em pull it to the house. I don't know how they knew it, but they knew I was gonna make them pull somethin' heavy. It was Old Blue and Old Roxy—my best. Man, that was some powerful horses. They started pullin' and went to their knees and when they

got up, they got it outta there—me and them both. I sho' was in
trouble that day—but they saved us both. They was just natchel
good horses.

I used to be leadin' cattle when the cows began to get rowdy. You had
to sing to 'em. It was a sound—a moanin'. They hear that voice and it
would settle them down. You could get their attention—they'd raise
their head up and you could get them in control. Somethin' cattle is
afraid of is thunder and lightnin'. They get away from you too far and
that's when you got to sing to 'em. You gotta be close to 'em—close
enough to where they'll raise the horse's tail up ever now and then.
That sound means a whole lot. Everybody can't lead cattle—you gotta
know when to give and you gotta know when to take. Some people
give too much. I will, too, but then you come to yourself. Tighten
down on 'em slowly and keep on singin' to 'em. When you get that
sound there, then you can control 'em. You can see 'em settle down.
That's why they wouldn't let me cook; I could sing to 'em. First thing
they tell me when they get the steers out is, "Go in the lead, Dan."
I used to love that—leadin' those cattle. It was kinda like church.

Nat: *Yeah, just everyday life. The same old seven and six.*

"I hardly ever go off this ranch. I was fifteen or sixteen before I saw
a town. I've worked here most of my life; never worked for nobody but
Welder. Cowboyin' was a dangerous business back in those days, but
I didn't want to pick that cotton. I wanted to be a cowboy. I learned from
Boo [Fred Terrell] and Uncle Tom. We had some good days and some bad
days, but I'd like to see them all again."

Dan Youngblood
"Tea Cakes"
"Wood"
Tophand and Farmer
Welder Ranch, Vidauri
1918–1987

"These ranches were strength to us. It was our backbone—like leanin' on
somethin'. You didn't worry about nothin'. It seems impossible, the things
we done. We'd do it and leave the sun hangin'. There wasn't no eight-hour
days—it was from can't to can't and no coffee break. It hurts when you
look back over—now guys are makin' more than we did, gettin' better
breaks, and can't even do what I can do now and I'm an old, broke-down
man. We had to come on with the come on—wudn't no ifs about it. You
had to put out. That was a sweet life; I wouldn't take nothin' for it.
It couldn't be beat."

Nathaniel Youngblood
"Little Baby"
Tophand
Welder Ranch, Vidauri

These Ranches Were Our Homes

After you stay on a place so long, you'd get attached to it, especially when the people you worked for were real nice. We took care of y'all's stuff like it was ours. These ranches were our homes. Not all of us felt this way, but most did. For many of us it is like we own that place. Whenever we go away, we don't feel at home until we come back. These owners believe in their land, and we pick up that feelin' from them. We felt we had a part in these ranches. Sometimes after two or three drinks of whiskey, these ranches did belong to us. We took our jobs seriously. People don't feel that way now. This attitude was passed down to us by our fathers. We helped each other out—the ranchers and us hands. The owners were out there with us. You know, many of us never gave the land much thought in our workin' days. Our concern was for the cattle and other animals. Now when a bunch of us gets together, we often talk about land and the fact that there ain't gonna be no more made. The world changes, people change, and what you think about changes when you get older.

Mike Adames, Mike Adames, Jr., Willie Brown, Alex de la Garza, Johnny de la Garza, Sam de la Garza, E. J. Garza, Charlie Hernandez, Clayton Isaiah, Jesse Jones, Horace Joshlin, Quinn Love, Henry Morrow, Abel Perez, Mike Rivas, Nick Rivas, Victor Rodriguez, Leo Scott, Monroe "Bailey" Shaw, L. V. Terrell, Henry Tijerina, Julian Tijerina, Porfirio Urbano, McKinley Williams, Rev. Mack Williams, Jesus Ybarbo

It's Go and Get It!

We were called cowhands on the ranch. In cities and in the movies was the only place you ever heard the term "cowboy."

You can tell a real cowhand by the way he sits a horse. If he sits proud, he's good; he understands, he pays attention, and watches others who know.

Cowboyin' gets in the bloodstream and flows down through the generations. All that a rodeo cowboy knows is ropin' and bronc-ridin', and that all happens in eight seconds. A real cowboy knows it all—ropin', ridin', and knowin' cattle, all day long.

A cowman works with his brains, and a cowhand works with his hands, but a cowhand has to be smart, too. He has to have real good common sense, patience, and be an all-around man. It takes more than boots and a hat to be a good cowhand. It's go and get it—ridin' and workin' a hundred and fifty head of cattle before breakfast. You don't sleep late; you gotta get on the road while the coyotes are howlin'.

Being a cowhand is like cookin'—two who know what they're doin' are better than fifteen who don't. To be a good cowhand, you gotta learn to roll with the punches, stay calm, and accept responsibility.

The life of a cowhand is to know horses and cattle. It's come on—one kicks you in the head and you don't think a thing about it cause you're cowboyin'. We worked hard back in them days, but it was a good life.

Pete Brown, Sonny Brown, Ananias Cook, Richard Harris, Clayton Isaiah, Jesse Jones, Coleman Joshlin, Joe Keefe, K. J. Oliver, Abel Perez, Monroe "Bailey" Shaw, L. V. Terrell, Earl Ward, Bill Welder, Dennis Williams, Rev. Mack Williams

From Can't to Can't

We used to eat breakfast at three in the mornin', have lunch when we could catch it, and supper around eight or nine. Long day, wasn't it?

Yeah, but that's the enjoyable work in life. We've been asked many a time: When do you folks sleep? Cowboys get less sleep than anybody.

We been gettin' up all our lives. It's just like drinkin' water to us. We were raised to get up.

We started out when you could see and quit when you couldn't see.

We worked from sun to sun and after sometimes.

Back in the old days, it was dark when we started out. The horses would have to guide us.

Posthole digger near Aransas River. Photo by Roger Fleming.

Tick dipping at Mexican Water Hole, ca. 1922.

Greta shipping pens, ca. 1920's.

We were dippin', brandin', and doin' fence work from see to dark, even if it was rainin'. Then we'd shuck corn for the horses.

Monday was the baddest day and Friday was the longest day.

These young boys now don't know up from down, or what a long day means. Back in the old days, we had done a day's work by the time these youngsters start their breakfast. It took longer to get our work done.

God, work was fun back in those days. It was you and me and take it— knockin' cattle back, cuttin' three or four out of the herd, and when that happened you better be ridin'.

Longhorn cattle in Salt Creek pasture, 1923.

When you had a big bunch of cattle, you had to talk to them. Those old-time cattle were wilder than today's. You had to be quiet and calm when you worked them.

They were small, with long tails that dragged the ground—mean and wild. We had to drive them in a trot to hold them together. You couldn't kill them, but they could sure kill you. Nowadays, they don't hardly even work cattle. You honk the horn now and they come to you.

Back in our younger days each cow crowd had their own sounds they worked by. Workin' or drivin' a herd was high-level business. Everyone had their job. We all had special positions around the herd and every job was important, but the point man at the front of the herd was special. You were really cowboyin' when you worked your way up to the front.

The work we did in this area was real different than other areas. Cowboys from other places didn't know how to work here. I guess they weren't tough enough. We've seen a lot of them come through, but very few stayed.

Pushing the herd, 1930's. Photo by Dennis O'Connor [II].

Cattle herd, Tom O'Connor Jr. [III] Ranch, Refugio, Texas, 1920's.

We've seen a lot of changes. The young people don't run ranches like they used to. The old people ran them better. They had more stock and they were easier on their cattle. They couldn't hold the light for their daddies and granddaddies.

Cattle are funny beasts—you have to know how to handle them. The boss always cut the herd and he knew how to do it.

The most important thing is learning how to read a cow's mind. You gotta figure that out every day. Things change every day in cow work.

Breakin' a mill or makin' a sweep is tough work.

Open herd work, 1930's.
Photo by Dennis O'Connor [II].

Dehorning and
castrating, 1930's.
Photo by Dennis O'Connor [II].

You pray to God your horse don't step in a gopher hole. He has to be light on his feet. He better be a stepper. Cow work is like a ballet. Everyone knows how to move and flow with the cattle. If someone messes up, it can go real wrong. There are days when everythin' works right and days when nothin' goes right.

We worked out in the open. We didn't know what a pen was. Dippin' and shippin' was the only time we used pens.

We went down that rope a many a time, muggin' calves in a wet duckin' jumper to keep cool.

How to brand properly? You burn until the hide is the color of a new duckin' jacket. If you have a choice, work a cow away from the sun and into the wind. The effect that weather has on cow-workin' would fill an encyclopedia.

There's a lot more brush now than there used to be. Just the boys at the Melon Creek Ranch knew brush work in the old days. Brush work needed different cowhands and different horses.

The bushes were crawlin' with cattle back in the twenties, thirties, and forties, and a bird couldn't get through that thicket, it was so bad.

Our brush riders were tough. They could even outride the *Kinenos* because their brush would break, ours wouldn't.

A cat couldn't make it through our brush. It made tough men and tough horses.

That's ranch life—the cowboy life. Sun up to sun down. If you didn't get up before daylight and quit after dark, you weren't a real cowboy. That's the way it was.

Buster Bickford, Pete Brown, Sonny Brown, Willie Brown, Bill Charleston, Ananias Cook, E. D. "Rusty" Coward, Rafael de la Garza, Freddy Fagan, Bud Harvey, Clayton Isaiah, Jesse Jones, Coleman Joshlin, Horace Joshlin, Will King, Tony Lott, Quinn Love, Bobby McCan, Tom O'Connor, Jr. [III], K. J. Oliver, Abel Perez, Camillo Ramirez, Romulo Ramirez, Simmie Rydolph, Leo Scott, Monroe "Bailey" Shaw, L. V. Terrell, Milam Thompson, Julian Tijerina, Earl Ward, Rev. Mack Williams, McKinley Williams

Salt Creek Ranch, 1930's.
Photo by Vincent Fritz.

FOOLS ON GOOD HORSES: THE COWHANDS

Tom O'Connor, Jr. [III] and Rusty Coward cooling off, ca. 1925.

Little Bitta Ol' Barefoot Boys

It was pretty loose and free growin' up out here on the ranch. You could go where you wanted to. We didn't want to go to town for anything, unless we were told not to. Then we couldn't get to town fast enough to go to Jecker's store and buy a Delaware Punch and a pack of cigarettes. We used to have lots of fun comin' up as kids.

From the time we were little boys. We made our own toys and played with them like we were imitatin' our daddies. We all knew one another when we were kids, playin' cowboy together. We made balin' wire spurs, and rode tree limbs when we were too young for horses. We smoked a lot of cedar bark cigarettes, too. We gave our mama's chickens and turkeys hell—dippin' them in the water troughs and practicin' our ropin' on them. We killed a many a rooster tyin' him down.

Our stickhorses were made of willow and seeney bean limbs. We had lots of fun makin' those horses, and makin' animals out of river mud. We would tie our stickhorses to the fence by their twine bridles, and then we watered them. Some of them we made into pintos by peelin' the bark, and some were just plain colors. Kids don't play now like they used to. We spent our childhood runnin' around in the river

"You know, I bet there were days when Rusty and I rode twenty miles or more playin' cowboy. When we got home, we would jump in the tank at the house and cool off like the cows did."

Tom O'Connor, Jr. [III]

bottom, fishin', and huntin', and ridin' our stickhorses.

Our corrals were made of mud and twigs, and no chicken could get away from us—we ran and roped everything that moved. Window cord and fishin' line made good ropes. It's a booger to get a rope off a turkey's neck. We could rope a cat as good as some people could rope a cow—heaven help mama's yard animals. They would see us comin' and scatter and run; they'd be lookin' for somewhere to go.

We were just little bitta ol' barefoot boys playin' around the ranch— swimmin, shootin' marbles, and ridin' tree limbs so we could be cowboys. Brandin' corn cobs was one of our favorites. We made our brandin' irons out of balin' wire.

Anaqua, Morrowville, Kemper City, Tivoli, Austwell, and the River Ranch. These were some of the schools we went to. We loved to get out of school. We played hookey a lot so we could play cowboy. Ridin' and ropin' milk cows taught us a lot, too. We loved to play cowboys, but we would also hide and bushwhack each other—we were the Three Musketeers. Chinaberries were bullets for our homemade guns, and sardine cans were our wagons and cars. Horned toads pulled our wagons, and we would sometimes get them to smoke cigarettes.

We were always barefooted—we didn't know what shoes were. We were pretty artistic in our time, makin' toys and entertainin' ourselves. We loved to camp down in the river bottom, and eat rabbits and gars. Boys and girls weren't allowed to play together in the Mexican culture, but the blacks and whites were. The girls played church a lot. Kids weren't allowed around the grown-ups either. Mainly, we just played the same games as all kids do in the country and waited to be cowboys. We had to find something to play with, and we did. If children had to do this now, they might be a lot better off. Kids are weaker now but no wiser. Livin' in the country teaches you a lot about life. We were always showin' out in front of the girls. Ridin' and bulldoggin' hogs was great sport. Anything we could get on, we would ride. We had to make our own play. We'd be rich if we had a penny for every mile we rode on stickhorses, hogs, and tree limbs.

Some of us didn't get to play much as children. It was work from sun up to sundown. Others, especially those that grew up at McFaddin, got to ride Shetland ponies all the time.

We just about all carried food to school in a molasses bucket lined with a flour sack dishcloth. Our sandwiches were made of lard, or sausage and eggs. We had to be grown before we could wear long pants, but we always ate good as kids. We walked along the Santone river with a bucket in one hand carryin' our lunch. We'd stop by a gum tree and get chickadee—that was our chewin' gum.

We loved to ride Shetland ponies, and some of us were lucky to get to ride Matt Jones—Jesse's daddy. He was tougher and meaner than any horse. Gettin' to ride in a buggy was a lot of fun, too.

Children used to have curfews when we were young. Kids aren't controlled now. We had to go to Sunday school and church. We were given chores and jobs when we were young—pumpin' water for the animals and shuckin' corn. We didn't have much leisure time. We only got to play when the grownups were gone.

It's a hard job to raise children now. The ages didn't mix back then. The older kids couldn't teach the younger ones too much mischief. Discipline was strict, and stealin' was not allowed. All the folks were our bosses. There was a whole different attitude about discipline then. If parents were tough now, things would be better. We didn't go out until we were fourteen

FOOLS ON GOOD HORSES: THE COWHANDS

or fifteen — no honky-tonkin'. The old folks were strict. Kids are not so naive now, the way they were back then. It was better raisin' back then — no stealin', no drugs. We played or worked all day long. Youngsters are born smart now. In our day, kids used to have to stay off to themselves. They are smarter now, but they don't have as much fun. We didn't know what TV was, and we were lucky if we heard a radio. A real treat was to get to go to the movies. We came home and played cowboy after the movie was over.

We watched the old heads work cattle a lot — that's how we learned. We took turns bein' the boss. Back in those days, people sat on their porches. We sang, wrestled, and had races. We're proud of what our parents taught us — to work and be honest.

Buster Bickford, John Brown, Pete Brown, Sonny Brown, Willie Brown, Kai Buckert, Ascension Campos, Bill Charleston, Ananias Cook, E. D. "Rusty" Coward, Alex de la Garza, Candelario de la Garza, Elias de la Garza, Johnny de la Garza, Rafael de la Garza, Freddy Fagan, E. J. Garza, A. M. Groll, Jr., Franklin "Bud" Harvey, Mose Henderson, Charlie Hernandez, Jesse Jones, Horace Joshlin, J. Y. Lott, Tony Lott, Quinn Love, Rufus Moore, Henry Moore, Thomas Michael O'Connor, Tom O'Connor, Jr. [III], Frank Perez, Jr., Camillo Ramirez, Romulo Ramirez, Mike Rivas, Nick Rivas, Tom Rodgers, Victor Rodriguez, Elvin Scott, Leo Scott, Monroe "Bailey" Shaw, Wallace Shay, Ed Steward, Jr., L. V. Terrell, Milam Thompson, Henry Tijerina, Julian Tijerina, Manuel Tijerina, Porfirio Urbano, Rev. Albert Wade, Will Weathers, Leo Welder, Rev. Mack Williams, McKinley Williams, Jesus Ybarbo, Dan Youngblood, Nathaniel Youngblood

The Movie Cowboys

"I never fooled around no movies — my movies were down amongst them cattle and those people on the Santone River."

Richard Harris
Foreman
Murphy Ranches

Sunset Carson.

Buck Jones.

Hoot Gibson

Bob Baker

Life Ain't Never That Easy

We would come back to the ranch and try to do the things we saw in the movies. There was a many a tear-up tryin' to teach those horses tricks, like lettin' us jump up on their backs and ridin' them fast. It was ten cents admission, and five cents for popcorn, and you got to see the cowboy heroes rescue girls, shoot lots of people, ride like hell—wide open and never rest a horse. You know, they didn't have a whole lot of time to work cattle, they were busy with the ladies.

If there ever was any cow workin', we would watch close to see if they did it right. That was about as bad lookin' a sight as a show cuttin' horse. Not even close to real life, but we loved it anyway.

They was runnin' and shootin' and fightin' all the time, but each one had his little special characteristics. Jack Holt always caught rustlers. He was hired by the ranchers' association to stop cattle thieves. In *The Colorado Kid* one time, they showed a hangin'—it was the first time anyone ever saw that.

Sunset Carson, the Durango Kid, Lash Larue, Charles Starrett, and Hoot Gibson—they could shoot all day and never run out of bullets. You know, Tom Mix was actually a cowboy before he became a movie star. He always rolled his hat. Bob Steele was so easy to hate, and Bob Baker was always singin' about bein' "forty miles from water." Wild Bill Hickok was good with a pistol and always had a little smile around his mouth. He rode a paint horse named Sonny. Trigger spent all of his time on his back legs, and we loved it. Tom Mix dressed so fine with those high heels and silver spurs. He knew how to dress right. Colonel Tim McCoy was higher-classed than all of them. Many a good cowboy star had to drop out when the singin' started.

I don't know that we ever related our movie heroes to the ranches, other than to try to do some of the things we saw on the screen. This never worked out very well, but we kept on tryin', and would learn somethin' new every week to kill ourselves with.

Buck Jones was a fist fighter, and Lullaby Johnson was tall and rough, and when he walked in a place everybody got quiet. Everybody in the movie house would get quiet, too. We would get real involved in the pictures. One time at the movie in Refugio, a local lawman got so excited during the film that he shot the screen out and had to pay for it. We were such country kids when we saw our first movies. We were spurrin' the chairs and hollerin' at the screen. I guess we thought it was real for a while—or maybe we wanted it to be real. Life ain't never that easy. We should have known.

John Brown, Candelario de la Garza, Elias de la Garza, Johnny de la Garza, E. J. Garza, Clayton Isaiah, Coleman Joshlin, Will King, Quinn Love, K. J. Oliver, Frank Perez, Jr., Mike Rivas, Nick Rivas, Leo Scott, L. V. Terrell, Henry Tijerina, Julian Tijerina, Earl Ward, Rev. Mack Williams, Jesus Ybarbo

Drugstore Cowboys and Rodeoers: Jerks in Fuzzy Hats

Rodeoers are usually make-believe cowboys. The two professions don't mix too well, they are so different. Rodeo cowboys aren't a whole lot like what comes off these ranches. The good ranch hands are a lot tougher; they know the dangers and how to handle themselves.

A real cowboy stays on his horse any way he can—the other kind just has to make his eight seconds and that's usually only for ropin' and bronc ridin'. A real cowboy knows it all.

You throw a rodeo cowboy in O'Connor's brush and you got somebody you're gonna have to go get. They're big hats and big boots—they never stepped where a cow stepped.

Western fashion is about jerks wearin' leather coats, chains, two-toned boots, and fuzzy cowboy hats.

They don't know what they're using or what they're usin' it for. Real cowboy clothes are a necessity—not fashion.

Many rodeoers can't make it on ranches. Out here, when we ride a horse, it's for dear life—any way you can manage to stay on him.

Don't try to class us with rodeoers. A rodeo cowboy's gonna get kilt down here. He's not set for the action on a ranch. Ain't nobody gonna help you out there but the good Lord. Our cattle were too wild for rodeo cowboys.

Many of us had to rodeo to make ends meet and that was a long eight seconds, but anybody can stand on the street corner and talk big.

Let's see them make one day with us out in the brush.

John Brown, John Cliburn, Ananias Cook, E. D. "Rusty" Coward, Elias de la Garza, E. J. Garza, Jesse Jones, Coleman Joshlin, Quinn Love, Henry Morrow, K. J. Oliver, Abel Perez, Frank Perez, Jr., Rumaldo Perez, Mike Rivas, Simmie Rydolph, Leo Scott, Leo Welder, Rev. Mack Williams

Devilment: When the Boss Was Gone

Most of our shenanigans the bosses never saw. Times have changed now. We were together all the time, and we had fun. There was lots of devilment out there when no one was looking.

We made the horses pitch so we could midnight-rodeo. If we had ever been caught, that would have been the end of it.

Anything would jump up in front of us, we would rope it and the race would be on.

We had our rodeos ourselves when we'd catch the boss gone—ridin' the milk cows. We'd hem them up, get on them, and learn to ride.

We got pretty good at breakin' a calf's neck so we could have some fresh meat, too.

Yeah, there was lots of devilment—shootin' dice in the church and ropin' hogs from them good horses. We could have killed those horses.

Wonder if the bosses really missed what we done, or did they just turn their backs when the show was goin' on?

Pete Brown, Sonny Brown, Willie Brown, Bill Charleston, Ananias Cook, Bud Harvey, Clayton Isaiah, Jesse Jones, Will King, J. Y. Lott, Tony Lott, Quinn Love, Rufus Moore, Nat Nixon, Abel Perez, Suey Richardson, Simmie Rydolph, Elvin Scott, Leo Scott, Monroe "Bailey" Shaw, L. V. Terrell, Jesus Ybarbo, Dan Youngblood, Nathaniel Youngblood

FOOLS ON GOOD HORSES: THE COWHANDS

"Lookin' for trouble, that's a foreman's job."

E. D. Coward
"Rusty"
Foreman
O'Connor Melon Creek Ranch

"A good cowman has to be a good cowhand, but a good cowhand doesn't have to be a cowman."

Dennis Williams
Foreman
O'Connor Brothers Ranches
Rancher

Earl Ward, 1918–1986.
Photo by Louise S. O'Connor.

"You develop an instinct about taking care of yourself out there or you'd soon be dead. You don't have to be rough, but it sure helps 'cause the good part is the rough part. Why do I do it? Stupid, I guess. I wouldn't say I love it, but I'd miss it if I couldn't do it."

Earl Ward
Itinerant Cowhand
Foreman
O'Connor Ranches
1918–1986

BOSSING

The Foremen: It's Our Responsibility

I think that we would want just as much for the land and cattle as the people who own it. Sometimes I think we want more. The land and the animals are our responsibility; that's what we are here for. Sometimes if we see abuses, it is like a personal affront to us, just as if it was ours. It is possible that foremen are as equally attached to the animals as the land. We treat both as if they were ours.

Kai Buckert
Joe Keefe
Wesley Vivian
Earl Ward
Dennis Williams

The Totem Pole: The Bosses' View

A good boss knows his men well. You have to be firm but understanding. You have to realize that you know more than your workers or you wouldn't have the job.

It's important to know your men well, to talk to them and know each one's name and his strengths and weaknesses.

A boss has to maintain his superior position. Being one of the guys doesn't work. It affects you emotionally to get down with the men, and it affects your judgment.

It's easy to understand a cow and horse; a man is a different story.

Men don't like to be chewed out in front of others. They don't like to be pushed around. You get a lot more work out of a man by being kind.

Two men can't ride the same saddle. It just doesn't work. The man in charge must be in complete control and be able to see the whole picture.

It takes a while to gain respect and establish an identity. You learn the men by working with them, and you aren't necessarily the most popular fellow around.

The cowhands are your eyes and ears. If you have a good rapport with them, you can have twenty-twenty vision.

A ranch owner designates authority to the foremen. If we're good, he doesn't have to worry. The boss should tell the foreman to do something, but not how to do it.

It's kind of like the army. There's a pecking order, and foremen are second on the totem pole.

Pete Brown
John Cliburn
E. D. "Rusty" Coward
Joe Keefe
Tom O'Connor, Jr. [III]
Bill Welder
Leo Welder

*"What's a cowhand? He's a fool
on a good horse."*

K. J. Oliver
"K"
Itinerant Tophand

*"A good cowhand is like a good
bird dog: there's an instinct
born in him."*

Ananias Cook
"Frog"
Tophand
Welder Ranch
Vidauri
1909–1984

The Tophands

A tophand is a man who can handle any job. He is looked up to by the others. He is a leader, a good hand that everyone could depend on. Often the tophands are put on salaries instead of hours or days.

They know a whole lot about cattle and they ain't lazy. He likes his job and will learn.

Tophands are always on a horse. They're responsible for the water, the land, the fences, and the cattle.

After you got good at all this, you were a tophand, but some never made it all their lives.

Ananias Cook, Clayton Isaiah, Jesse Jones, J. Y. Lott, Tony Lott, Quinn Love, Abel Perez, Frank "Pancho" Perez, Jr., Leo Scott, L. V. Terrell, Manuel Tijerina, Dan Youngblood

"I'll tell you about that ranch life. It was tough, but I never thought about it that way. If it rained, it just rained. Mosquitoes couldn't get too bad to stop us. When I was a cowboy you were just out there—horses fallin' on you, calves fallin' on you, your bones gettin' broke up. If I hadn't started preachin', I'd still be there. If I could recall my days back, I'd go to that ranch rather than anywhere I've ever been. I like that life."

Rev. Mack Williams
"El Coyote Prieto"
Tophand
O'Connor Peach Mott Ranch

"I was born down on the Santone River. I wanted to be a cowboy. I loved the rough stuff, ropin' bad bulls, and stayin' in camp. That's when life was good."

L. V. Terrell
Tophand
O'Connor Ranches
1916–1989

"Monkey see, monkey do—that's how I learned."

Porfirio Urbano
"Lapo"
Tophand
McFaddin Ranch

"I work cattle for a livin'. Someone has to do this job. It's what I've done all my life."

Manuel Tijerina
Tophand
O'Connor Ranches

"I guess I was born crazy. I'd ride any animal I could get close enough to kiss."

Sonny Brown
Tophand
Traylor Ranch

FOOLS ON GOOD HORSES: THE COWHANDS

"I was born on the Santone River. Goin' to Redlew was like goin' to New York. I was twenty years old before I seen a picture show. We pounded out the way for these young boys."

S. W. Lott
"Tony"
Tophand
Welder Ranches
Vidauri

"It was cowboyin' or balin' hay and I didn't want to work behind a mule. I like to ride. I was a pasture rider. The registered cows were my special job. I knew each one by heart."

Henry Tijerina
Tophand
O'Connor Ranches

"Guero's [Abel Perez] the last of the great brush riders; there aren't any more like him. The copters do that kind of work now."

E. D. Coward
"Rusty"
Foreman
O'Connor Melon Creek Ranch

"When I first started goin' out on the cow crowd, I couldn't sleep the night before, I was thinkin' about it so hard. It was a good life. It didn't seem like work, it seemed like play."

Leo Scott
Itinerant Tophand
Rancher

"I was born among cowhands and horsemen. I guess it must run in my blood. I love workin' with horses and cattle, but my favorite thing is breakin' and handlin' horses."

Frank Perez, Jr.
"Pancho"
Tophand
O'Connor Ranches

"I don't build fences, I don't fix windmills—I just work cattle."

Camillo Ramirez
Tophand
O'Connor Ranches
1910–1983

"There was somethin' about those days in cow camp. It was fun. It seemed like it would go on forever. If I could ride again, if I was able, right quick, I'd be back there workin' cattle."

Jesse Jones
Tophand
O'Connor Ranches

"If you was raised up on it, you can't get it out of your blood no way. I don't care what you do or where you go; you see a cow, it takes your attention. If you was born and raised on it, you gonna die with it in you. You get a thrill out of it. It's in my blood, it's my life."

Pete Brown
Tophand
Foreman
Traylor Ranch

"I grew up here on the Santone River in a cowboyin' family. My grandpa, John Summers, went up the trail. I thought about farmin', but cowboyin' was in me. I knew how to work cattle, so I stuck with it. I like it; it's all I ever done."

Quinn Love
Itinerant Tophand

"You gotta be able to read a cow's mind. That's the most important thing."

Romulo Ramirez
Tophand
O'Connor Ranches

"I like cow workin'. I love to hear a cow bawlin'."

Mike Adames, Sr.
Tophand
McFaddin Ranch

"I loved it; it was joy — a joy out of ridin' horses. It wasn't for the prestige. I just enjoyed it. I'd still be out there if I hadn't started preachin'."

Rev. Coleman Joshlin
"Cokie"
Tophand
Welder Ranch
Vidauri

"We ain't no account now, but we enjoy thinkin' about what we've done. What makes it sweet, we can do it a little till yet."

Rufus Moore
"Slim"
Tophand
Welder Ranch
Seadrift

"We felt like brothers. We helped one another; it made it easier to work. We would depend on each other like a family, we were that close. That feelin' stays forever. It don't never change."

Nick Rivas
Tophand
O'Brien Ranches

"I was raised on a horse and worked cattle all my life. I love to ride, rope, and rodeo. That's why I wanted to be a cowhand."

Mike Rivas
"Midnight"
Tophand
O'Brien Ranches

"Why did I cowboy? My Daddy was a cowboy. I started when I was eight, herdin' remuda. *That's what I love."*

Elvin Scott
Tophand
McFaddin Ranches

"This here's a hard story—workin' for fifty cents a day—mostly ranch work. I had a raggedy saddle with both stirrups broke, but I stayed with it. Been cowboyin' all my life."

John Brown
Tophand
O'Brien Ranches

"I enjoy this kind of work. I like workin' with horses and cattle. There are a lot of other jobs I can do, but I'd rather live and work at a ranch. I dream about cow-workin' every night because I can't cowboy no more. I got hurt."

Elias de la Garza
"Liza"
Tophand
O'Connor Ranches

"Sometimes I get the feelin' I own this place, I've been here so long."

Elizardo Hernandez
"Charlie"
Foreman and Tophand
T. M. O'Connor Ranches
1911–1985

"I had other choices in life, but I wanted to ride them horses."

McKinley Williams
Tophand
O'Connor Ranches

"Give me a horse and a saddle and I'll go back to the Santone River and ride. I love that."

J. Y. Lott
"Fry"
"Slim"
Itinerant Tophand

"Hot or cold, we were there. If I hadn't gotten hurt, I'd still be out there. I I miss bein' a cowboy."

Julian Tijerina
Tophand
O'Connor Ranches

"It growed up in me. I can't explain it. I just inherited it. Harveys have always had cowboyin' in their blood."

Franklin Harvey
"Bud"
Tophand
Traylor Ranch

"I sure did like it — a bunch of men together in those days, workin' cattle. It was fun. It made me happy."

Jesus Ybarbo
Itinerant Tophand
Caretaker
O'Connor Cemetery

"I love to ride them bulls. When you come outta the chute and that hide starts rollin', it feels like he's fallin' in love with you, and by the time it's over, all you can hear is your bones crackin' and your spurs ringin'."

E. J. Garza
Itinerant Tophand
O'Brien Ranches

"I don't say much. I'm just a bull roper and a brush knocker."

Ascension Campos
Tophand
O'Connor Ranches

"We took care of the land and animals like they were ours. We took it seriously. Most people don't feel that way now."

Candelario de la Garza
"Sam"
Tophand
O'Connor Ranches

HORSES: A Fringe Benefit

"I felt a lot better when I was on top of a hoss."

E. J. Garza
Itinerant Tophand
O'Brien Ranches

We cared so much about our horses, we wouldn't let nobody fool with 'em.

We had some cow ponies out there was so good you could shut your eyes, throw your rope, and know you was on horseback.

Some of us loved our horses so much we couldn't quit the ranch. We stayed workin' there to make sure nobody hurt 'em or stove 'em up.

A good horse was the fringe benefit that made up for low pay. A famous sayin' among cowhands at the time was "As long as O'Connor got horses an' cattle, I don't need nothin'."

It was a good feelin' when it was comin' up to cow workin' time 'cause we got to ride the horses. Our horses were like our companions. You was sick all day if you didn't have a good horse.

Every time you saddle a horse, it's your happy day. You feel good when you straddle one. Nobody loves an old horse better than a cowhand. It was the only excitement we had.

We used to talk to our horses, tellin' 'em what we were goin' to do, callin' 'em bad names— tellin' 'em what we were thinkin'. We used to talk to 'em with our hands too—through the reins.

Not all horses were good. Some were no-account, rough, and lazy—but when they were good, you really loved 'em. Sometimes they could save your life in a tight situation.

A typical Coastal Bend cowboy rig.

A lot of us liked our horses better than we liked most people—we liked 'em better than anythin' out there.

There is nothin' worse than seein' a horse mistreated. To watch a man take out his frustrations on a horse is a sickenin' sight. You have to discipline a horse, but beyond that, it's abuse.

The greatest pleasure in the world was ridin' a good horse. It feels so good, it makes you proud.

You have to love a horse for him to work properly. I guess we get to know animals well because we live around 'em.

"A good hoss was our bread and butter—you depended on him for your life. Sometimes a good hoss was better than havin' another cowhand with you."

Clayton Isaiah
Tophand
O'Connor Ranches

There is a difference in the relationship between a man and a horse, and a man and cattle. With a horse, you can have a friend. A horse becomes a part of you.

A horse can be an equalizer between the young and the old. An old man can step up on a good horse and ride right with the young guys.

We used our horses for everythin'. If a man isn't a fool, he can learn from a good horse. A good horse keeps his mind on his business. He's like having another good hand with you.

Some are even better than people—they got a whole lot of sense.

A lot of us would have never made it without a good horse. They kept food in our mouth.

A horse back then meant to us what these pickups mean to kids now. It was our transportation. It did a day's work for us. If you weren't ridin' a good horse, you got the blues. The better man had the better horse, you were taller than the man on foot.

The horse was the most important thing around. He has to be quiet around cattle. Some horses are better at certain jobs.

Ridin' a bad horse is the hardest day's work you can do. A good horse makes it easy. A good cow horse watches a cow like a policeman watches a drunk on the highway. A tired horse is a dangerous animal; you have to know when to rest him.

Horse breaking.
Photo by Dennis O'Connor. [II].

When you're on a horse you're in control. Horses were stronger back then. You'd kill one today if you worked him like we used to.

I guess most cowhands like mares the best. A mare appreciates good treatment, like a woman.

There is just somethin' about your horse—you can talk to him. A good horse will make you love him. He's dependable and can make a hard day easy on you. You gotta have a horse that can step, one that knows what you're doin', what you intend to do. A horse can outsmart a cow and, pound for pound, they're a strong animal. Horses get used to their environ-

FOOLS ON GOOD HORSES: THE COWHANDS

Quinn Love on a good horse, 1948.

ment and get good at handlin' what they have to deal with.

You know, those old-time horses were mostly Spanish. They were a lot tougher than they are now. You could ride 'em all day long and they'd pitch you off at night.

A workin' cow pony is a totally different animal than a show horse. They have to be much smarter and much calmer to work on a ranch. For example, a cuttin' horse that works a show arena is a completely useless animal. It would destroy a real herd of cattle in a minute. All show animals are generally useless on a ranch, but a cuttin' horse is the worst.

On a ranch, there are certain horses for certain jobs. We used our horses for everythin' and they had to do everythin', but they were always better at some jobs than others. For instance, you had to have a special horse for the brush—not just any horse could take that kind of beatin'. A good brush horse is smarter and tougher than the rest.

We all had our favorites for certain jobs.

A horse that was used for herd ropin' had to be very calm and would sit back well.

It makes you feel good to be given a special job because you had a good horse. If a man has a whole lot of cattle but you haven't got the horses, you would have to find somewhere else to work. A good horse is the main thing on a ranch. It advertises your ranch. Back in the old days, a cowhand would go to the ranch that had the best horses. That's how important a horse was.

There are lots of stories down in this river bottom about horses that would point and flush game. There is even one story about a retrievin' mule. There were horses that would bite cattle to make 'em work properly and horses that you only used on Sunday.

There are horses that were great swimmers and horses that could stop traffic on the highway when they were workin' cattle.

We've all been throwed every way you can imagine—on our heads, our faces, our backs.

If you ain't been throwed, you ain't been nowhere. It didn't bother us—it was part of our business. We really had fun ridin' horses. You can get a thrill out of somebody gettin' pitched off.

We've all bought more ground in our workin' days than the O'Connors own all put together. That's the life of a cowboy.

Buster Bickford, John Brown, Pete Brown, Sonny Brown, Kai Buckert, Bill Charleston, Ananias Cook, Alex de la Garza, Candelario de la Garza, Johnny de la Garza, E. J. Garza, Richard Harris, Bud Harvey, Clayton Isaiah, Jesse Jones, Coleman Joshlin, Joe Keefe, Will King, Henry Clay Koontz [IV], Quinn Love, Bobby Martin, C. K. McCan, Henry Morrow, Tom O'Connor, Jr. [III], K. J. Oliver, Abel Perez, Frank Perez, Jr., Mike Rivas, Nick Rivas, Leo Scott, Monroe "Bailey" Shaw, L. V. Terrell, Milam Thompson, Henry Tijerina, Julian Tijerina, Wesley Vivian, Earl Ward, Rev. Mack Williams, Jesus Ybarbo, Dan Youngblood

THE CATTLE: Telling the Grandmas Good-bye

"As long as a cow thinks she's doing what she wants to, she's happy."

Dennis Williams
Foreman
O'Connor Brothers Ranches
Rancher

You have to have feelings about a cow. You have to know how she feels to be able to do what you want to do with her.

There is a kind of bond you form with them when they have been on the ranch as long as you have. You have to reserve a special place in you for a cow. There's a part of you that's just there for cows. You got to have that, and if you don't have it, you're never gonna get it and you shouldn't work with them. You gotta be born with it.

You know, it wouldn't be that bad being an old cow, as long as you had plenty of water and grass. You may get hot and you may get cold, but your fur coat and the oak trees pretty much take care of that.

A cow is a family-oriented animal. They get used to each other—they have their buddies. All a cow needs is something to eat and drink. A cow knows what tastes good, and that's what she'll eat first. A cow has a big responsibility. She has to eat enough to keep her going, plus make enough milk to be sure her calf does well. When her number comes up, she can say, "Hey, I'm something. Look at what I got standing beside me." You can tell

Cattle at Copano Creek pens, O'Connor Melon Creek Ranch, 1920's.

a cow that has a good calf standing beside her. There is a strong bond between them. A cow that has a bad calf isn't interested in it, she isn't proud of it. If you see a bunch of calves together with one cow, she's baby-sitting. Each cow baby-sits voluntarily.

Cows don't relate to people unless they are dependent on them for food. They get accustomed to your presence and get to know one person from another. They know your habits. After the calves are sold, your lonesome days start in. The cows get so quiet. They don't have to look out for anything but themselves for a while.

These old grandma cows have been a part of you for so long that when you have to get rid of them, it's like some part of you is going with them. You really feel that way. There are some cows that especially make you remember them. When you have an old cow like that around and she has to go, you know you have to do it, but it hurts. She ain't there no more and becomes just a memory. The cowhands will often talk about certain memorable old cows among themselves.

You get a real affection for them. You hate to see them get down in the winter. An old Brahman cow can get down and she'll give you that look that she ain't gettin' back up, and you might as well break out the .30-30 and do it.

I feel almost weak about shipping those old cows—like you do when you are going to black out. I don't even want to punch one. I'm thinking, "Go on, Grandma, so I can be nice to you. It's the last time I'm ever going to see you." It's hard to make people understand the feelings you have for animals. You just have to get them where they are going and don't look back.

You have to be easy with a grandma cow. She has one speed when she

A cattle herd,
O'Connor Brothers Ranches,
Refugio County, Texas,
ca. 1920.

gets to that age, and everyone learns to respect that. You can't feel sorry for every cow that leaves this ranch, but sometimes I think I care more about those old cows than I do about most people.

Armour Joe Keefe
Straw Boss
O'Connor Brothers Ranches
Rancher

The World's Best Chemists

One thing about cattle—you never know what they are goin' to do. There were some bad cattle out there in our time.

You would have to sing to them to calm them down, and then sometimes they would still stampede on you. You can't make cattle do what you want them to do, you gotta give them time and make them think they are doing what they want to do.

Cows are a lot smarter animals than bulls and a lot more dangerous to work. Cows don't close their eyes when they come at you like bulls do. That makes them a lot more dangerous to handle; but, at the same time, they are gentle creatures. They blend in well with nature and the land. They are peaceful animals when you leave them alone. They are herd-oriented and they love their calves.

Cattle aren't as crazy and stupid as a lot of people think they are. It's kind of like what people thought about the Indians when we first got here. They weren't stupid either, they just didn't want to be pushed around and made to do what they didn't want to do—to go against their nature and their culture.

A cow is the best chemist in the world. Turn her loose in a pasture and, with her God-given instinct, she will eat the most palatable grass there. She eats each one in the order of their value to her. They are a machine that can turn grass, a useless commodity, into beef, a valued product for man.

I guess we all get more attached to our mother cows that we do to our steers. Steers are like migrant workers—in and out. Those mother cows spend all their useful lives with us. We know them like they were members of our family. It is a very personal relationship.

Young cattle are silly, but the older they get, the smarter they get. The fancier they get bred, the stupider and easier to handle they are. Now, you take those Longhorns and Spanish cattle—they were as bad as hogs. They would get in the fields and eat the cotton and corn. They were small with long tails that dragged the ground. They were mean and wild. You had to drive them in a trot—they couldn't be handled slow. It looked like you couldn't kill them; they weren't at all like the ones we have today.

The people outside thought we were crazy, but the man you worked for knew you gave him every bit you had. There's a loyalty between a cowman and a cowhand that money can't buy, and we both have a loyalty to the stock. We did what we were supposed to do, and we felt real bad about losing an animal.

I guess we all like the country life—elbow room. We like to feed the animals and see them grow.

John Cliburn
Rafael de la Garza
Coleman Joshlin
Thomas Michael O'Connor
Tom O'Connor, Jr. [III]
K. J. Oliver
Camillo Ramirez

Romulo Ramirez
Nick Rivas
Monroe "Bailey" Shaw
L. V. Terrell
Wesley Vivian
Dennis Williams

"God, that was some tough times. You aren't going to get any mercy, so you don't give any mercy away."

C. K. McCan, Jr.
"Kerry"
Rancher

Initiation Rites: You Gotta Ride Him or You Gotta Leave

When you were new on a ranch, they were goin' to see what you were made of. They were goin' to give you somethin' hot. They wanted to see if you were a cowhand, or if you just thought you were one. This wasn't just meanness, they couldn't depend on you until they knew you were safe. A man's life could depend on your ability. Someone who was scared or couldn't ride could be deadly to everyone.

A bad pitchin' horse was the main initiation tool. We'd put a guy on four outlaw horses, and if you could ride them, you got your own. Sometimes we would even highlife a horse to see what a man was made of. The fellas who were already there didn't want someone new to outshine them, so if you were good, you better stay good. You better know how to work hard and take teasin'.

If you couldn't handle those two things, you better hit the road. If you turned out all right, you had it made.

Mike Adames, E. D. "Rusty" Coward, Clayton Isaiah, Coleman Joshlin, Quinn Love, Rufus Moore, K. J. Oliver, Abel Perez, Lee Powell, Simmie Rydolph, Monroe "Bailey" Shaw, Leo Scott, L. V. Terrell, Porfirio Urbano

Makin' History

Very few people don't grow up wantin' to be cowboys. It was a good life. It was hard, but you were happy. It was a lot of work and a lot of fun. We spent a lot of time hopin' daylight would hurry up and break so we could

Open herd work, O'Connor Duke Ranch, 1930's. Photo by Dennis O'Connor [II].

run cattle. Many a night we went to bed thinkin' about the good times ahead. Ridin' horses and ropin' calves—that's what it was all about.

It didn't get too tough when you were young. There was nothin' greater than being a cowboy. We had so much fun on those ranches. The hard work didn't bother you.

You always tried to be ready when that cow-workin' started. That was Christmas. It was money, fun, talkin', lying', and hoorawin'. It was hard work, true enough, but we didn't pay any attention to it. We went out and done it, and then went out at night, and was back on the job the next day.

What was so thrillin' about cowboyin'? It was fun! A fast horse is like racin' a car. We loved the excitement. There is somethin' in the cowboy life that you can't get out of your system. It's deep in our blood. If we weren't workin' cattle, somehow we weren't satisfied. If you're brought up around cattle and horses, you get attached to them.

It's a lot of fun to work cattle. When the people you work with know what they're doing, then it makes hard work into fun.

We listened, worked, and watched under people who knew what they were doin'.

The way we worked in the old days made it fun, too. The main thing you appreciated was your horse. We felt like brothers. We helped one another and it made it easier to work. We would depend on each other like a family. We were close. We were for one another. Cowboys today are all for themselves. They're jealous-hearted of one another. We teased each other, but we really respected each other's abilities. That feelin' stays forever. It don't never change. Even today when we meet on the street, we're glad to see each other.

We laughed a lot in those days. We were young, I guess. Somehow, things don't seem as much fun when you get older.

We did a lot of things just for the fun in it. There was a lot of joy out there among the cow crowd. You could hear us for miles comin' down the road laughin' and hoorawin', just a bunch of guys makin' each other laugh. We played while we worked. We kept bad things off our minds.

Guess we were kinda crazy. We would laugh at a man about to lose his life. It seemed like it wasn't no fun if you weren't getting killed. Maybe we didn't know any better, but it does seem like we would have had more sympathy.

Today it isn't like it used to be. The fun isn't there any more. In those days every day was good. No matter what we did, we made fun out of it. Nowadays things are different. Modern times have ruined the cowboy. It took the wind and fire outta him. In the old days, we weren't thinkin' about gettin' off work.

They took the fun outta cow work when they quit campin' out and put the horses in trailers. A bunch of men singin' and ridin' along talkin' to cattle was fun; that's where you made good horses and good cowboys. If there was any way to stop things and go back to the way they were before World War II, that would be great. It was just you and your buddies, and nobody had anythin' to say about it.

We didn't have no money, but we made a livin', and we made fun outta our work. Most of us couldn't pick enough cotton to make a pillow, so we got good at workin' cattle. The more you handle cattle, the more you learn.

You could call it a hard life, but we made so much pleasure out of it that we had a good clean life. Everybody had respect for a good cowhand. Guess we kinda made history with our lives.

Pete Brown, Sonny Brown, Jesse Jones, Clarence Preiss, Camillo Ramirez, Romulo Ramirez, Nick Rivas, Simmie Rydolph, Monroe "Bailey" Shaw, L. V. Terrell, Julian Tijerina, Rev. Mack Williams

"It didn't matter to me what color a cowhand was, as long as he was good at his work."

E. D. "Rusty" Coward
Foreman
O'Connor Melon Creek Ranch

Pitching horse on Roche Ranch, Refugio, Texas, ca. 1939.
Photo by Ora Louise Beaty.
Courtesy of Institute of Texan Cultures.

Ridin' Old Buckshot—A Story of Pride

One time, Mr. James [Welder, Jr.] bought fifteen hundred head of steers from around Inez at the Keeran Ranch. We went up there in the truck and they was meetin' us with the steers. Each one of us roped a good horse and then drove them steers from Inez to Mr. Ed Pickering's ranch at Victoria. It was Boo [Fred Terrell], me, and Irving Gipson. We got there way before dark and got the cattle all bedded down.

Mr. Ed Pickering said to Mr. Jim, "Say, Jim, I got a little sorrel horse out here. If you got anybody can ride him, I'll give him to you."

I was sittin' there with a great big plate of beans and some tasso. I sat my plate down, 'cause I knowed he was goin' to call on me. Mr. Jim said, "We can ride him, can't we, Tony?" I said, "Yassuh!" He sent Boo and Irving after the horse.

Now here comes this horse, his tail straight in the air. Mr. Pickering said, "That's him in the front—Old Buckshot." Now, I looked at that. He was a roan. I roped him, and he was lookin' away—didn't pay me no attention. I bridled him, then led him up to the fence and put the blanket on him. I couldn't saddle him alone, so Boo got on him and bit his ear and on went the saddle.

They called out all them old people—them old cowboys and owners—Mr. Dennis [O'Connor II], Mr. McCan, all of them came out to see that horse rode. Mr. James asked me if I wanted his spurs, but I didn't. I wanted my old star-rowel spurs that I tied down under my foot. They twisted his ear, and I got on and got straight and the horse didn't even hump up.

Then Mr. Jim said, "Hook him, Tony" and I hit him. That horse went crazy. He had me all over him. Buckshot finally slipped and fell and when I rode back to Mr. Jim, he told me to pass my hat. I got about thirty dollars out of that ride.

I was rich that day—not so much from the money, but because Mr. Jim thought enough of me to let me represent his ranch.

S. W. Lott
"Tony"
Tophand
Welder Ranch
Vidauri

Friends Are Better Than Money

We been knowin' each other since we were about this high. We done everythin' together. If you live and work together with people, you get to a place where you understand each other. We were good friends, we looked out for one another. We knew each other on sight from long distances. A stranger among us stood out.

It made you feel good to know you were goin' out with a bunch of good guys—they were like your brothers, like family.

L-R, Elvin Scott, Pete Brown, Norman Davis at Riverside Park Youth Rodeo, 1950's.

"We had Spanish, whites, and colored in our cow crowds. We were friends—we all come up like brothers. There wasn't much friction between the races down here. It was a brotherhood."

McKinley Williams, Horace Joshlin, Will King, Richard Harris

Salt Creek cowboys, 1930's. L-R front, Abel "Guero" Perez, Felipe Rodriguez, Dofus "Poorboy" Oliver, Winford "Shorty" Green, Fritz "Cat" Green, Levy Green; L-R standing, Edward "Corazon," Romulo Ramirez, Sam Green, "Bubba," Tom Green, Ira "Bill" Green. Photo by Vincent Fritz.

Cowhands are rough men, but we got along well together. We had to. We knew each other and respected each other's territory. We understood one another.

We have more money and more conveniences now, but we don't have the friendships. Sometimes you're better off without the money, but havin' friends. Back then we could depend on each other.

The dangerous work created a strong feeling. We were close.

Ascension Campos, Ananias Cook, Candelario de la Garza, Johnny de la Garza, E. J. Garza, Clayton Isaiah, Jesse Jones, Henry Morrow, Rufus Moore, Suey Richardson, Nick Rivas, Simmie Rydolph, Monroe "Bailey" Shaw, Elvin Scott, Leo Scott, Ed Steward, Jr., L. V. Terrell, Henry Tijerina, Julian Tijerina, Porfirio Urbano, Rev. Mack Williams, Jesus Ybarbo, Dan Youngblood, Nathaniel Youngblood

The Owners Were the Law

We all knew what the bosses wanted. That was part of our job. Workin' with a man who knew what he wanted made it easier—when they give and take a little bit.

You want to know how we handled the bosses? We didn't handle them—they handled us.

He makes the first step; you adjust yourself to what he wants from there. You ain't gonna find no two or three alike. You have to learn what they want.

Back in the old days, when the bosses knew what they were doin', they had rules. And they had to know more than we did.

They were strict—never mean, just strict. As long as you did right you were okay.

We respected The Man and would fight for him like a bunch of bulldogs. We stayed our distance, but we had a lot of fun with the bosses, too.

We were close in a way. We were well taken care of. Those ranches were our homes, and those owners were the law.

John Brown, Ananias Cook, E. J. Garza, Clayton Isaiah, Jesse Jones, Coleman Joshlin, J. Y. Lott, Tony Lott, Quinn Love, K. J. Oliver, Nick Rivas, Simmie Rydolph, Monroe "Bailey" Shaw, L. V. Terrell, Will Weathers, Rev. Mack Williams, Dan Youngblood

"We don't have no leaders no more."

Leo Scott
Itinerant Tophand
Rancher

Calf doctoring, early 1900's.

Ordinary Working People

You know, cowboys are just ordinary workin' people who love nature and would rather be punchin' cattle than anythin' else.

They don't like to walk, and they work cattle so they can ride that horse. You didn't show your face if you couldn't ride. Nobody, not just cowboys, wants to cut wood, dig postholes, or work in the field. But a cowboy is worse than anybody—he just wants to ride.

Cowboys are supposed to be the biggest liars there is, but things happen to us that you wouldn't believe. There wasn't nothin' we wouldn't do and nothin' we haven't seen.

Recreational alligator roping, 1949.

Honesty was important among us and so was our reputation. You had to be a good person along with being a good cowhand.

Ranchers and cowhands are a different kind of people. They are dedicated to their jobs and don't watch the clock—free spirits and fun-lovers.

Anythin' we did, we was proud of it, because we knew we had done somethin' well that other people couldn't do. Even at that, at one time or another we all tried to get off these ranches. That town life was glossy. Now everybody wants to come back to the country. Maybe it was because we were the only ones who knew we were special. Back then, we weren't considered heroes by others and we didn't brag about it but among ourselves. Even cotton pickers were proud of their work in those days. Everyone had pride in what they did. We tried to be the best—we just tried to do our jobs.

The people outside thought we were crazy, but the man we worked for knew we gave him every bit we had.

In those days, we thought if you weren't a cowboy, you wasn't nowhere. We used to run away from school to join the cow crowd. If you weren't a good cowhand, you couldn't stick. You were left in camp to do women's work.

There's somethin' you've got inside of you and you get a good feelin' about doing it. It's somethin' nobody can take away from you.

Cowhands are full of fun and devilment. You never see mean boys workin' the ranch.

Tom O'Connor [II] fishing on Copano Bay, early 1900's.

We liked to be on top of some animal. That was our recreation—ropin' deer and coyote, ridin' cows and calves, huntin' an' fishin' for food.

When we had time off, we enjoyed it—drinkin' a little bootleg whiskey and hanging out in Lewis's Bend on Saturday and Sunday.

We spent a lot of time workin' in the country by ourselves. We talked to our horses a lot.

John Brown, Ananias Cook, Candelario de la Garza, Johnny de la Garza, E. J. Garza, Clayton Isaiah, Jesse Jones, Coleman Joshlin, J. Y. Lott, Tony Lott, Quinn Love, Tom O'Connor, Jr. [III], K. J. Oliver, Mike Rivas, Nick Rivas, Leo Scott, Monroe "Bailey" Shaw, L. V. Terrell, Milam Thompson, Henry Tijerina, Julian Tijerina, Dennis Williams, Rev. Mack Williams, Jesus Ybarbo, Dan Youngblood

Non-Cow Work—Dirt Men and Housework

We only worked cattle at certain times. After the cattle leave in the fall is when you get into maintenance work. There were many different groups of workers on the ranch. The dirt men and the cow crowd were the main ones. There was a fence crew all the time, and we baled hay when the time came.

Cutting cane on the O'Connor Melon Creek Ranch, 1914.

Tossing hay, 1930's. Photo by Dennis O'Connor [II].

Cotton being hauled down Guadalupe River, Tivoli, Texas, 1911.

Filling a silo, ca. 1910.

We just took our hands and got things started—posthole diggers, windmills, you name it, we did it. Men even did the housework on these ranches in our time—there weren't a lot of women around. On a ranch there are lots of different kinds of work a man can do.

It's all ranch work—even gardenin'.

Most of us hated the dirt work, when we were off the horse. We hated the posthole diggers, the hay-balin', and cleanin' the fresnos most.

Ananias Cook, Alex de la Garza, Rafael de la Garza, Richard Harris, Clayton Isaiah, J. Y. Lott, Tony Lott, Nat Nixon, Camillo Ramirez, Romulo Ramirez, Leo Scott, Milam Thompson, Rev. Mack Williams, Dan Youngblood

"A hard life? No, ma'am—work don't hurt nobody. I just did too much of it. Worked steady too long."

Richard Harris
Foreman
Murphy Ranches
1891-1988

"I'd hate to see daylight come 'cause I'd have to catch old Becky. We had to make a livin'— we didn't steal down here."

Monroe Shaw
"Bailey"
Itinerant Tophand and Well Digger

"If you make plans to do something, some old cow will change them every time, and if she doesn't, a contrary boss man will."

Armour Joe Keefe
Straw Boss
O'Connor Brothers Ranches
Rancher

"We didn't get up by no clock; we got up by the moon and the stars. There ain't no gettin' through on a ranch—there ain't no gettin' through to it."

Quinn Love
Itinerant Tophand

"I've got too many frosty mornin's on my back."

Dan Youngblood
"Tea Cakes"
"Wood"
Tophand
Welder Ranch
Vidauri
1918-1987

The Other Side of the Coin

I guess the time has come to get down to the other side of the coin.

It's come on—you get kicked in the head, and you don't think nothin' of it cause you're cowboyin'. We've all been hurt a many a time.

It wasn't romantic. It was hard, hard work. At the time, we didn't think much about it, but now you realize—when we were workin'—it was a little bit rough. Up at three in the mornin' for fifty cents a day.

We'd all be millionaires if we had got overtime.

By anybody's standards but our own, it was a hard life. Sometimes when we were workin' the silos, we wouldn't even quit to eat. We'd just grab a plate and keep on workin'. Loadin' hay was so tough, we'd break the equipment just to get a rest.

You ever put out a brushfire with a saddle blanket, or skinned cattle standin' on ice for a week at a time until your fingernails and forehead come off? It was so cold one time, Sam Upton froze to death at Twin Mott.

Our income was from two hundred to a thousand a year. You were exposed to the weather back then. When it rained, it rained on the cowboy. When it got cold, you got cold. You slept on the ground and it felt like a featherbed, while you was praying to the good Lord that a rattlesnake didn't bite. We had to ride rain or shine, heat or mosquitoes. Oh, we used to have some rough times and we could tell some tough tales in those days. Uncle Tom [Ball] could tell tales about sleepin' out when it was so cold his slicker would stand up.

The Depression wasn't tough on us. We had jobs. Maybe that's why the work didn't seem so rough to us. Some people starved to death. At least we didn't have that.

I guess it was tougher than we thought as kids. It wasn't a gravy train. You had to be made out of some pretty good rawhide to do those days—but nothin' really fazed us back then. We weren't heroes, we just did our work and went home. Your clothes wore out and there wasn't anythin' glorious.

I don't see how more of us didn't get killed out here. Bad things happened on ranches—bad horses and bad cattle and people who didn't know their business.

We used to night-herd—stay up all night and watch lightnin' dancin' on the cattle's horns. You could even get killed by rustlers out here if you messed with them. Lots of cowhands got killed out here ropin' and runnin' cattle. If you're goin' east and the cow's going west, somethin' bad is gonna happen.

We never went to the hospital or quit when we were hurt—not then. We thought it was part of life. We thought we had it better than the older folks.

Pete Brown, Ananias Cook, Alex de la Garza, Elias de la Garza, Richard Harris, Charlie Hernandez, Jesse Jones, Coleman Joshlin, Will King, Vincent Linney, J. Y. Lott, Tony Lott, Quinn Love, Nat Nixon, K. J. Oliver, Abel Perez, Frank Perez, Jr., Tom Rodgers, Victor Rodriguez, Simmie Rydolph, Leo Scott, Monroe "Bailey" Shaw, L. V. Terrell, Milam Thompson, Julian Tijerina, Manuel Tijerina, Porfirio Urbano, Wesley Vivian, Rev. Mack Williams, Jesus Ybarbo, Dan Youngblood

Vaccinating at Salt Creek Ranch, 1920's.

The Remuda, 1930's.
Photo by Dennis O'Connor [II].

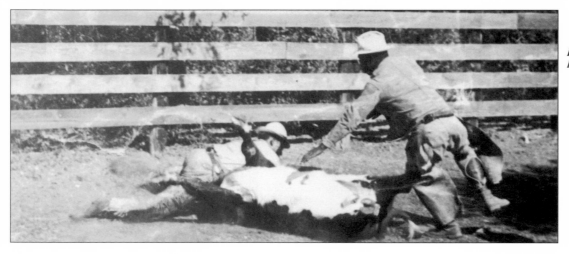

Pen work, 1930's.
Photo by Dennis O'Connor [II].

Banded rattlesnake at Coleto Creek, Victoria County, Texas, 4'6" long, 3" diameter. "This is the snake we ate, 12/7/18," J. D. Mitchell to Thomas O'Connor [II].

Milam's Sermon

When I was a young man cookin' in cow camp, I read the Bible a lot, and I used to wonder at the goodness of God as I watched the boys workin' cattle with their horses.

Cattle and horses are mentioned many times in the Bible because they are important for man. God knew that we would need these animals for meat, milk, and work, and so He made them right along with man to help him. In Exodus, God tells Moses to "gather thy cattle," and in Isaiah He prophesies that man shall "nourish the young cow".

Man, cows, and horses have always been together, because God showed man how to work horses, and He was wise enough to make horses faster and smarter than cattle to help man as he began to herd and care for these animals. The men who worked these animals were called herdsmen in the Bible.

As man began to own more and more cattle, it was necessary for him to get help carin' for them. As the rich man in the Bible entrusted his many goods to his steward, the bosses on these ranches had to have help with their big herds of cattle, and so they turned them over to us. But we were faithful stewards, unlike the one in the Bible, and this is our story— the story of the cowboy.

Milam Thompson
Itinerant Camp Cook

CHAPTER FIVE

KITCHEN BOSSES: THE COOKS

Milam Thompson
Photo by Louise S. O'Connor.

KITCHEN BOSSES: THE COOKS

"I learned to cook by dependin' on that little soft voice in me — an inward spirit. I started out a cowboy when I was around fifteen years old. One day the cook didn't show up and I was told to pitch in and do dinner. I didn't know how to boil water. I just had to depend on the spirit to guide me. I was scared. I didn't know nothin' about cookin'. I called on that source that has taken care of me through life — God. I cook by revelation."

Milam Thompson
Itinerant Camp Cook

Cooking for the cow crowd has always been a very important job in the ranching world. Many of the old cooks are highly respected, if not feared, by the cowhands, who would have been in deep trouble without their services. The cooks became almost legendary figures to the cowhands, even though most of them came from the same families and backgrounds.

All ranch cooks have different stories about how they started in their jobs. Some were trained at an early age by their mothers or by someone else, while others learned to cook by the seat of their pants and the grace of God. Each has a least one funny story about his or her worst mistake during the learning process — stories about everything from three-crusted camp bread to pudding that was so bad it had to be thrown under the woodpile so no one would see it and "hooraw" them about it. Some became cooks by choice, largely because they were not good at cowboying. Others recall being shanghaied to help out for a few days and then, five or six decades later, still cooking for the cow crowd.

On a typical ranch there were ranch cooks and camp cooks. The ranch cook worked in the kitchen at ranch headquarters, cooking for the cowhands when they were not off working cattle. The camp cook followed

Mose Henderson and Nat Nixon with chuck wagon, Welder Lease, ca. 1950. Photo by Roger Fleming. Courtesy Institute of Texan Cultures.

the cow crowd, cooking out of a chuck wagon or, later, out of a camphouse. The camphouses were built at the camps that grew up around dipping sites after dipping laws were passed, making it necessary for cowhands to spend frequent and regular periods of time at these camps dipping cattle. On a modern ranch, however, the distinction between a ranch cook and a camp cook no longer applies. Since cowhands now put in a regular day's work, the cook simply packs up their noon meal, which is then flown or driven to where the work is scheduled for that day. The old traditions of feeding the cow crowd are quickly vanishing.

Charlie Williams and chuck wagon.

*"Call one, call two, call the captain,
and the whole damn crew."*

**Charlie Williams
"Tippy"
Camp Cook
O'Connor Ranches**

All the cooks had their rules, but some were stricter than others. Many had reputations for being cantankerous, solitary, and generally fearsome creatures, while others were easygoing, cheerful, and fit in well with the cow crowd. Regardless of the cooks' temperaments, the cowhands could not seem to resist teasing and harassing "Cookie." They learned each one's limits fairly well, but occasionally one of them would miscalculate and go too far. When this happened, life in camp became less than ideal. A mad camp cook could make everyone's life miserable.

Cow-working, horses, and women were the major subjects of conversation around the cooking fires. Dominoes, monte, kangaroo court, and practical jokes were the entertainment. Religion was not strong among the cowhands until their later years. There was an occasional preacher among the cooks who tried desperately to bring religion to the camp. More often than not, this lofty mission was a miserable failure.

Women cooked in the kitchens at ranch headquarters, never in cow camp, but their stories and the foods they prepared are essentially the same as those served up by the male cooks. Beans, rice, potatoes, tasso, and dried fruits were the cowhands' staple diet. A good camp cook could work miracles with these basic provisions. Stories of legendary cowboy stews made from tasso are still strong in the cowhands' memories.

The old camp cooks were superb chefs. Their style of cooking will soon be lost forever.

*Chuck truck.
Photo by Dennis O'Connor [II].*

The Camp Cooks: Cookin' from the Ground

Women people have to take measurin' spoons—a cup o' this, a cup o' that. These men people, they don't do that. They just go in there and pour out. They know what they're doin'. You can't really say men are better cooks than women—they're just different.

We didn't have no stove to be peepin' in, either. We cooked from the ground. You didn't have nothin' like canned goods you could open and fix. You had to pick your food from the ground and clean it. Cooks have it easy now. Our work was harder than the cowboys'. We had longer hours.

Camp food, Refugio County, ca. 1950.
Photo by Roger Fleming. Courtesy Institute of
Texan Cultures.

It was tough any way you take it—more hours, the same pay.

You feedin' a bunch of men, you don't realize what a responsibility you got. They come in cold and they want their food. You forget what you're doin' and you have to go around them. That makes you a little cranky sometime. Just before you serve is a real busy time. You have to keep your brains and eyes workin' right. If a person is busy, someone shouldn't be cuttin' him off.

Our flunkies were real important to us. They kept the fire goin' and did what we asked them. That was more than we could get from the cowboys sometime. They loved to tease us.

John C. "Bear" Bland, Mose Henderson, Nat Nixon, Sidney Rydolph, Milam Thompson

A typical camp house,
ca. 1920's.

"The camphouse system was developed after the turn of the century. Before that, the cowhands slept on the ground and around the wagons. Because of the new dipping laws, in 1922, the ranchers needed to have large dipping vats, and camp areas were built up around these vats. All of the cattle on the ranches had to be run through the vats every fourteen days. A tremendous amount of time was spent in camp during the dipping days."

Thomas Marion O'Connor [II]
Rancher

Tasso on the line.

Life in Cow Camp

When you were in camp, that's where you stayed. There was nowhere to go, so you spent your time talkin' and lyin' around and playin' games and tellin' jokes. You went to bed early and you got up early. Camp was great in the summer—three meals a day around the fire. It could get a little hairy in winter, though.

Back before the days of camphouses, the chuck wagon would be set up by a lake or a creek. The camp system worked well. The camp was moved around to where it was needed, givin' a central gatherin' place for all the activities.

Camp was fun for everyone, but we made our own fun. We stayed there rain or shine, workin' herds, roundin' up and brandin', castratin', vaccinatin', until the work was done. We'd be sleepin' by a big old fire. The bosses could bathe, but the hands only took spit baths. We used baking soda for deodorant and charcoal to clean our teeth. We were really gross in camp if the truth be known. The language out here was horrible, it was

Cow crowd at Salt Creek Ranch, 1930's. Photo by Vincent Fritz.

unexplainable, but that was everyday life, one of the things that happened. We acted like hogs and dogs a lot of the time—typical men when the womenfolk aren't around. Sometimes we acted more civilized and sensitive, sittin' there at daylight trying to figure out what the owls were sayin'. We could act both ways.

Often we camped around stock pens or wells, and there was always a rick of wood for the campfires. The cooks kept a fire burnin' all night. Camp was really basically sleepin' and eatin' and sometimes there was very little sleepin'. A lot of those old cowboys would get up and walk in their sleep

Horn clipping. Photo by Dennis O'Connor [II].

and never know it. Some would wake you up hollerin' at cattle. Some of the men snored so loud they might as well have been talkin'. You were asleep, but you could hear them. You knew you were out there; you were sensitive to any little sound. The cattle constantly lowed in the background—it was like a permanent symphony.

There were rules in camp: Only the bosses could drink whiskey. We weren't allowed to look in the pots, the cook would get real mad. Everybody had their own sleepin' gear and a place to sleep, and we better not ride or walk too close to the fire and kick up dirt around the food. The old hands told the young ones what to do and they better obey.

The wagons had wide wheels and a canvas sheet over the bed that held the sleepin', cookin', and workin' gear—everythin' we needed.

Cattle people are fun, happy people. They lived by tellin' tales; what else could you do? There was lots of devilment in camp—hoorawin' and lyin' and playin' jokes on each other.

We would hide things from each other a lot, put things in each other's boots, and tell great ghost stories. About 90 percent of the conversation in camp was about horses and the rest was about women. There wasn't much singin', maybe a Jew's harp once in a while. There wasn't much to do, lyin' to each other and jokin' for two or three weeks. You're in bad shape in a cow crowd if you can't take teasin'. Many didn't care if their lies were

Branding in a chute.

believed as long as they were able to tell the tale. Layin' out there looking at the stars, and nowhere to go. We fought mean horses and ran wild cattle. You could hear us for miles comin' down the road, just a bunch of guys hoorawin' and laughin' to get things off each other's minds. That's what kept us goin'.

It was never lonely in camp, but out ridin' by yourself you could get lonesome.

The card games were monte, poker, coon can, 7-up, and cotch. There were some hot domino games, too. Beans and matches were used for

Orion Linney at chuck wagon, Salt Creek Ranch, 1930's. Photo by Vincent Fritz.

money. We sat around the fire and talked about the old-timers and what happened back in their days—Alan and Monroe Benson and how they could ride. Lord, they was cowhands! There was always a story or two about a horse that ran his heart out.

At the McFaddin Ranch we had music in camp. Lee Powell played the guitar and old Fred Rivas played the accordion. Charlie Avery sang in Spanish—"El Rancho Grande", "Quatro Milpas", "La Panchita."

Kangaroo court was great entertainment. Someone who had messed up that day was tried for his mistake and sentenced.

The night before cow camp started was big fun. The wagon was loaded, we got our horses and gear ready, and always there was jokin' and laughin' and fun.

The old camphouses were very primitive, usually two or three rooms at the most and no electricity and only a wood stove to keep you warm. But in bad weather they were an improvement over the open skies.

In camp, we hunted a lot for meat. They only butchered on Sundays. Tasso, beans, hoe cakes, dried fruits, biscuits, coffee, eggs, rice, potatoes, and cowboy stew were about it for camp food. But there's no better food in the world than the food in cow camp. It was unbelievable what those cooks could do with the limited food and primitive conditions. They were the first ones up and the last ones to bed and they could get cantankerous after several weeks in camp. Cookin' must have an adverse effect on people;

Camp houses at Mexican Water Hole, O'Connor Melon Creek Ranch.

cooks are almost all famous for being cranky.

I'd like to be in cow camp one more time. We enjoyed workin' together, helpin' each other, and teachin' each other our knowledge. It was a family feelin'; we were friends. Cow camp was good.

Comin' back to family life after cow camp wasn't hard to do. You didn't tie them together. They were two different lifestyles.

Camp cooks and chuck wagons—all that really happened. Some people don't believe we done all this but we did. That was a good life—good fun—everyone was happy. Shootin' dice, stayin' outdoors, talkin' about the

Duke Ranch camp house with tasso on the line, 1930's

day, what happened among the cow crowd. That's where the fun came out in camp. Some of us would like to see it go back to that time. Some younger ones want to start up cow camp again, but can it ever be the same? It couldn't have been as much fun as we remember, kind of like war stories. It was romantic in a way, but it was hard work, too.

Mike Adames, Buster Bickford, John Brown, Pete Brown, Sonny Brown, Willie Brown, Kai Buckert, Bevans Callan, Ascension Campos, Bill Charleston, John Cliburn, Ananias Cook, E. D. "Rusty" Coward, Candelario de la Garza, Johnny de la Garza, Freddy Fagan, E. J. Garza, Franklin "Bud" Harvey, Charlie Hernandez, Clayton Isaiah, Jesse Jones, Coleman Joshlin, Horace Joshlin, Joe Keefe, Will King, J. Y. Lott, Tony Lott, Quinn Love, Rufus Moore, Nat Nixon, Thomas Marion O'Connor, Tom O'Connor, Jr. [III], K. J. Oliver, Abel Perez, Lee Powell, Clarence Preiss, Camillo Ramirez, Romulo Ramirez, Mike Rivas, Nick Rivas, Rufus Rogers, Simmie Rydolph, Elvin Scott, Leo Scott, Monroe "Bailey" Shaw, Ed Steward, Jr., L. V. Terrell, Milam Thompson, Henry Tijerina, Julian Tijerina, Porfirio Urbano, Wesley Vivian, Earl Ward, Will Weathers, Leo Welder, Rev. Mack Williams, McKinley Williams, Jesus Ybarbo, Dan Youngblood

Layin' Religion on the Shelf

I came to Texas from Louisiana durin' the Depression. I always heard them talkin' about Texas and I wanted to see what it was. I came down here to see the hookin' bulls. I'd never seen a prairie or a ranch before, and I didn't have any idea I was bein' hired to cook for a bunch of cowboys.

When I got here, I couldn't believe my eyes. These cowboys was as foreign to me as Sputnik. I thought they were nuts—actin' like a bunch of monkeys with terrible table manners. I couldn't fill them up, but at the same time, they was complainin' about my food. So I just finally had to lay religion on the shelf and tell them how it was goin' to be in my kitchen. I was goin' to run that kitchen and they was goin' to follow my rules.

They give me so much trouble sometimes, I nearly be ready to quit. I thought ranches were penitentiaries—like slavery times. I was gettin' up at two, three o'clock in the mornin' and cookin' three big meals. Durin' the heavy work times, I'd just bring my pillow and blanket and stay here. I had to keep my kitchen shiny.

Finally I got them in line because I wasn't scared of nobody. I held that kitchen down for eight years. By the time I left here, I loved this ranch and I loved my cowboys. It got to be home and family.

Gertrude Patterson
Ranch Cook
Welder Ranch
Vidauri
1889–1987

"I've done all kinds of work, but I couldn't ride a horse so I stayed with cookin'. It was a lot of fun—go to bed late, get up early. I learned pretty quick not to let them give me trouble. I was boss of that kitchen. Didn't nobody meddle with my pots and pans. You gotta have some kind of rules around a bunch of cowhands."

John C. Bland
"Bear"
Itinerant Camp Cook

Mose Henderson and Nat Nixon at Vidauri, ca. 1950. Photo by Roger Fleming. Courtesy Institute of Texan Cultures.

"I was no account on horseback and I didn't know one end of a cow from another—but I looked at the rest of them cowboys. They was havin' plenty of fun while I was helpin' Nat [Nixon] do the cookin'."

Mose Henderson
"Rat"
Camp Cook
Welder Ranch
Vidauri

"I learned to cook when I was a kid, at home on Sundays, me and my brother. We'd fix up a little cake—throw it together some kind of way and eat it up before Mama got home. From then on I started cookin' for all these ranches."

Sidney Rydolph
Itinerant Camp Cook

"When I was a young kid my mother wouldn't let me go out with the big men. She made me stay home and she taught me how to cook and season. Down the line, all that come in handy. While the rest was cowboyin', I was cookin' and doin' road and fence work. Sometimes the cowboys could be aggravatin' when you were tryin' to cook, but they were a lot of fun, too."

Nat Nixon
"Fog"
Camp Cook
Welder Ranch
Vidauri

"I came to the O'Connor ranches in 1947. After all these years here, I feel comfortable doing' the cookin'—feedin' my cowboys."

Steve Rubio
Ranch Cook
O'Connor Brothers River Ranch

"I drifted onto the McFaddin Ranch many years ago on my way to Bay City. Mr. McCan asked me to help out a few days; that was fifty-five years ago. I been here so long, I dream about Mr. Claude. I see him real plain—workin' cattle—so natural-like."

Lee Powell
Camp Cook
McFaddin Ranch
1904–1984

I Have Rules

"I been twenty-five years in this kitchen. Started out helpin' Bessie Holmes, and when she passed, I took over. This job is easier now. We used to get up so early. Then the cowhands would be eatin' at two in the mornin'; now we feed at six. All the work is easier now, less hours, and better equipment.

"I have rules. They can't look in the pots and they can't go in the icebox. Food from the ranch kitchen is important to everyone. If you give them beans and meat, you got it made. I'm gettin' a little sluggish now that I'm gettin' old, but it's still family out there. I enjoy it."

Ludie Youngblood
Ranch Cook
Welder Ranch
Vidauri

"I've done it all on these ranches but fly helicopters. What trapped me in this kitchen was when my father-in-law got sick. Mr. Rusty asked me to cook for a few days until he could find somebody. I guess he's still lookin'—that was almost five years ago."

Bobby Martin
Ranch Cook
O'Connor Melon Creek Ranch

Up at Four

"I'm proud of my work on these ranches. I was up at four and had breakfast ready by five every morning. The cowhands would be out there yellin' at them cattle in the dark, but when they got in, I'd have it ready for them. They loved to talk about their work and who got throwed off a horse that day. They didn't give me no trouble; they were nice to me, but I did have rules about muddyin' up my kitchen. I never used recipes, I cooked in my head. When I took a notion to cook, I'd use my brains and my nose. They were my recipe book. Everybody liked the way it ate.

"I've cooked so much in my life, I'm tired of it now. But there was a time when I could feed two big tables at once. I fed them well and never wasted any food. When I got through with my day's work, I'd watch those cowboys. They loved the work they were doin'."

Cinderella Terrell Avery
"Daisy"
"Dady"
Ranch Cook
O'Connor Duke Ranch

CHAPTER SIX

THE OLD HEADS:
LEGENDARY HEROES OF THE COW CULTURE

Richard Harris. 1892–1988
Photo by Louise S. O'Connor.

THE OLD HEADS: LEGENDARY HEROES OF THE COW CULTURE

"I works cattle now through dreaming."

Richard Harris
Foreman
Murphy Ranches
1892–1988

The people I interviewed in previous chapters are my heroes—the cowhands, the ranchers, the foremen. They are the survivors, all that is left of a dying culture.

During more than one thousand hours of taped interviews, the "old heads" in this chapter are referred to and talked about over and over. "Old heads" is an affectionate term used by the interviewees when they refer to previous generations of cowhands and ranchers. This chapter includes the individuals, from empire builders to fence builders, who lived and worked on these ranches, or in this area, from about 1880 to 1970.

These men and women lived and worked at the tail end of the pioneering days. The women kept house without electricity, running water, or modern conveniences. The cowhands and ranchers rode a more open range. They lived and worked before the days of gooseneck trailers and cutting chutes.

These are the people the interviewees in this book consider the real cowmen and cowhands. The "old heads" are their heroes.

The Solomon of the River Bottom

Louis Power was the finest cowman anyone ever saw. He was foreman of the Duke Ranch, and his name was a household word around here. Anytime a bunch of people started talkin' cows, his name would come up. He was managin' O'Connor land even before the Coward family. He knew a lot about cows and taught us younger ones what he knew. All of us owe our knowledge of cattle and ranchin' to him. He was an honest man, true in everythin' he did. He didn't play around with his cowhands, but his word was his word. He was straight—he made you want to be like him. We still live by his teachin's and his rules to this day.

Often he would study things out at night, but he never did say anythin' till mornin', then he gave it out. He was a smart man—kind of like Solomon in the Bible. He was wise.

John Brown, Willie Brown, Jesse Jones, Rosie Terrell Jones, Dennis M. O'Connor [II], K. J. Oliver, Monroe "Bailey" Shaw, Milam Thompson

Louis Power—An Interview

I live on the O'Connor Duke Ranch now, down on the Santone River, but I was born in Refugio County on the Melon Creek back in 1875. I've spent all my life on O'Connor land, and I never really knowed anyone but O'Connors to live on this land, back to the original Mr. Tom. I used to see him sittin' on the gallery of his house on Dry Bayou as I went by. I must have been about twelve years old when he died.

I started ridin' when I was about eight or nine years old and I been workin' cattle since I was fifteen. I been with the O'Connors all my life, except three days when I worked for Mr. Will Hynes. I started out workin' under Mr. Pat Lambert, their foreman. Then I worked under Mr. Findlay

Simpson, Mr. Phillip Hull, Mr. John Pope, Mr. Hynes, and now I'm foreman of the Duke Ranch.

I never really have knowed how big that ranch is. I started out bossin' the country east of Melon Creek and west of Copano Creek from 1904 until they divided the land in 1907. After that I went to the Duke Ranch for Mr. Joe O'Connor except for a couple of years—1912 to 1914—when I farmed for Mr. Tom O'Connor [II]. I planted a little cotton and corn on two tenant farms belongin' to me and Mr. Bissett, and then I went back to Mr. Joe at the Duke Ranch.

I've got lots of remembrances. I knowed Mr. Jim Coward, and I remember a man named Junek, who lived near Melon Creek. He looked something like Spanish and had a long beard. They called him "Unicorn." I can remember the 1886 storm—I was livin' at the Shelly Pasture then. I remember when they built the fence between O'Connor and Lambert around 1905 or 1906.

*Louis Power.
Photo by Dennis O'Connor [II].*

I used to work all up and down Copano Creek. Around the 1880s they drilled an artesian well at the head of the creek. Before that, it was just a flat.

I remember all this as well as yesterday.

**From an interview with Louis Power
by Verlin Vandenburge, c. 1941**

Louis Power.

A Mighty Man

Louis Power was the half-breed grandson of the *empresario* James Power. He was a big man with blue eyes and a copper-colored skin and had very Irish facial features, especially the big nose.

The first I heard about him was when I was a kid. All the old cowhands dated everything from the time when Louis Power was running the outfit. He ran the cow crowd that divided the cattle after Grandpa Dennis died in 1900. How he came about having that job, I don't know.

Louis was a real cowman, not in terms of running the business end of a ranch but in knowing how to handle a cow. He knew what an old cow would be thinking tomorrow. He was, in my estimation, absolutely without peer. He taught me what I know about cattle. I mean, not just penning them or running them through a chute, but things like looking at an old cow and knowing if she could make it through the winter up here on this Duke Ranch. His thoughts and concerns were dominated by those cattle and the well-being of his cowhands.

There are very few men in this world I respected more than Louis Power. There are just some people who have a certain presence. He was very quiet-spoken and unpretentious, but you knew, if you knew straight up about a cow, that he was just about the best in the world. At what he did and what he knew, he was tops, and if you didn't think so, you didn't know cattle.

Louis was a large man, quiet, slow-moving, and easygoing, but he was an authority figure. He could handle cowhands. When he spoke, they jumped. When I took over the Duke Ranch, I was an inexperienced kid. I had to lean heavily on Louis. Right away I learned how much he knew and realized how much he could teach me. That's why he was so important to me. But above all, I just respected him as a man.

Louis couldn't read or write, but he kept his accounts in a black book. He had his own peculiar marks that only he understood. He never let anyone see this book. A day or two after he died, I was up at his house sorting things out to send to his family. I thought about looking at that book just to see how he did it. As I reached for it, I thought about how I didn't have the guts to ask him about the book when he was alive and that it would be cheating to look at it now. I threw the book into the fire, burnt it up, and to this day I don't know what was in it.

Even though I was just a child and he was an old man, he always treated me with respect—not subservience, just respect. He knew cattle so well because his world was that herd of cows. Was it instinct? There's no doubt about it.

Other people also have that talent, but in Louis's case it was something more. He spent a lifetime studying cattle. I think that's why he was so knowledgeable about them.

In my experience, he was one of a kind. I never ran across anybody just like him. He was a mighty man.

Tom O'Connor, Jr. [III]
Rancher

Alonzo "Lonze" Edwards
Houseman
Yardman
O'Connor River Ranch

"He was the real boss around here."

Their Real-Life Heroes

I guess we wanted to be like the old cowhands. They were the best at their jobs that ever lived.

They were good teachers, too, and we all respected them. We would just stand and watch them give out the best they had, and that was pretty good. Willie Jones, the Tijerinas, the Bensons, the Fagans, the Averys — these were some cowhands. Tom Ball, Joe Tillman, and old Pancho Perez were legends in this river bottom. You never get a group of old cowhands together, you don't hear those names.

They were tough, too. You know, Jim Avery lived with a bullet in his head . . . Aunt Alice shot him.

Some of these old-timers were in positions of real power on these ranches in their day. Take old Lonze Edwards, for instance. He was the boss. You had to go to him for information. There was no use goin' to the white man if he said "No." Seems like there was thousands named Rodriguez, de la Garza, and Tijerina, too. Terrells was good horsemen, and all them Harveys was some cowhands — Alfred, Tony, Pat, and Bull — all cowboys, and so was their fathers, grandfathers, and great-grandfathers before 'em.

There were even a few women like Mary Kroeger and Aunt Rittie who could work right with the men.

We ain't nothing compared to these men. They were the real heroes — the best that ever lived at ridin' a horse and handlin' a cow.

Mike Adames, John Brown, Ananias Cook, E. J. Garza, Jesse Jones, Quinn Love, Henry Morrow, Abel Perez, Lee Powell, Mike Rivas, Nick Rivas, Tom Rodgers, Leo Scott, Monroe "Bailey" Shaw, L. V. Terrell, Porfirio Urbano, Rev. Mack Williams

"Why do you have to be dead before somebody remembers your name?"

J. Y. Lott
Itinerant Tophand

"These men were the giants when it came to cow-working."

K. J. Oliver
"K"
Itinerant Tophand

"Those forefathers, they were tough. Nothin' didn't get too bad for 'em."

Horace Joshlin
Cook
Manhattan Cafe
Cowhand
McDowell Ranch

Jose Serrata
Tophand
O'Connor Melon Creek Ranch
1895–1975

My Life History

I was born on October 2, 1895, and raised on the Charlie Fox place near the Catholic cemetery. I started workin' for Fox when I was ten years old. In 1914 I was nineteen years old and I quit workin' for Fox. Then I started workin' at the Melon Creek Ranch for Mr. Thomas O'Connor in 1915.

In 1917 I went into the armed forces and returned in 1919 on June 27, and in July I started workin' for the O'Connors again. Ed Coward was the big boss at that time on the Melon Creek and Salt Creek ranches. These were the men that worked with me: Monroe Benson, Alan Benson, Hilario Deases, Alberto Serrata, Mark Williams, Tom Hynes, Oliver Harper, Alan Heard, and Manuel Vela, and also Mr. Simpson from the San Antonio River worked when Ed Coward was boss. This was when Mr. Ed Hall and Jimmy Hall and Mr. Henry Kroeger lived on the Salt Creek Ranch. Mr. Bernie Coward, he was a hardworkin' boy.

In 1929 Mr. Jimmy Coward took charge of the camp at Telegraph Well durin' the dippin' time. Walter Garza was the cook. Our campin' place was right in front of the big barn. Mr. Tom O'Connor, Sr. [II], had a dog named Jake, a real good cow dog. Mr. Tom had two buggy horses, one named Jerry and the other Old Tom; he was ridin' Old Tom.

One evenin', we were workin' in the Eustachio Pasture when Mr. Tom killed all the wild steers. The dog picked up a pale red, unbranded muley steer. It was between ten and twelve years old. We started runnin' steers from two o'clock that afternoon until six—Rocha, Mr. Jim, and me. Jim Coward was ridin' a horse named Jack Johnson; I was ridin' a gray horse named Bad Dog; Rocha was ridin' one named Whiskey Brown. We roped that wild steer, the three of us, between Black Mott and Barlow Flat. By the time we tied that steer to a tree, it was draggin' old Jack Johnson. That was a BIG steer.

The rest of the boys were runnin' another bunch of steers. They used to say that Mr. Tom couldn't ride a horse, but he was a real cowman that day.

These men worked with me at Salt Creek Ranch: Romero Rocha, Chico Rocha, Pancho Rocha, Ignacio Rocha, Mercario Serrata, Old Man Esteban Cisneros, Jose Beltran, Jim Santiago, Will Elliot, Dick Avery, Fred Harris, Crescencio Fuentes, Jose Cisneros, Sam Shaw (cook), Findlay Simpson (San Antonio River), and Victor Basaldua.

The Bend, Lamar Camphouse, Cavasso Creek, and Twin Mott Lake were the camphouses on the Salt Creek Ranch. Copano Creek was the only camphouse O'Connor had. At Black Mott we had a big old mesquite tree for a camping place. All the country was open at the time. I started workin' for Mr. Tom, Jr. [III], when his daddy died, and for Mr. Dennis O'Connor [II] and Rusty Coward. The Cowards were all good foremen, three of them. Pete Navaido was the *remuda* man in those days.

Jose Serrata
Tophand
O'Connor Melon Creek Ranch
1895–1975

Elias Jackson
"Bud Lias"
General Handyman
O'Connor River Ranch

"One time everyone was teasing Bud that he was going to be drafted into the army. Bud allowed as how Martin [O'Connor] wouldn't let them do that. Someone suggested that Martin couldn't tell Uncle Sam what to do. Bud replied, 'I don't know who Uncle Sam is, but he ain't never seen Mart when he was mad'."

Tom O'Connor, Jr. [III]
Rancher

Photo by Dennis O'Connor [II].

LEGENDARY HEROES OF THE COW CULTURE

Sam Ricks
Camp Cook
O'Connor River Ranch

"He was an old cowhand. When he got too old to ride, he started to camp cook. His biscuits were hard as a rock. He was famous for cookin' the worst food on earth."

Charlie Williams
"Tippy"
Camp Cook
O'Connor Melon Creek Ranch

"The Old Deacon used to change his call to dinner from time to time. When we started getting 'all right, you dogs, come and get it', we knew he had been in camp too long."

Will Upton
Ranch Cook
O'Connor River Ranch

"My sole memory of him was as cook for the River Ranch. He was a real character. There are an endless number of stories about him. He seldom went to town, but when he did, he looked like a senator—he was the same size as Uncle Martin, and inherited all of his clothes. He usually sat on the porch and rocked while his flunky did the work."
Tom O'Connor, Jr. [III]

Harrison Williams
Itinerant Cowhand

"He was right next to Louis Power as a cowman."

Tom Rodgers
"Tom Ball"
Camp Cook and Tophand
Welder Ranch
Vidauri

"It was said he could walk barefooted on the campfire coals. When someone
suggested that he wear shoes, he would reply, 'What are you talking about? I got
the shoes on God gave me. I don't need no others'."

Leo Welder
Rancher

Jim Coward
Foreman
O'Connor Melon Creek Ranch

"Mr. Jim wanted holes dug deep—whether it was for fence posts or water troughs. They could never be too deep. The day we buried him, we both walked up to the grave and looked in. Then we looked at each other. I said to Terrell, 'He's gonna come back and haunt somebody—that hole ain't near deep enough'."

Abel "Guero" Perez
Tophand
O'Connor Melon Creek Ranch

Oscar Gipson   **Alan Benson**   **Irving Gipson**
"Monk"   **Tophand**   **"Iron Gall"**
Tophand   **O'Connor Salt Creek Ranch**   **Tophand**
Welder Ranch   **O'Connor & Welder Ranches**

"Alan looked like an Indian. He was a cowboy from his heart."

"Monk's favorite working song was:
Santone River ain't no place for strangers, ain't got no business around here."

"Irving was a left hander, but he sure could rope."

Orion Linney
Foreman
O'Connor Salt Creek Ranch

"Big, slow, quiet, and honest. He never yelled at his men."

Ygnacio Rocha
"Nasha"
Tophand
O'Connor Ranches

"Nasha had a lifelong problem with whiskey—but only on the weekends. Rather than disturb the bosses every weekend to have him bailed out, they got him a charge account at the Victoria, Refugio, and Goliad county jails. The sheriffs would keep him overnight, sober him up, and send him back to the ranch for Monday morning roll call. His bills would be sent to the ranch for payment every month."

Tom O'Connor Jr. [III]
Rancher

Frank Perez, Sr.
"Pancho"
Tophand
O'Connor Ranches

"He walked up from Mexico with his saddle across his back and became a legendary horseman on these ranches."

Fred Terrell
"Boo"
Tophand
Welder Ranch
Vidauri

"He's the one made this Vidauri Ranch."

Steve Odem
Tophand
McDowell Ranch

"A good man, he took care of his business."

Lester Long
Foreman
O'Connor River Ranch

"He was a man with a great sense of humor."

"Little" Henry Lott
Tophand
Welder Ranch
Vidauri

"He owned a horse named Get Him At The Gate."

O. G. Copeland
Foreman
O'Connor Duke Ranch

"His men liked him."

Antonio Rodriguez
Tophand
Welder Ranch

"A good cowhand."

Victor Moraida
Tophand
O'Connor River Ranch

"He worked for O'Connor Brothers all his life."

Wilson Lott
Tophand
O'Connor River Ranch

"He and Fred Spriggs were the only ones who could stop a stampede."

Rafael Casas
Jose Casas
Cowhands
McFaddin Ranch

They walked this river bottom so long ago that no one remembers knowing them — **L. O'C.**

Charlie Lara
Tophand
McFaddin Ranch

*"He was so old, he worked for James McFaddin. He was a helluva cowhand.
He could do things nobody else could learn."*

C. K. McCan, Jr.
Rancher

Hennon Collins
"Quinta"
Camp Cook
O'Connor Duke Ranch

"He found someone killing the ranch hogs in the river bottom one day, and duly reported this to his boss, Mr. Boyd. Boyd was angry about the hog killing and said to Hennon, 'Why don't you just go kill him.' Quinta did exactly that, and it took fifteen years to get him out of jail."

Will Elliot
Pasture Rider
O'Connor Melon Creek Ranch

"He was pasture riding when I met him; I guess he still is . . ."

Violena Elliot

Will Elliot was considered the consummate pasture rider by all who knew him. Before the days of mechanization, the pasture riders were the eyes and ears of the boss. A good pasture rider was invaluable. They would go out every day and observe the land, the cattle, the fences, and the water supplies, doctor the animals, and repair the windmills and fences as they rode the land. From the day he went to work on the O'Connor Melon Creek Ranch as a young man, Will spent almost every day in the saddle. It has been estimated that he covered approximately forty miles a day until he retired as an old man in the mid-fifties. The statement above came from an interview with his widow conducted almost thirty years after his death. — **L. O'C.**

"Stuttering" Bill Leonard
Mayor of Mexican Water Hole
O'Connor Melon Creek Ranch

Bill was bitten by so many rattlesnakes that he was no longer affected by them—he had developed a complete immunity to the venom long before he reached old age. He lived by himself out in the middle of the Melon Creek Ranch at Mexican Water Hole. He was always there to greet and entertain anyone who stopped by. —**L. O'C.**

Logan Upton
Ranch Cook
O'Connor Melon Creek Ranch

"Logan only cooked one type food at a time—either all potatoes, all meat,
all vegetables, etc. It was said if you ate with him long enough, you would
eventually get a balanced diet."

Jim Lewis
Tophand
O'Connor Ranches

"When we were working cattle, he would always say, 'Bring me a hot iron and a sharp knife, boys. We got work to do'."

Jim Santiago   **Valley Elliot**
                                 "Buckskin"

Tophands
O'Connor Melon Creek Ranch

"Jim was tough as a mule. He went right back to work after he had his fingers cut off by a roped bull."

"If Lester Roloff could yell as loud as Valley, the whole world would know we was sinners."

Monroe Shaw
"Bailey"
Itinerant Cowhand and Well Digger

Ralph Lott   Will Elliot
Tophands
O'Connor Melon Creek Ranch

*"Will loved to set fires and watch them burn. One day as he was riding
along, he struck matches and tossed them out in the grass. Naturally
the whole pasture caught fire. When he got home, Mr. Jim [Coward] asked
him if he had seen any fires in the lower country, because he thought he
could see smoke coming from down near the bay. Will's reply was 'No sir.'
As he turned and walked past me he said, 'I said, "No sir," but I didn't say
that I didn't look back'."*

Tom O'Connor, Jr. [III]

Walter Garza
Itinerant Camp Cook
Power, Hynes, and West Ranches

"A good man, and a good cook."

Mercario Serrata
"Mac"
Tophand and Remuda Man
O'Connor Melon Creek Ranch

"He was pure Indian — a pasture rider and a remuda man. He took good care of his horses."

Ed Coward
Foreman
O'Connor Melon Creek Ranch
with
Mary O'Connor [Braman]

"He was the exact opposite of his brother Jim — small, wiry, and he worked cattle much faster."

Henry Dunman   Ike Dunman
Tophands
Fagan Ranch

"Henry could break that brush!"

"Ike was killed by a horse. It kicked him so hard, it drove a Prince Albert can into his side."

Willie Jones
"Hawkeye"
Tophand
O'Connor Ranches

"My brother was a quiet fella, he watched over things and never told you
nothin' wrong. People looked to him. You couldn't pull nothin' over
on him; that's why we called him Hawkeye. He was dependable, a good
roper, a good rider, and a good teacher. He was respected and liked by all."

Jesse Jones
Tophand
O'Connor Ranches

Matthew Jones
"Matt"
Tophand
O'Connor Ranches

"A powerful man—one of the best that ever rode this country."

L. V. Terrell
Tophand
O'Connor Ranches

Bosh Heron
Tophand
Welder Ranch
Vidauri

"A good rider."

Romero Rocha (left)
"Chico"
Cowhand
O'Connor Ranches
Chauffeur and Cook
for
Kate S. O'Connor
(with Jose Serrata)

"Chico was a patient, loyal man, and a good cook."

Gilberto Perez
Cowhand
O'Connor Duke Ranch

"A good cowhand."

Monroe Benson
Tophand
O'Connor Salt Creek Ranch

"He was the best rider in Refugio County."

Butler Williams
Tophand
O'Connor Ranches
(with Elma Ross)

"He was some cowhand!!!!"

Dick Avery *(second from left)*
Tophand
O'Connor Ranches

"He could set a hoss! He could even ride old Polecat."

Spencer Cook
Tophand
Welder and O'Connor Ranches

"Spence taught me everything I know about ranches."

T. Michael O'Connor

Willie Terrell *(on horse)*
"Luck"
Tophand
Armour Fagan Ranch

"I went to school with him in Lewis's Bend. He was a good man."

S. W. "Tony" Lott

Elmore Joshlin
Tophand
McDowell Ranch

"He was foreman of the St. Charles Ranch. He ran all that Lucas country."

J. D. Mitchell
Naturalist

Mitchell discovered the method of dipping cattle that brought about the eradication of the Texas fever tick. He studied and photographed on all the ranches in this area. — **L. O'C.**

Clarence Lott *(far left)*
Cowhand
O'Connor Melon Creek Ranch

"In his younger days, he was a good rider."

Lawrence Williams
Camp Cook
O'Connor Melon Creek Ranch

"He was born on the Nine Mile Ranch, near Little Sarco Creek. He fed us well."

John Scott
Cowhand and Farmer
Fagan Ranches

"He lived on the Fagan Ranch for many years, and farmed back when you could make a living farming. On the side he worked on our ranch breaking horses and mules."

Freddy Fagan
Rancher

Lucas DuBois, Jr.
Rancher

"He was a horseman and a member of Waller's Texas Cavalry in the Civil War. He raised horses more than he raised cattle."

Sabas Urbano
Pasture Rider and Farmer
McFaddin Ranch

*"He was gassed in the First World War, and pretty much retired after that.
He was a real old-timer."*

William Scott
Cowhand
McFaddin Ranch

"A good rider and good roper. He was rough in that saddle."

Jim Brown
Itinerant Cowhand

"An all around cowhand in the Victoria area."

Eddie Lewis
Cowhand
O'Brien, Hynes, and Shelton Ranches

"We tied him naked to two trees out on the highway one day 'cause he was foolin' with us."

K. J. Oliver
E. J. Garza

Edward Harvey
"Bull"
Tophand
Traylor Ranch

"He was an all around cowboy—a veterinarian of sorts. He could cure a fistula on a horse by cutting something in his nose. He promised to tell how he did it, but he died with the knowledge in him."

Charlie Parks
Rancher
Parks Ranch

Charlie Lewis
Cowhand
Parks Ranch

"Charlie Parks employed Charlie Lewis from the time he [Lewis] was very young.
They were good friends, they were really thick."

Andy Spriggs
Itinerant Cowhand

"They say he was a cowboy. He cooked for the Texas Rangers, too."

Henry Rice
Farmer and Rancher
Goliad County

"He was with the O'Connors all his life. When he retired, they gave him a farm."

Claudie Greenwood
Tophand
O'Connor Ranches

"He was one of the very top hands in the outfit."

Steve Rubio, Sr.
Farmer
O'Connor Ranches

"He was a good man and a good farmer."

Andrew Youngblood
"Johnny Beat the World"
Cowhand
O'Connor Duke Ranch

"He gave everybody he knew a nickname. He kept the whole world laughing."

Paul Lott
Cowhand
Welder Ranches

Steve Holliman
Former Slave
Fiddle Player

"Paul was an old man when we were coming up. He just sat down in the river bottom most of the time."

"Steve could stop anything from bleeding, and he could tell a great ghost story, too."

Vivian Power, "Nig", "Yaller" (far left)
Ranch Cook
O'Connor Melon Creek Ranch

"Nig" was not known for being excessively energetic. Many of the cowhands whom he cooked for say they would come in to eat and find him lying on a bench in front of the fireplace, stirring the pots flat on his back. — **L. O'C.**

Thornton Williams
aka John Thornton
Cowhand
O'Connor Brothers River Ranch

*"He came into the Salt Creek country when he was nothing but a boy.
He went up the trail, then he came home and took care of those O'Connor
boys (Tom [II], Joe, and Martin)."*

Phil Snowden
Foreman
O'Connor Brothers River Ranch

"He could think like a cow."

Roll Call

Photographs of the following people are not available, but they were mentioned just as often and are just as important to the history of this area as the others. — **L. O'C.**

Oliver Andrews
Antonio Andrada
Aunt Rittie
Charlie Avery
Garner Avery
Jim Avery
Walter Avery
Pete Barber
John Barefield
Jose Beltran
Dan Best
Mose Best
Joe Best
Ernest Blackley
Sam Blue
Billy Bowlegs
Sim Brown
Stella "Cat" Brown
Frank Butler
Charlie Cantu
Inez Cardenas
Geronimo Cardenas
The Chofala Boys
Mead Collier
Raymond Cunningham
Alonzo Cunningham
Valentine Conrad
Thurman Dawson
Jesus de la Garza
Jose de los Santos
Ed Doss
Albert Duke
Frank Dunman
Joe Dunman
Charles Simon Dykes
Doc Edwards
Emmet Fagan

Armour Fagan
Ben Fox
Alex Fry
Charlie Fry
Juan Garcia
Ishmael Garza
Martin Garza
"Dry Bones" Gibson
Bowlegs Giddings
Gertrude Gipson
J. P. Gipson
Bubba Green
Ben Green
Levy Green
Mandy Harris
Henry Harvey
Will Harvey
Alan Heard
Freddie Lee Henderson
Santiago Hernandez
Oliver Hopkins
"Doc" Hubbard
Phil Hynes
Mary Jones
Deelie Joshua
Tom Joshua
Adolphus Kay
Red Kay
Marion Keyes
Charlie Lasso
Pedro Lasso
Cornelius Lewis
Jack Lewis
Walter Lott
Tettie Lott
Vera Lott
Vivian Lott

Cicero Miles
John Mitchell
Doc Powell
Uncle Major Powell
Peter Power
Caesar Ramon
Amos Raspberry
Fred Rivas
Adolph Robinson
Joe Rodriguez
Elijah Scott
Marcellino Severino
Han Shaw
Love Shaw
Cornelius Simms
Louis Sitterle
John Sommers
Lizzie Lott Sommers
Fred Spriggs
Ed Steward
Roy Steward
Tom Steward
Frank Taylor
Dennis Terrell
Ernest Terrell
Henry Terrell
Prince Terrell
Andy Tillman
Joe Tillman
Jim Tippin
Lynn Tucker
Albert Williams
Jim Williams
Duke Youngblood
Jackson Youngblood

CHAPTER SEVEN

THE POWER BEHIND THE THRONE: THE WOMEN

Gertrude Patterson, 1889–1987
Photo by Louise S. O'Connor.

THE POWER BEHIND THE THRONE: THE WOMEN

"I came to Texas from Louisiana to see the hookin' bulls. When I got here, I couldn't believe my eyes. These cowboys were as foreign to me as Sputnik, like a bunch of monkeys with bad table manners. They give me so much trouble sometimes, I nearly be ready to quit. Finally, I got them in line 'cause I wasn't afraid of nobody. I held that kitchen down for eight years."

Gertrude Patterson
Cook
Welder Vidauri Ranch
1889–1987

Although this book is principally aimed at the rancher and the cowhand, women and family life were the backbone of the entire operation, as they are in any culture. Daily life, the keeping of the home, and the rearing of children went on, whether the ranchers and cowhands were at home or were out in the cow camps, sometimes for a month at a time. The women had more time for themselves when the men were away and would often use this time to indulge their love for fishing, quilting, and just enjoying the company of other females.

The women ran their homes with an iron hand and were the chief disciplinarians for their children. Since the men were gone much of the time, or left home early every morning and did not return until late at night, the children often looked on them as strangers.

The women kept their modest houses and dirt yards impeccably clean, and took great pride in their vegetable gardens and domestic animals. Their homes were often clustered together in a small neighborhood-like community, usually a short distance from the main ranch headquarters.

Even though they had enough room to raise their own food, it was still necessary to purchase staples from the ranch or community store if they lived a great distance from the nearest town. They were often given meat when the ranches and their neighbors butchered, but kitchen staples like flour, salt, coffee, and sugar had to be purchased. Trips to town were infrequent for the women, often they would get to town only once or twice during the year.

Church was the social center for everyone on the ranches, but it was especially important to the women. They had their own female communities within the ranch structure, and the church was often the center of their social lives—more so than the men, who were in contact with each other every day and who created a social event out of their work, their mealtimes, and their camp life. Not only did the ranches provide churches for their people, but often there was a cemetery on the ranch or in a nearby community, or on an adjacent ranch for burial of the deceased workers and members of their families.

The midwife was an honored member of female society on the ranches. Often curanderas and herbalists were used for the medical needs of the women and their children, but in more serious cases, the town doctor would be summoned.

Most of the owners' children were sent to town to school or, in some cases, off to boarding school, but education was provided on the ranches for the workers' children. School was usually conducted in a building especially constructed for that purpose or in a building that was used for church on Sundays. If the ranch was in proximity to a town or community such as Kemper City, Anaqua, or McFaddin, the children were sent there for schooling. The children were playmates on the ranches as well as classmates in school.

These ranches were a microcosm, a self-sufficient social unit that often required only minimal contact with the outside world to survive. As the radical changes brought about by World War II began to break up these ranch communities, many of the families moved to town. Most of the women I talked to are not happy with this breakup of their community. They feel that they have lost control of their lives and their children, and do not like the effects of town life on their families. They also do not like to hear other women deny or ridicule their past lives and their upbringing on the ranches. They have a great sense of pride in their rural heritage and believe that the close-knit ranching communities gave them a sense of family and a set of values that has remained with them, and strengthened them, all their lives.

South Texas Women

"The strongest women in the world live in South Texas. You show me a strong man and I will show you seventeen strong women. It is still a masculine world down here. In order to survive, women must be tough and unique.

"Out of the Mexican tradition of matriarchy, women here have learned to use and manipulate the system to their advantage. They are soft, feminine, and elegant on the outside, but on the inside they have backbones of steel."

Lawrence Wood
Rancher

No Roads and No Electricity: The Foremen's Wives

"When I came to this ranch it was pioneer days, and only forty years ago. The roads were terrible and there was no electricity. There wasn't even any butane or propane. I was raised in a German family, and we were taught to be clean and work hard, so ranch life didn't bother me at all. I even lived through the seven-year drought, when the whole ranch was on my front porch. Life here was a challenge—it was going to be our home. It still is in my heart."

Wilma Nelson Copeland
Ranch Manager
O'Connor Goliad Ranch
1910–1989
Wife of O. G. Copeland
Foreman
O'Connor Duke Ranch

"Being married to a ranch foreman is like being married to a doctor: you never know when or if he will be home."

Dorothy Turman Coward
Wife of E. D. "Rusty" Coward
Foreman
O'Connor Melon Creek Ranch
1917–1984

"Orion was foreman at the Salt Creek when I married him. The first day at the ranch, I realized there was no electricity and an outdoor privy. I walked in the house and said to myself, 'My God, Nita, what have you done? Will you survive?' I had never lived in the country in my life; it was quite an adjustment. I learned to ride, hunt, and work cattle, and I grew to love it dearly."

Anita Sommer Linney
Wife of Orion Linney
Foreman
O'Connor Salt Creek Ranch

"I began living on the ranches as a bride in 1912. There was no electricity or modern conveniences, but it really wasn't all that tough. I had a lot of help.
"Being a foreman's wife was fun. Jim loved the ranches so much he was always happy. I learned to fish and shoot snakes and ride horseback. Ranch life was a good life around good people."

Eulalia Marmion Coward
Wife of Jim Coward
Foreman
O'Connor Melon Creek Ranch

THE FOREMEN'S WIVES

Wilma Nelson Copeland, 1910–1989

Dorothy Turman Coward 1917–1984

Anita Sommer Linney

Eulalia Marmion Coward

When in Doubt, Scrub It: A German Upbringing

We grew up in a small town, where everyone knows your business. We were born into a German family in Gillett [Karnes County], Texas. On our grandmother's side, the family originally came from the Black Forest region in Germany; our grandfather's side came from Prussia. They were members of a military clique, and one of them married a housemaid—that's why he was kicked out of Prussia and had to come to the United States.

Daddy was a ginner, and he owned a gristmill. He also did windmill work, sold pipe, and did some blacksmithing. Both sides of our family were master farmers, as were most Germans.

We were almost a pioneering family in the Gillett area, and Gillett was a pioneering farm community. It was cleared of mesquite by Mexicans from Mexico using grubbing hoes. The wood was then used in the gin's boilers. God only knows how many cords of wood Daddy bought a season. Cotton was the cash crop in the area, and everyone planted corn for animal feed. Molasses was the summer cash crop.

We had a normal childhood. Being German, we were taught to be clean. If Mother found us loafing for one minute, she would find something for us to scrub.

The woodshed was our playhouse. We were raised Catholic, and so playing church was one of our favorite games. Often we would imitate the Baptist and Methodist revivals, shouting and rolling around on the floor. One of our favorite pastimes was to go to the shed, where Mother kept an old sow. She would be our church organ. One of us kicked the sow and made her grunt, while the other one sang church songs. Often we would get in a fight over who got to play the organ. Oh, the grand finale was something to hear. "Beulah Land" and "When the Roll Is Called up Yonder" were two of our favorites. Mother always took a nap, and the neighbor kids would come over and we churched.

We were so fascinated by the telephone office, with its headpieces and flibberting lights, that we had to construct our own telephone office. A collapsible drinking cup was our phone. Everyone had one in those days for travel. The top was our earpiece, and strings from the flour sacks were the telephone lines.

As children, we amused ourselves. We could find any little thing and figure out how to play with it. You know, where children grow up with chinaberry trees, a chinaberry culture develops in their play activities. They were used by the boys in their slingshots and toy guns, while the girls used them more for playing house and cooking and making jewelry. Chinaberry beads were glamorous things!

We had a mania for bottles, and collected them from everyone. They were used in our apothecary. We don't know where we learned this word, but that was the name of our drugstore. Baby Percy and Castoria were big items in our store. We would soak crepe paper in water to create colored liquid to put in our "medicine" bottles.

We had a normal girlhood, but when our younger brother Jake came into our lives, his was anything but normal. We used him for a living doll.

We dragged him around and incorporated him into our play until he was old enough to make us stop.

Christmas always came from Sears and Roebuck, and our tree was never put up until Christmas Eve. One Christmas, the packages were delivered to Daddy's office as usual. They were fur neckpieces for each of us. Jake was with Daddy that day, and he couldn't get home fast enough to tell us we were getting "woo-woos" with glass eyes. He always called us "the girls." He was great at imitating people. Mr. Potts, the high school principal, and Dr. Cook, the town doctor, were two of his best.

We used spools and thread to make trains, and helped the boys make bird traps. We never hunted — we just helped clean them. Neither of us could stand to kill things. We climbed trees and made doll clothes with the few female friends we had. Mostly, we played with boys.

Mother made us do chores. We fed the chickens, gathered wood, and chopped kindling. We also brought in the wood, milked the cows, and helped Mother dry the dishes after she washed them. We had a huge garden, and we canned everything. There was plenty of work to do around our house. If it was dry, we chopped weeds; if it was wet, we pulled them; and if there wasn't anything else to do, we cleaned the windows again. The walls and ceilings were cleaned every six months. Mother never wanted servants — she did all the work herself.

The afternoons were free. The women would visit in the afternoons and do their handiwork while they talked. This visiting time was very important. You were considered white trash if you worked in the afternoons.

We grew up with a rigid set of rules about what was proper and what was not. Saturday was shampoo day if the weather permitted. We washed our hair in emulsified coconut oil and rainwater. It was the only soft water around. If you had dandruff, then you used Packer's Tar Soap, and you had to dry your hair in the open to get rid of the smell. Everyone had long hair, and was that a "botheration," as the old folks used to say. Granny Patton had short hair, and everyone made fun of her.

Saturday night was bath time. We had the first bathtub in town, and we had running water in the bathroom and an oil heater. Were we ever fancy! There was no heat in the houses because it was believed to cause tuberculosis. It was the most dreaded disease next to pneumonia. Diphtheria, whooping cough, smallpox, croup, typhoid, and flu could be deadly also. It is hard to believe how feared these diseases were before inoculations and antibiotics. Both of these came in after World War II. We lived through the flu epidemic of 1917 or 1918, whichever it was. Whole families would have it. They closed the schools. Mother nursed everyone and never caught it, but so many people died in the Gillett area that they ran out of coffins. Daddy made coffins lined with muslin and helped bury the victims. There was nothing to cool the fever at the time, so the patients were wrapped in wet sheets and towels — and ice packs when ice was available. Mother used castor oil and chicken noodle soup for everything. She always swore that they saved us from the flu.

There were herbalists in the black and Mexican communities, but we never

Wilma Nelson, Ruby Nelson, ca. 1915.

used them. Mother just stuck with her patent medicines.

The rules governing our dress were strict, too. We wore drop-seat teddies that buttoned down the back. They were made of unbleached muslin. There was also two-piece underwear. You could wear either one. Black sateen bloomers, a full slip, black ribboned stockings, and a dress finished our outfit. Bras and corsets were also worn. We couldn't wait to wear a corset! Flat-chested was the fashion. You dare not have a bust. This was a fashion issue, not a moral issue. And did the boys make fun of you if you had a bust! Now is that crazy? This occurred during the flapper era. As soon as you developed a bust, you had to flatten it. You were never seen in public bareheaded or without your gloves, either.

Pregnancy was never discussed, and a pregnant woman was never seen in public. A lot of women died in childbirth. Most women had nothing but midwives. Sex education was never mentioned in the homes or in the schools. It was considered immoral to do so. We never knew our brother was on the way. Sidney Hutchinson said he never knew women had ankles until after World War I.

Wednesday was washday. It was a ritualistic performance and a status symbol in the community. Lye soap was shaved so it would melt, and the laundry was boiled fifteen or twenty minutes in a big black pot. A broom handle was used to stir the clothes, and then it was all put through two rinses. The second rinse had blueing in it. The clothesline was in the sun to further whiten the clothes. We usually started the day before. The clothes were rubbed on a washboard. That is the hardest work a woman can do. Clothes must be hung in a certain order, and you never hung anything on the fence. Only white trash did these things. You were gauged as a house-keeper by the way your laundry was hung. Back in those days, there was pride in being a housewife. Clothes were washed in a certain order and hung in a certain order. First, the fine things, then the dirtier things, and then the colored clothes. The clothes were never mixed up on the line. Shirts were hung together. White towels were not hung among the colored towels. The set of rules was endless, and Thursdays were ironing days.

The daily schedules were very rigid. We did not often deviate from them. Friday was reserved for housecleaning. Between shampoos and baths on Saturdays, we baked for Sunday and finished the housecleaning. Our floors were scrubbed with lye for bug control. On Sunday we always had a cake. Red-checked tablecloths were used for everyday, and Sundays we brought out the white linen cloth, starched to the nines, the best silver and china, and the food was special. Sunday was always special whether we had guests or not. We always dressed up. Roast beef, buttered parsley potatoes, dried fruit, corn, carrots, pickled beets, green beans, stewed raisins, noodles, sweetened rice, noodle cream, ambrosia, and coconut cake—to name a few— was the menu. There were almost no cookbooks in those days. The women had the recipes in their heads. There was a lot of improvisation. For example, new peach leaves were used for almond flavor. Tomatoes with cream, sugar, and cinnamon are something you don't see anymore. Ice cream socials were popular, as were community barbecues on the creek.

A clean chick sale was a sign of pride. Ours had a half moon on the door. There were no indoor plumbing or sewer systems then. There was always some lye in the outhouse, and when we finished with the laundry water, we used it to scrub the privy. The outhouses had to be clean or you were trash. Not only was everything clean, but nothing went to waste, either. When we butchered a hog, all that was lost was the squeal. Daddy was a fix-it artist, so everything was saved. The work ethic was very strong in our lives. Everything was scheduled, and the houses were expected to be as clean as they are now with modern conveniences.

There was a telephone office, a post office, a drugstore, and a confectionery in town. On Saturdays we could go to town if all the work was done. German people are industrious, and every minute had to count. We were always stockpiling for a bad year. You were trashy if you didn't pay your bills, and there was no need for welfare. People took care of their own. Men were expected to support their families. Nobody was ever in need. All of our clothes were sewn at home. Domestic was five cents a yard, and patterns were made of newspaper. Women handed their patterns around. They also did a lot of fancy work. Everything had to have a scarf and crocheted edges. All the women sewed—it was very important to be able to do this. Winter nights were a great time to sew.

Both of our parents were extra special people. They came from a good heritage. They were pioneering stock who started from nothing. This must explain their frugality. Our grandmother did everything by hand. She spun wool, made hats out of palmetto, and tailored men's clothes. We came from a family that was highly self-sufficient.

Oh, my goodness, the rules we lived by! Girls didn't wear trousers, and they didn't ride astride. Even with all these rules, we couldn't wait to wear corsets.

Neighboring was practiced in farming and building. The barter system was used. Food was traded, but the staples were all bought at the town store.

We were two of the first women in the area to go off to college. There were lots of rules governing our behavior, even at this age. Discipline was very strict at home, but no one ever laid a hand on us. We didn't have any fruit on our peach trees until we went off to school. Mother tore off so many switches trying to make us mind that the trees couldn't bear fruit. Boys visited girls in their homes in the presence of their parents. If a girl didn't come home at night, she had to marry the boy. There were lots of changes after World War I. Until this time, women kept the home fires burning. They reared the children and kept the house. Women didn't go out in the world. Ma Ferguson was a real shocker! Schoolteaching, bookkeeping, postmistress, and telephone operator—these were acceptable jobs for women. We never felt restricted, though. Daddy felt that we could do anything. He had confidence in us.

We had a strong religious upbringing, but church was not the center of social life in the German community. The Ku Klux Klan was strong. You went to Mass, and you went home. Weddings were a big deal, and the neighbors came in and helped prepare for the festivities. Gifts for the bride and groom were always practical. Baptisms were done when the priest came to town.

Houses were simple in those days—kerosene lanterns, iron beds, and curtains of heavy lace were used. The irons were heated on the stove. Then we got gasoline irons. It was later when electric irons were available. Sugar and flour sacks were used for clothing.

To think of what women lived through! Everybody took pride in their homes. Women vied with each other to see who had the cleanest clothes. You were the envy of the town if you finished your laundry by nine o'clock in the morning.

Before morticians, women prepared bodies for burial. Wagons and horses took the bodies to the cemetery. There was no embalming, so you couldn't wait long to bury. The men sat up with the body. Women wore black veils for six months after the death of a family member. Men wore black crepe armbands and had a black bow on the door of their place of business. No one ever thought of going anywhere during the mourning period.

Nothing was ever too clean for Mother. She even washed her milk. Daddy's idea of life was, if you needed something, do it yourself.

So we lived by our parents' mottoes. Daddy always said nothing was so bad it couldn't get worse, and Mother always said nothing could be too clean.

Ruby Nelson
and
Wilma Nelson Copeland
Manager
O'Connor Goliad Ranch
and
Wife of O. G. Copeland
Foreman
O'Connor Duke Ranch
1910–1989

The Mexican Women: *Madre de Dios!*

Life was pretty much the same for all of us women in the Mexican community. We washed, ironed, cooked, raised gardens and children, and went to church. Often we did work in the fields and hunted and fished for our food. Life is a lot different now than it was in our day. We didn't have much money, but everything was cheaper to buy then. Life is going by real fast now. When we were young girls, we were never allowed around the boys. We could not even watch them play. The boys were close friends and the girls were close friends, but they never mixed as children. Even when we married, our husbands were very strict. We had no freedom—we were not permitted out of our homes without our husbands, not even to visit between our homes during the day.

In those days it was work, work, work all the time. There was no radio, telephone, car, refrigeration, or electric stoves. We had to chop the wood for the woodstoves. We grew up with respect for God, our country, and our elders. We grew up with strictness. Married women were never allowed around unmarried girls, and children were never allowed to sit around when the grown-ups were visiting.

Petra Ybarbo and her husband Juan, parents of Jesus Ybarbo

Group at de la Garza Ranch, 1947, Alex de la Garza, center.

There was a community barter system. The women would trade household items among themselves. There was a strong community among the women. We helped each other. There was little time for recreation or play. We only got to visit on special occasions.

When we were young, children didn't speak their piece. Parents were strict then. There was no divorcing in our day. When we married, we knew our obligations, and if we didn't want to keep those obligations, we didn't marry.

Interior of St. Anthony's Chapel, O'Connor River Ranch.

It was a hard life back then by today's standards, but everyone helped and no one thought of it that way.

Our children were delivered by *parteras*—midwives. We used lots of herbs and natural medicines to stay healthy or to treat diseases. We sometimes used *curanderos*, but the church didn't like it much. The priests thought it was superstition, but they didn't preach against it.

There were strange customs in the Mexican community, with all the strictness about boys and girls being around each other. There was a custom of boys and girls running away to marry. Everyone knew the boy was

THE POWER BEHIND THE THRONE: THE WOMEN

coming to steal the girl and acted like they didn't know, then everyone got upset when the boy stole the girl.

We always had to go to church and school. We learned our prayers, and not to lie and steal. Our homes were simple wood frame houses, with iron beds and homemade furniture.

There was a lot of sharing and neighboring in those days.

We didn't show our bodies to anyone. We wore long dresses, long socks, and long hair. We sat properly and we didn't wear makeup.

We all loved the boys, but we couldn't look at them. We would communicate with them by sign language when the grown-ups weren't looking. There is a time for everything. You look at each other, you love each other. Then you decide to marry and our parents negotiated the deal. There was a lot of talk about arranging the marriage.

In our days, boys would come to the house or write a letter if they wanted to court. The boy would find someone to come to the girl's father and ask permission to marry after the courtship. They could not see each other until they married. They barely saw each other and they had to write letters. Our mothers usually knew, but the fathers didn't. Our fathers were always the strictest. We saw good marriages come from this method of courtship. There was really love there even though there was no real dating.

If the family had any money, there would be a marriage celebration.

Our mothers taught us what little we knew about sex and our bodies. Mostly we were taught modesty. When we came of age, we had a *quinceviera*—a celebration for approaching womanhood.

Hut of Antonio Rodriguez, guardian of St. Anthony's Chapel, early 1900's.

Girls never rebelled against the female role. We did the jobs women were raised to do. The wife did what her husband said. He was the boss.

When the men were gone, we had permission to get together. We sewed, quilted, talked. We had a great time and we got some rest. We would teach each other and help each other. We enjoyed their absences.

As long as our husbands had a job, we didn't think anything was hard.

When we got up in the morning, we kissed the hands of our mother, our father, and our grandparents, and said "Good Morning." They would say, "God give you a good day. How was your night?"

First communion group at St. Dennis Church, 1953, O'Connor River Ranch.

In those days people were not afraid to help one another. Now they are, because there is no love. Now everything is modern—children are not reared right. In our time, a child was brought up with love and fear.

Our religious beliefs were passed down to us from generation to generation. We would never play church—that was considered irreverent. We never went to bed without saying our prayers. The big star at night is the Prayer Star. The seven stars are called the Seven Virgins—they can show us the road to heaven. We were taught to praise God, His Mother, and the saints. Shrines and saints are used so we can be praying constantly. Often, when we were young, we had no priest, so certain men in the community would conduct services such as burials and Lenten services between the priests' visits. This was a very big privilege to be allowed to do this.

In the Mexican community we have a power called mother wit. The hand of God touches someone and lets her know what is going on. It's like a dream. God puts something in your head and you know about it before it happens.

World War II brought about many changes. We live in a new world now. You can even see people killing their own children—and other things we never saw before. People used to accept discipline, now they don't. Country people and town people have always been different, but in our day we were not introduced to new ideas and did not have foreign influences.

Education in our schools has caused much harm. Education does not give spiritual feeling and understanding. People do not pay attention to good

Eulalia Coward with her class at Twenty-four Farms School, O'Connor Melon Creek Ranch, ca. 1920's.

things any more. Educated people don't seem to know what is best for them. Ambition is killing us all. *Madre de Dios*, things are strange now.

Agapita Roderiguez Garcia, Florentina Williams Lara, Susie Moreno Perez, Carlota Rocha, Maria Reyes Rubio, Margaret Rubio, Teresa E. Tijerina, Aurora de la Garza

These women are the wives of various cooks and cowhands associated with the O'Connor and McFaddin ranches. Their words were translated by Thomas Tijerina and Teresa Escalona Tijerina. —L. O'C.

THE POWER BEHIND THE THRONE: THE WOMEN

"Until death do us part—
if I have to kill her myself."

Monroe Shaw
"Bailey"
Itinerant Tophand
Well Digger

"I was married on Saturday,
carried her home on Sunday,
and caught a mean horse
on Monday morning."

K. J. Oliver
"K"
Itinerant Tophand

Raisin' the Kids

If you had a big family in those days, you were rich.

Everybody had big families, and the young ones minded the old folks whether they were their parents or not.

The old cowboys left their women to take care of the home. The women did a good job, too. They worked together, makin' soap, quiltin', cookin', and makin' lard. They had their own community.

The men and the women each had their jobs. Back then, the women stayed home and raised the kids and ran the home. Everybody did what they had to do, and that's how it was.

The marriages worked out fine—the men were always out with the cow crowd.

We seldom saw our daddies; they left before daylight and came back after dark. I guess our kids never saw much of us, either.

Women were strong in those days, born to the outdoor life. They ran the home and were the bosses there.

The women had their own social life. They played cards and fished together when we were gone. At least this was the way it was in the black community.

The Mexican women did not have so much freedom, but they still were friends.

The fathers were the disciplinarians. Many of us obeyed our daddies as long as they lived—they were strong.

Family life back then was excellent. The mother stayed home and everybody sat down to the table and said grace. The children said verses from the Bible and everyone had chores. Now they have nothin' to do and they eat all over the house. Women leavin' the home has created many bad problems.

Now we are afraid of our own children and grandchildren, but you dare not discipline one. You'll get hauled off for child abuse.

Ananias Cook, Clayton Isaiah, Jesse Jones, Coleman Joshlin, Quinn Love, K. J. Oliver, Abel Perez, Camillo Ramirez, Romulo Ramirez, Simmie Rydolph, Leo Scott, L. V. Terrell, Milam Thompson, Porfirio Urbano, Rev. Mack Williams, Dan Youngblood

Alice Cook on porch of her childhood home, ca. 1920's.

The Black Women: Of Mother Wit and Cowboys

Just to think how many used to be out here and all have gone away. Girls used to be kept in control in our day. Our mothers disciplined us; our daddies were hardly ever here. They were off workin' cattle and livin' in camp.

We grew up in old wooden houses. When the wind was blowin', those old houses would sing to us. Woodstoves, iron beds, outhouses, and a Victrola— that was what our homes were like.

Everyone was together in our day. Whatever one had, the other had.

We were allowed to play with the boys, but we were told to keep our skirts down and to be careful if we wore patent leather shoes. Sometimes girls were held too close when they were growin' up, and then they overreacted when they were turned loose. Back in our days, children were closely watched.

THE POWER BEHIND THE THRONE: THE WOMEN

225

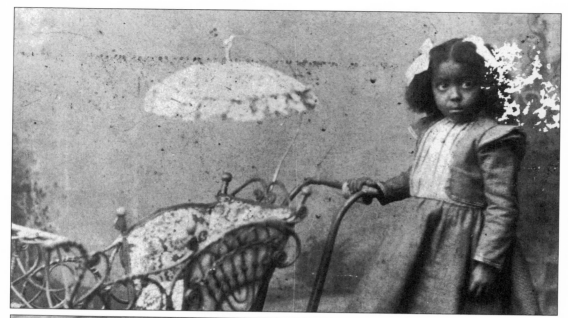

Maude Williams Brown.

Evelyn Youngblood, second from right.

Lucille Youngblood on right, at Mt. Pilgrim Church, Refugio.

THE POWER BEHIND THE THRONE: THE WOMEN

Mandy Harris, midwife, mother of Richard Harris.

Nowadays, other people's values are controllin' our children. We still want our children to have our values, but not the lifestyles we had. We don't want them to have the hardships. Keepin' one and changin' the other doesn't work. We are losin' our children.

Cowboys weren't heroes in our day. It was the town girls that loved the cowboys. All us country girls would get so mad when the town girls tried to take our men away.

The men were gone a lot, and while they were gone we would gang up and play cards.

Midwives had a very unique position in our community. They were the female heroes. They acted kind of like godmothers to the girls they delivered. There were always some older women around, too, who were gifted with mother wit. We would go to these women for advice and to learn about life.

Women had lots of control in the black community. It was a strong, matriarchal society. The men would try actin' macho like the Mexican men once in a while, but we were strong enough to stop that.

People stayed together back then better than they do now. That doesn't mean that adultery wasn't widespread, but people just didn't divorce much. At least immorality was kept under the covers back then.

You know, the men really did have as much fun as they remember.

Back in our day, women chose more carefully in their men. We married when it was time to marry. Now, they don't seem to love one another. That's why there is so much separatin'. Women were brought up to be a certain way and stay where they were supposed to be. It never really occurred

Church group, Victoria, Texas. ca. 1940's.

to us to want to do men's work. The men were havin' more fun, but what could we do?

We loved our daddies. We thought they were kings even though we never saw them. Cowboyin' was their life and they loved it.

We played a lot of church and the boys were playin' cowboy.

There was no cursin' or swearin' in our homes. We were taught to speak correctly, how to behave around boys, and we were not allowed to associate with loose girls. Many of us were educated and then had to come home and marry uneducated men. This caused a problem in a lot of marriages.

THE POWER BEHIND THE THRONE: THE WOMEN

Cotton-picking time, 1940.

Group at Mt. Pilgrim Church, Refugio, Texas, early 1900's.

School class, Refugio, Texas, 1940–41, Mrs. G. A. Smith, teacher.

THE POWER BEHIND THE THRONE: THE WOMEN

Lola Gibson Adams, right.

Pearlie Pleasant.

All of us chopped and picked cotton in our time. Our families were large and our lives were happy. Once a month only, we would get a treat.

We played dolls, sewed, made mud cakes, and had a lot of funerals for our pets. We told ghost stories and helped our mothers in the house.

It was church every Sunday. Back then the feelin' was more real. Children couldn't join the church until they had been tested. Sometimes we would nearly starve to death on Sunday before Daddy would stop prayin' over the food.

The world has changed and churches have changed. The world offers more than the church does now. Parents don't go to church any more and kids' friends have more influence than both parents and churches. We are driftin' away from bendin' our knees because of lack of oppression now. An easy road makes you think you don't need God. Everybody wants to be a chief. Nobody wants to be an Indian.

Children get too much too easy now. Back when we were growin' up, our parents didn't have it to give.

Our mothers were strict about housekeepin'. They taught us how to do it. Our yards and our houses were clean—only trash didn't keep things cleaned. Our laundry was hung a certain way.

Most of our families were brought into this area as slaves way back in the 1700s and 1800s.

Women were more aggressive about gettin' an education than the men. Men provided the money for the women to go to school. They wanted the women to go also because they didn't like to be indoors teachin' and they generally didn't like to study. Men depended on the women to do the readin' and takin' care of business matters in the family.

Material was ten cents a yard back then. A $1.98 pair of shoes was expensive. You know, shoes like that used to cry, especially in church when you had to carry the collection down to the front. We used to always say the shoes were sayin'. "A dollar ninety-eight." Shoes don't cry like that now. Most of us had patent leather shoes that our mothers would shine with a biscuit or hog lard.

Everyone used to think of funny things to do all the time. There was a lot of fun and happiness in our families.

Mother saved pieces of soap and melted them down in water and scented our lye soap.

Sugar was cheap, so we made a lot of candy. When Mama left, we made peanut brittle out of sugar syrup and horse corn. Mama used to get so mad at us. All the little things we wanted to do we would do when Mama went to town. We were always cookin' behind her back or doing somethin' we shouldn't. Anythin' we were forbidden to do, we wanted to do.

"Beans and biscuits most every day, I'd as soon be eatin' old prairie hay." That was one of our favorite songs, and that was what we ate along with cornbread. It was all eaten off blue granite plates.

The old people had dreams—our parents and grandparents. They wanted us to be educated and to better ourselves. Most of us did this because it was instilled in us. The old people were contented with their lives, but they had dreams for their children.

July Fourth boating trip.

Isaac Spriggs, youngest son of Dave and Minnie Spriggs.

We were all taken care of in those days—no worries, no bills. Our food was taken care of and our burials, too.

Slavery was gone, and in a way we were very secure on these ranches. June 19 was when we found out in Texas that we had been freed from slavery—that was several months after the slaves were actually freed by Lincoln. This holiday meant a lot to the older people. Some of the younger people don't want "Juneteenth" celebrations, but they were great. These things happened. Why not admit it?

All these ranchers and cowhands cared about the cattle. It was their life. They were proud people, warm and rough. They had guts and were full of love and laughter. There was lots of community. We were one big family until after World War II. Exposure to the outside world wasn't necessarily good. Lots of things would have been better and sweeter if it had stayed the same. A lot of people are ashamed of growing up on ranches. That is pitiful. We have so much more heritage than those who didn't.

Most black girls played with the boys, unlike the Mexican culture. The Spanish girls were kept inside—almost locked up. We shouted and fell out and had many a baptizin'. We would say anythin' came to mind. Nothin' Biblical—we would preach about horses and cows. We preached about things we knew about. It didn't even make sense. We used green grapes and chinaberries for collection money.

We played lots of games in our day. We walked grasshoppers on strings, made mud cakes, and used lightnin' bugs as rings and on our caps for headlights.

It was a lot of fun in those days. We made our toys out of things we found—we used nature as our toys. We used grape leaves for lettuce and jar lids for pans. We'd build a house under the trees and use old boxes for furniture. When they killed hogs, we used the bladders for balloons. We used crushed rose petals for lipstick and cheek rouge. Sugar and cocoa was our snuff. We had cedar-bark cigarettes and blew bubbles with spools and soapy water.

We counted railroad cars coming by and made kites out of newspaper or brown paper and grapevines. We played doctor and used herbs for medicine. Some of our play medicine wasn't any crazier than what the grown-ups really used. Mare's milk and sheep-turd tea were whooping cough remedies. You wonder how they knew to use these things. Many of these remedies came from Africa and the Indians.

We grew up with lots of superstitions and folklore. The old people said they never really believed in those things, but they sure used them.

Back in the old days, churches didn't have pianos or organs. There were no song books because no one could read, and they had to make up the music and words as they went along. Old-timers sang when they were worried. Those old One Hundreds put the music in you anyway without a piano.

Motherless children used to have a hard time. People were especially hard on orphans for some reason. There was no protection then for children, especially the black children. It was partly economics and partly cultural.

Matty Tillman Jones.

Maybe it came from survival laws in Africa. Stepparents were sometimes hard on children in their care. It was hard to feed all the children in large families. All this was a real problem back in those days.

One of the things we remember most is how our mothers would come home from the big houses they worked in and make us use the highfalutin' manners they used in the big house. They would do really creative things like make napkin rings out of harness rings and the napkins out of flour sacks.

The manners were taught to us when we had meals. We were taught to use finger bowls when we ate greasy foods or finger foods. We were taught proper food service such as serve left, remove right. Mothers taught us to use the silverware from the outside in and to watch somebody else if we didn't know which one to use. Never lay the knife on the table and always have the blade facing in.

We were taught manners—yes ma'am, thank you, excuse me, may I please—and we really caught it if we talked with food in our mouth.

For Christmas we had ambrosia, fruitcake, and homemade wine. Sunday dishes were chicken and cobbler. Our Christmas trees were yaupons decorated with popcorn, paper chains, and moss.

Our mothers treasured their oatmeal glass that came in oatmeal boxes. Towels came in the washing powder. Every house had an ice cream churn and a butter churn.

People miss so much that grow up in town. Our children don't even believe the things we tell them. But you better believe it—life was good out here in the country.

Althea Lewis Burns, Alice Youngblood Cook, Laura Evans, Dorothea Gaskin Green, Dorothy Scott Harris, Sadie Cook Hillyer, Rosie Terrell Jones, Irie Youngblood Nixon, Evelyn Elliot Youngblood, Ludie Hynes Youngblood, Helen Magruder

These women all grew up on ranches and shared a mutual upbringing in the ranching culture. Some left the ranches when they married; others are still there.—L. O'C.

Lucy Gibson Bunton.

Style Is Ruinin' the World

Women are different now. Our lives were more innocent in that river bottom. We were big kids before we quit believin' in Santa Claus. It was a large community fifty or sixty years ago. These ranches have just gone down. Hardly anybody lives here now. It used to be like a little town all around this river bottom and even out by the prairies—McFaddin, Lewis's Bend, and Vidauri. Now there's nothin' to talk to but the cats. It's lonesome out here now. There probably won't be any cow-workin' out here before long. The old cowboys are gettin' too old to work and the young ones won't.

Them days back yonder are way better than now—they done somethin' for you. We respected the church, our elders, and the sick.

Nettie Rice Hicks.

Elvira Terrell.

Sarah Wofford Wade.

Aunt Martha Perryman, McFaddin, Texas.

"She lived so long she saw the stars fall."

Church ain't nothin' like it used to be down in that river bottom. It was a place to worship God and be together. Now churches have a lot of style to them—people are just there to check your clothes and leave. Style is ruinin' the world.

Emmaline Youngblood Henderson
Wife of Mose Henderson
Cook
Welder Ranch
Vidauri

Cinderella Terrell Avery
"Daisy"
"Dady"
Ranch Cook
O'Connor Duke Ranch

Gertrude Patterson's mother.

If You Want the Truth. . .

My people come from Africa way back when. They wound up in Louisiana as slaves and farmers. They farmed on halfsies. My mother was a Christian who raised seven children and I never heard her cuss an oath in her life. She always advised me to live Christian and pray.

I was a tomboy—swingin', jumpin' rope, and makin' dolls. We tended chickens, swept the yard around our log cabins clean with broomweed. I was raised to keep a clean yard and a clean house. Our furniture was homemade and our mattresses was straw. Everyone made quilts in my time. We were taught all that—cookin' and sewin'. The men hunted for the food and the women cooked it.

Now, if you want the truth, I'll tell it to you.

Boys and girls was raised different back then. You didn't go with no boy until you were old enough. That boy better keep his distance. Society was tougher on girls than on boys when I was young. We listened to the advice of our older folks. We minded our mothers. We used to have a mama on both ends and one in the middle. We didn't get by with nothin'. Everyone took care of everyone's children. My mama used to knit socks. I can knit, but I can't turn a heel. That's the old-time way to do it.

We also grew up with aunties and uncles—the older, wiser folks who taught the younger people. They taught us how to do the things we would need when we grew up, the household work, and whatever it was the boys needed to know. They taught us manners, fidelity, how to live, and how to carry ourselves. They knew how to tell us how to be somebody and what would be our downfall. Lyin' made a rogue out of us and they said never to do that. They were for honesty, marriage, and love. Our aunties taught us how to treat men and how to live a good life.

Men were men back when I was growin' up. There aren't no men now—no Christian men, anyway. Don't get me to talkin' about men here. They want you to work and take care of them and feed them and give them money. I ain't gonna take care of no man. I never have and I never will. If he can't take care of me, I'll just stay like I am. I'll live without them and trust in God. I got my chickens and two birds, and I ain't interested in men. Men are adulterous critters. You should try talkin' to your man about fidelity, and if he won't quit, you shouldn't throw yourself away because he does. Now that's the truth, too. I knowed a man at home named Mr. Will Sullivan. He had seven wives—seven women for one man. They treated each other just like sisters. I don't know what he was. In them days, I was a child and I used to think about it. Miss Annie was his real wife and they all took care of her. They never had an argue. Back in those days, children didn't know nothin' and I never could figure that out.

When I was young, I would sit down and try to map things out. I know what life is. I come up the hard way, but I made it over, thank God. Women's lives was tough back then—we couldn't do like they do now.

Unmarried pregnant girls was throwed in the trash in my day. Women didn't have sense enough to get mad about the double standard back then. Men got away with more. I didn't understand about being shamefaced when

Gertrude Patterson on left, Juneteenth at Vidauri.

I was young. I had two cousins who told me about it, and along with my mother they led me into the light of it.

My advice to young girls would be, if a boy walks up to you, tell him to get out of your face, 'cause he don't mean you no good. He just wants to get your name in the air. Men will try to talk you into doin' wrong and then blame you for it. It ain't like it used to be when I was growin' up. Then you had to be somebody. Now you get recognized for bein' bad. In my day, you couldn't go nowhere with a bad girl. I never will forget it — there was a rough girl lived on the tracks. We had to walk around her. I felt sorry for her. She wasn't married and she had a baby. Now it's fun to be bad. Times have done changed. People gonna get weaker but not wiser.

I got good mother wit. Even if you can't read and write, like me, you will have good judgment. The Lord shows you things before they happen. It's kind of like common sense and psychic powers. I knew my son was goin' to die, and I went and lost all my senses. I haven't got them back yet.

Women had to learn how to do their work back in those days. I learned to milk early in life. I even taught everyone at the Welder Ranch how to milk the right way. I did the same for Louis Power, too. I won't use tin buckets for milk, it will give you ptomaine poisonin'.

I loved biscuits as a child. My mother made the best ashcake bread you ever tasted. At hog-killin' time, my mother would put on hog backbone and ribs and boil 'em. We raised sweet potatoes and when we dug 'em, we would lay 'em on the jamb of the chimney to cook.

We would get up and eat ham bones and sweet potatoes and parched peanuts. We didn't know what eatin' breakfast was. We got up and went to the fields — without breakfast. But we had the two other meals, and what was left over wasn't throwed away. We didn't know what buyin' meal was — we ground our own. Everybody shucked two or three bushels of corn every Saturday. We'd take it to the mill and grind it when we finished. We had homemade bread and sorghum syrup, and sometimes that was all we had. Sometimes we wouldn't have a mouthful of food, so Mama would go out and get that half-green corn and grit it and feed it to us. If you spit in Mama's fireplace, you just had it, 'cause she baked her bread in the ashes. Them old iron pots did some good cookin'. We bought flour in barrels and Mama saved the ashes in that barrel, and in the spring of the year she made lye for her soap.

Acres and acres and acres of ribbon cane — I stripped so much ribbon cane. The stalks would grow as high as that door, and us children would bring the cane home and bury it, and it would be good for Christmas.

Things were different in Louisiana than in Texas. The people was different and the rules was different. There was lots of us from Louisiana out here at the Welder. Now, you want the truth: Louisiana is harder on black folks than Texas. I was raised up with the white kids and we always got along. When one would call me "Nigger," I'd just tell them that they had hair like an old horse's tail. We played together, and they wanted their hair wrapped just like we wrapped ours. We wrapped all that slick hair in little strings. Their mamas would laugh and laugh and then take the strings out.

THE POWER BEHIND THE THRONE: THE WOMEN

Jemima Youngblood at Vidauri.

My mother was born after the freedom, but she remembers all about that Ku-Kluxin'. It was rough back when I was young in Louisiana. Seemed like they wanted to put us back in slavery—they used to call us monkeys. That's why I decided to come to Texas. Here we are all like one. There never was no problem on these ranches about race. You can't get to heaven hatin' nobody. I want to have friends when I leave this world.

I come to Texas during the Depression when there was old Hitler, Mussolini, and the Kaiser. Times was tough then like it is now. It used to be good times out there; that ranch was excitement to me. Mr. Welder didn't like people around that ranch that didn't work there, and he made me keep the kitchen locked. I had fun keepin Tom Ball [Rodgers] from stealin' sugar and shortenin'. He was always tryin' to outsmart me.

Quinine, turpentine, and country doctors—we didn't have no drugstores. The country doctor came in on a horse with his saddlebags full. He would take out his knife and dose out that medicine in little papers.

It was a time out there at that ranch. Lord, those cowboys was somethin' else. I couldn't fill them up and them complainin' all the time about my food. So I just laid religion on the shelf and told them, "You damn fools ain't used to nothin' nohow. You don't know what good food is." I made up the same thing I made before and added a little tomato sauce and they et it then. Many a time I had to run them out that kitchen with a butcher knife. I was gonna break 'em up and I finally did. I had to give 'em hell but I got 'em in line.

They expected me to feed armadillo out there, but I wouldn't eat it—not me. We called them "grave robbers" at home. Those cowboys worked— be comin' in at eight or nine at night, get off those horses, eat, and get right back on.

The last quilt Jemima [Youngblood] and I pieced was the Sweetgum Leaf. The fabric came from the Vidauri mercantile. The backing is made out of salt sacks. We saved cotton sacks for the mattress covers. A lot of women helped Jemima and me, but mostly I had to get in their face and get them told about how it was done. Jemima and me did the best quilts around.

I tell you it was hard times when I first came here. I was scared of cattle, and they called me everythin' but the right thing, you hear. It was because I was from Louisiana. Lots who came from Louisiana had this happen. They used to give them a hard way to go. But Miss Rachel Power stuck by me, she was my friend. She got me a job with Miss Emma Huddleston. I really didn't want to live in Refugio—I wanted to go to *The Valley*, but I wound up stayin' and leasin' my place from Miss Novella Thomas. It was an old brooder pen. I bought it for fifteen dollars and lived in it until I got this house. Finally Miss Emma and I had it, and I had to lay religion on the shelf again. I had to give her a sermon on black and white separa- tion in heaven and hell. I had to go home for our graveyard workin' in Louisiana about that time, and I never did go back no more to work for her. When I came back, I went to work for Miss Madie Mitchell. I kept her place spotless shinin' before she and I finally had it. We all died friends at the end of our lives.

Gertrude Patterson and Ed Doss.

I saved my money even with all this and bought my house finally from the money I made at Welder. It cost me $350 in 1942. That's the reason I ain't no account now—workin' hard to get my house. They talked terrible about me, said I was an old hoodoo, I was this, and I was that. I told them if I was a hoodoo, I would go to the bank and have myself a mansion. Why would I want to hoodoo them? They didn't have nothin', neither. All that comes from the Devil—and people who mess with it come from the Devil. Lots of people thought I was biggety and hateful—times have changed.

Courtin' is when you goin' with a man and he ain't sleepin' with you. You ain't layin' up like no man and wife, you just laugh and talk until you make it up you gonna marry. It wasn't like it is now—uh-uh.

This young generation comin' up here now—I just don't know. I only got a little education, but I think theirs has gone to their heads. Now they're intermarryin' and that ain't gonna work. The young people treat us old folks like dogs now. They cuss you out and tell you they will do as they damn please.

Everythin' I'm telling' ya'll—it's the flat truth, you hear?

Half-breed children used to be treated rough, and women who had half-breed children were treated rougher. Now, white men been goin' with black women since I been in this world. They have always mixed—just not publicly. The white and Mexican girls were the ones goin' for the black men. There have even been suicides over intermarryin'. It's all done got crazy. I don't know what I think about mixin'. I guess we'll mix in heaven and hell, so let's live happy and die in peace.

I used to make beer out there at the Welder Ranch, but Mr. Welder finally made me quit 'cause everybody got drunk and got to fightin'. I did make the best beer of anyone around. They tried to get me to make it when I went to Refugio, but I was afraid they'd put me in jail there.

You know, Mr. Welder told me trouble's easy to get into and a lifetime journey to get out of. Ed Doss made me so mad one time I nearly forgot what Mr. Welder said and was ready to kill him. We got in a fight over my car, and when he come in that door, I busted him in the head with my gun. Now you know how men are—they are the Devil sometime and Ed just pushed me too far. And so, bless your soul, everythin' worked out all right. I got myself together and my senses back, but I was so mad for a few days I could smell my own blood.

There were some wild times around there once in a while. Rough times made tough people. If you ever talked to a black child been through it, I have. I was raised by a stepdaddy I hated—he beat me. Some men are the Devil—ain't worth kickin' out the door. I've had enough of their ways. I'm stayin' in this shack by myself until God calls me. It's hard to find a good man now. There is so much separatin' now—husbands and wives goin' off leavin' each other. All anyone is lookin' for now is a good time. Don't nobody respect nobody no more. Men used to respect women then, but not now. I guess that's our fault, ain't it?

Children are bad now. I don't care what the law say, I wouldn't let no child of mine get by with nothin'. Look at what's happened since the law won't allow children to be chastised anymore.

In them days, when I was growing up, it was tit for tat—you had to be a man, you had to be a woman. In the old days, people pulled together, they helped each other. Now you get down sick and nobody cares. I've had some tough times, so I try to help others any time I can.

People think I've gone crazy—always bitchin' about Uncle Sam messin' with me. The gov'ment just keep me where I ain't got good sense. Dealin' with the gov'ment is kinda like bein' around an east wind all the time. An east wind is poison and it'll make you crazy. An east wind is a searchin' wind. It will search your body.

Town church ain't like country church. Town church is more for the money, country church is for God. Country church was so much better—you hear some good church out there. I laid out my race in church the other day. I let them have it. There is just sin everywhere. People done forgot there is a God. Evil, jealousy, and malice everywhere, and not just among the colored. It's among all nations. People don't care about you. They charge a fortune and don't do their job. I just get to cryin' and studyin' and moanin' and prayin'. The Lord is good to me—you have to trust in Him. I'll just stick with my religion.

On Sunday, we used to play church as children—copyin' the sermons and singin' like the grown-ups. We'd shout and sing. "Sail on, Noah" was one of our favorites. We made ourselves a church arbor out of fence rails and a pulpit out of boxes. We mocked the preacher. Anythin' came into our mind, we'd say it if it was right; we wouldn't say nothin' wrong. We was always hollerin', "Repent, repent." We didn't always understand the grown-up sermons, but we did our best, we did our version. We'd get happy and feel the spirit, and when we got overloaded we got up and let it out. We'd just shout.

This has been a back'ard year—looks like the Devil is aloose. It's gettin' rough. Man thinks he can run the world, but he can't run nothin' unless God lets him. The way I see it, the Lord gonna come down through this world like the '42 storm.

Gertrude Patterson
Ranch Cook
Welder Ranch
Vidauri

Midwifery

I was born and raised here in Victoria. Usually midwives run in the family, and my grandma, Ranie Bell, was one, and an aunt and a cousin. We were Indians and Blacks, but I don't know where we came from or exactly who we are related to. There were some strange combinations in that river bottom, and you don't know where those old people stopped at. I'd just as soon be barefooted as not. I guess that's the Indian in me. It's a good way to be. As long as I'm clean, I can make it.

I picked cotton and washed clothes as a child and got married before I knew better. I thought I was havin' fun, but I soon found out better, just like all ignorant people. I had my first baby all by myself. My husband had gone to work. I was fifteen years old. A neighbor finally came and helped me, but ever since, I been helpin' others have babies. My cousin, Neelie Bell, started me off [midwifing]. I must have been around eighteen.

At first, I was helpin' Dr. Ward with women after they had their babies. I asked him to teach me how to deliver babies. I got my equipment from Chicago—my clippers, scissors, strings, scales, ties, soap, gloves—everything I needed. My books came from the Chicago School of Nursing. I really can't tell you how long I worked with Dr. Ward—years and years— forever.

Midwifin' ain't what you think it is. You have to ask God to help you. I actually learned by lookin' and listenin'. I don't give medicine unless it comes from the doctor. If babies have a problem, then I take blood from the navel and they test it at the clinic. The doctors have taught me circumcision, too.

The earlier a woman starts with me, the better. When they come in early, I can talk to them about carryin' themselves, takin' care of themselves, rest, food, and exercise. I want them to go to the clinic, I insist, but they don't always do it. I have to have a health certificate, but we don't have to be certified.

Sometimes I seem to know more than the doctors do. I've found twins several times when the doctors didn't know it. One time, I delivered twins and one was dead. When somethin' like this happens, I have to call the police. No one has ever tried to sue when a baby dies, but lots of times they don't want to pay me.

Many women prefer midwives because they don't like the way doctors treat them. We're more personal—more human. We have more time to be with the mothers.

Remember those sugar-rationin' books? Times were tough, then. Now people on welfare complain about the food they get. Relief fed me when I was raisin' my babies. Now people are dressed in fine clothes with money in their pocket, goin' down to get food stamps. You can't tell me that's right.

I've only had one woman get in real trouble with me. She was havin' twins and wouldn't go to the doctor. It scared me, but I can handle big problems. I took her to the doctor. The babies were the prettiest things you ever saw. I've never lost a woman—ever.

The way babies are delivered today, I don't know how women survive. Nothin' is done the way nature intended it. No wonder women have so much trouble with birthin' now. That's why a lot of women go to midwives, so they can birth the way nature intended. Nature knows best.

Now you get to find out what all the rags and boilin' water are for: that prevents episiotomies. I really don't like that operation unless it's absolutely necessary, and hot compresses almost always prevent that.

I get lots of calls now to do abortions. I'm not about to do that. I'll go hungry to help you have a baby, but I won't get rid of a baby—uh-uh. That's murder, period.

When a woman first comes to me, I put on my gloves, check her, and listen for the baby's heart. You hear all kinds of things, but you can usually tell if it's a boy or a girl. The heart sounds are different. A boy's heart is faster. Women carry girls pointed in the front and back. Boys make you narrow in the front and wide in the back. You just carry girls and boys different, that's all. Labor pains on the left side is a girl, on the right is a boy.

I carry a lot of equipment with me. Sometimes I even carry diapers with me and have to use them. I work in some very primitive situations sometimes.

I can look in a woman's face and tell when she's pregnant. She looks different. She builds up, she looks like a rose, she twinkles. With a boy, you're smooth—he brings you out. With a girl, you wrinkle. Mothers always want to know whether they're having a boy or a girl; that's the biggest surprise in the world.

When they come to me, I tell a first-time mother what to expect. I explain that I don't give nothin' for pain. I make sure they want to do it that way. They have to know this will hurt, and if they can't handle it, they'll need a doctor. I never noticed a big baby being any more difficult than a small one.

My girls must exercise, eat well—lots of vegetables and lean meat, no salt, no Mexican food, no sweets. They have to understand that they will stretch— grow—and their bodies will change. I don't like smokin', and I don't like high heels. Lazy women have more trouble, that I know for sure. A bunch of nervousness when you're carryin' a baby is bad, and a bunch of drinkin' and hell-raisin' won't do, either. If you're calm, you'll have a calm baby.

I like havin' the fathers help but not the whole family around. Fussin' with the husband is bad for everyone.

Today there's a lot of problems with women wantin' to keep on doin' all the bad things like smokin' and drinkin' and honky-tonkin'. Women have quit being proud of being mothers and doin' their jobs. Growin' babies is a serious business. Women have forgotten about that nowadays. They just want to get rid of their babies.

I tell all my women, "When the fruit is ready, it will fall." I don't believe in inducin' labor or hurryin' up the labor. I tell them they have to push, move around durin' labor, and I promise I'll hold their hand. I also tell them the squattin' position is so much better. If they don't want to, I can't make them, but I sure let them know. I let my women walk, but they won't do that in the hospital. Most women that have had a midwife delivery and a hospital delivery prefer havin' a baby with a midwife. We're more sympathetic and more natural.

I was given tea and crackers after my children were born. I let my women eat whatever they want to.

Everyone I brought into the world I consider my baby. I'm their granny. It's like being a godmother. I love all my children. I've delivered thousands of babies. I've brought a many a little thing into the world and then wound up takin' care of them. I guess God gave me the spirit to do these things. I drove the school bus for thirty-five years and finally had to quit, but I've kept on deliverin' a few babies now and then. What do you do when

Laurine and Albert Cunningham.
Photo by Louise S. O'Connor.

women want you to deliver babies for nothin'? There are so many people like that, but what are you goin' to do? When they don't have the money, you do it anyway.

At one time I wore uniforms all the time. Now, only when I go to the hospital. Doctors and nurses didn't ever resent me, and I don't bother them unless I have to. I've been in the labor room with the doctors before when my women had to go to the hospital.

You know, I have to deal with the husbands, too. Some are good, some are bad. I've seen the men have mornin' sickness and labor pains. The worst I ever had was a drunk husband one time. That was a sight, but most men don't want to be around and most men don't need to be around. They just get in the way unless they're trained to attend. I do believe in Lamaze. It works for everyone. I like to go to the house and check out the family so I'll know what to expect when I go in to deliver. I've seen some bad situations in my time. I can tell if a husband is good. I even try to live with them for a while. Some of these men need my scissors used on them. They want to have all the fun, but when it comes time for birthin' and baby care, they're long gone.

Why they want all these children, I never know. They want them, but they don't want to be bothered with them. I've seen a lot of wife-beatin's in my time—a lot.

The men are ignorant, they want lots of babies and can't take care of them. They don't want to take care of them and they take it out on their wives. A lot of men are like hogs, that's all.

There are some funny things that happen once in a while, but I let the women do it if it makes them feel better. For instance, they would want scissors under the bed to cut the pain. Many wanted their herb teas when they were in labor. Many things like that were believed in, so they helped.

The older people knew more about this than I do. They boiled corn shucks for tea and hog hoof tea for pneumonia. It was so nasty. I never used these things much. I worked more closely with the doctors.

One thing you better pay attention to is the moon sign. It really affects childbirth. It will bring you on or stop you. It'll be in your sign. You have to get your almanac. It depends on where your blood is. I'm going to have to show you all these things.

My second husband Albert has spent a many an hour sittin' around waitin' on me and a baby. He wanted to go to school and be a doctor but he couldn't. He thinks my midwifin' is wonderful. I'm sick now and can't do much, but he wishes I could still carry on with my babies. We shared a whole lot of this together.

I did this because I love it. I love to help people.

Laurine Cunningham
Midwife
1914–1984

It Was Our Bread and Britches: An Oil-Field Wife

My daddy was an engineer and a nomad. He was always looking for the pot of gold at the end of the rainbow, so I grew up in a mud dugout on a claim in the New Mexico Badlands.

We lived in Oklahoma until I was four. Our house caught fire and everything we had perished, including my doll. My mother was able to get her sewing machine out and that was all. That started our moving all over the place.

Next, we rented a burned-out farm. There was a rabid cow and a rabid dog there. I'll never forget that sound. We stayed there a year, and then we started moving out to New Mexico by train. Daddy got his claim out there, and we started living in the mud dugout. He built a frame house over that later.

We were practically starving to death. He had been an engineer on the railroad back in Alabama, but he had some socialistic tendencies and thought the government owed him a living. That's how we wound up in New Mexico.

That was the winter of 1918—the bad influenza year. Even the cows began to die with it. When they died, Daddy and I would run out and skin them, because we could get money for the hides.

Christmas came and went, and we couldn't go to town—no mail, no

Oil well, Refugio County, Texas, ca. 1920's.

Christmas, and practically no food in the house. Mother took my sisters in the spring wagon with the team and went to town. She drove to the next claim, got fresh horses, and went on into town to get food. Food and water were precious commodities, and we shot a mudhen while Mama was away. I fried it, but we couldn't eat it.

My mother was a lady, but she could cope with any situation. She even pulled my father through the flu. She had a hard time. It was minus ten degrees and snowing.

We used lots of folk medicine—mullein leaf tea for coughs, and sassafras

Burning gas well, Refugio County, Texas, 1930.

tea in the spring to thin our blood. My mother used onions for cough syrup—she sliced onions, and covered them with sugar until they made a syrup, and then she added whiskey to them. Mustard poultices were common, too.

My mother and daddy were about as compatible as two stray bulldogs. She was from a good family, and she ran away and got married when she was fourteen. Daddy was ten years older, and was a very nice person until he got this bug about socialism. This was as bitter as gall to my mother, and she always seemed to have trouble following him around.

I was with Jeff from 1923 on. I lived in attics, tents, places you wouldn't believe. If he could stand it, I could stand it. Had a little oil stove in a tent—that was living high, but I had to bow my head to cook on it.

My horror was that Jeff would fall in an open hole. There was no safety in those early days. It was a nightmare, but it was a way of life. Either you accepted it or you left it. We couldn't afford to turn our back on it. It was our bread and britches.

One time when Jeff was drilling in West Texas, the other driller, who had four children, had made a tent with screen wire and canvas, and it even had a glass door. There was a lean-to attached with a sink and running water. We got this when they left. That was the winter of 1929. Then we went to Illinois in a Model A in one of the worst winters I ever saw. I lived many days in winter sawing up old derricks for firewood.

Hijacking in the oil fields was going on all the time. They hijacked a lot of rigs in those days for the money to pay the crew.

Jeff always slept twelve hours and worked twelve hours. If Betty and I were out of that tent, he couldn't sleep. It was a terrible winter. I really worried about Betty, so I would put her in bed with me. I was wrapped up in every stitch of clothes I had. One night I was standing at the door with a wool cap on my head and Jeff's wool socks up to my knees. I had my pajamas on under all this. He looked at me that night and said, "My God, if you was to die tonight, I wouldn't claim the body."

As soon as the lights would go out, the coyotes came up by the tent—all the way around it. Sometimes you could hear their teeth snapping. They would bump against the tent. We had gaslights there and when you opened the door you could see a ring of eyes reflecting in the light. You know, I never was afraid, though.

I never knew many wild women in the oil-field days. The family women were hardworking, underprivileged, depressed, unhappy, childbearing slaves. There was no rest in the oil fields or in the homes in those days. We never even got Sundays off. The school and the churches were the community life, but religion was not strong in the oil fields. There were lots of men in the oil fields who were very irresponsible with their families. They were often poor providers for their families—good-hearted, but they would give it all away to a stranger and let their children starve.

As much as we moved, most of the towns we moved into were not happy to see us. We had to be compatible with the crews. They were our only social contact. The townspeople wouldn't have us, but the churches would welcome us. We moved so fast we never grew roots. Betty, our daughter,

THE POWER BEHIND THE THRONE: THE WOMEN

"When I first came here,
I thought it was the moon.
It was a strange landscape.
I had a fear of open spaces and
bad weather, but I learned
to like it. I wanted to be
a cowgirl, but it's hard for
a woman to find a place on
a ranch other than as a cook."

Judy Pittman Welder
Wife of William Smith Welder
Agriculturist
Marshall, North Carolina

had it real tough. That was no life for a kid. She was in five schools her first year. I felt so sorry for her, but she wasn't demanding. It didn't seem to worry her. She was a great reader. It was company to her.

I married just a little past eighteen and I was a very optimistic person. I had obtained a set of Noritake handpainted china that I just adored. I had no idea in this world that we wouldn't soon have enough to retire or quit, or I'd be living in a good brick house and using my good china. I drug that all over the state of Texas—moved it in a great big box. I kept all my treasures in it. It had to be shipped on Red Arrow. I was hopeful every-day until we moved into Victoria that soon my china would catch up with me. By the time I reached the [O'Connor Brothers] River Ranch, I was thoroughly convinced there wasn't a prayer.

Victoria was our thirty-fifth town in ten years. It was tough. I had never lived in a modern house, only in the oil fields in tents and attics. When I hit Victoria, they made it known they didn't want oil-field people there. This wasn't peculiar to Victoria—that was the feeling just about everywhere.

When we got to the [O'Connor Brothers] River Ranch, it was the first time we had lived a year anywhere, and the first real home we had ever had. When we were living in the Humble Camp bunkhouse, the office was still there and the boarding house was still there. I was bored to death. I didn't have enough to do and Betty had started to school. I'd help the woman that ran the boarding house. I was always afraid of getting in trouble, because several people had been fired when they abused the ranches.

It's different times and different people now, and I'm sorry. You remember that Edgar Guest poem, "Live by the Side of the Road and Be a Friend to Man?" That was us—we really were. We fed every hobo and tramp that came by. We never locked the house.

There used to be an old man that came from Brownsville to Houston, and he pulled a little red wagon with all of his belongings in it. He went north in the summer and south in the winter, up and down Highway 77. When he came by here, he would go sleep under the flare by the pump house. He was a tinker and sometimes he wanted to buy ten cents' worth of sugar or something. He never begged. Someone ran into him pulling that little red wagon. They had to take him to the hospital. He never bathed, either. I bet those nurses couldn't believe it. It was said he had money and some property in Brownsville. He was highly insulted when anyone offered him money. We never really knew who he was.

Parson Weathers was such an interesting man—one of the most interest-ing I ever met. I had a friend that always read *True Story* magazines. One time she left a bunch of them at the house, and since I didn't read them, I offered them to Parson Weathers. He always came by to get our copy of the paper. He took the *True Story* magazines even though I jokingly told him I thought he might be too old to read them. A few weeks later, he came back and said he had gotten a lot of inspiration for his sermons from these magazines and wondered if I had any more! He was a very smart and understanding man, interested in current events and much loved by his flock.

When we first moved to the River Ranch, Dennis O'Connor [II] was the manager. I had bought some new lace curtains for the living room. I was quite proud of them, and they were nice — they nearly took a month's wages for six of them. I would hang them on the clotheslines for spring cleaning. They hadn't been out there an hour when I looked up and here were all the cows. One had horns and when she walked under them, they hung on her head and down her back like a bridal veil. I ran out the door screaming and she paraded off with the curtain flapping in the wind.

You know, I had never canned anything, and during the war, in order to get a pressure cooker, I had to agree to let everybody in the community use it. So the Marberrys, the Holemans, the ranch, us, and some other people used one pressure cooker. Since we had free gas and water, our kitchen was headquarters. Tom Holeman furnished the corn and the peas. We canned meat, butchered hogs, made our own lard, and put up 1,019 cans of corn one year. We used Continental tin cans.

Laura Hopkins and I were plane watchers during the war. She lived in a house made of railroad ties. We never did spot a plane. She always said she'd rather be an old man's darling than a young man's slave.

Life was tough then, but it was fun. We could have lived well on three hundred dollars a month at that time. I was a good manager and that would have been a fortune. Now it takes many times that for us to live.

I have always thought I should have been a man. I love the country. I never go to town, but I still think men have the easier deal.

You know, I wouldn't give anything for these experiences, but I sure would hate to have to go through them again. I couldn't endure it now, but then I accepted it. I thought everyone lived that way.

With the easy life now, we have a bunch of misplaced values. We're so materialistic. We don't care about family and freedom — the real treasures we do have.

Sophie Jeffers
Wife of T. A. Jeffers
Oil Gauger
O'Connor Brothers River Ranch
1904–1989

CHAPTER EIGHT

THE SUPPORT SYSTEM: THE TOWNSPEOPLE

Abel Perez
Photo by Louise S. O'Connor.

THE SUPPORT SYSTEM: THE TOWNSPEOPLE

"He's one that come outta' the book. You can't get no better. He make the hair stand up on your neck watchin' him. He's a cowboy!"

Clayton Isaiah
Tophand
O'Connor Ranches

L. V. Terrell
Tophand
O'Connor Ranches

Every culture must have its backup system. Many people, in different trades and professions, are necessary to keep the ranches functioning. Not all of these jobs were romantic, but all of these individuals provided essential services to the ranches. Many of them were in close and sometimes daily contact with the ranch people.

Seeds and grains as well as staples for the ranches were provided by the grocers in the towns. The sheriffs kept order while the blacksmiths and saddlemakers provided the ranches with necessary equipment. Until fairly recently, boots were a handmade, special-order item, much valued by their owners. The importance of the local shoe and bootmaker, as well as the bootblack, cannot be underestimated.

The large ranches, and even the small ones in this area, produced herds of cattle for market that were far too large to be sent to the local auction ring for sale. Cattle buyers would come in, purchase these vast herds, and ship them away to larger markets that were able to absorb such numbers.

Although the cowhands were superb amateur vets, it would often be necessary to call in a professional veterinarian if a prized animal was very ill. Midwives and herbalists were frequently used in the early days, and even into the middle of this century, but as there was a necessity for profes-

L-R, Bob Bunton and Bob Bunton, Jr., at Bob Bunton's Cafe, Refugio, Texas, 1922.

sionals with the animals, the services of a true medical doctor were often needed—and gratefully accepted.

Schoolteachers were needed to educate the workers' children on the ranches, especially if the ranches were too isolated from town for the children to be taken in on a daily basis.

Many people, especially those in small-town and rural situations, had not learned to drive cars, even as late as the middle of this century, so chauffeurs were often employed by the ranchers for their families and themselves. These chauffeurs are a great source of information about this culture. They spent many hours a day observing ranch life.

There were many other services provided by the townspeople, but these are the ones that the ranchers most often mention with respect, admiration, and appreciation. They are aware of their importance to and influence on the entire culture.

Gamblin', Dancin', and Great Food

Bob's Cafe was the cowboy hangout down in Frisco. They had gamblin', dancin', and great food. Bob [Bunton] was the daddy of all cooks. He never was no cowboy, but he could get stuff together in a hurry. He weighed over two hundred pounds and he could mess with that food.

He was the best fish man around. There was somethin' he could do with that fish that nobody else could. Little Bob was a good cook, too. They sold fried fish and potato salad for a dollar, and their specialty was oysters and bacon grilled with butter, salt, and pepper. We washed down chili and hamburgers with Lone Star, 3.2 beer, and Southern Select. Now that was some good eatin'.

It was the hangout place, and the ranch bosses would come by there and pick up men for their cow crowds. The cowboys danced to Bob's Victrola, and sometimes he would have big dances and hire an orchestra. It was rough around there on Saturday night, and many a man walked out that door didn't know who he was.

Bob was generally easy-goin', but after a long weekend he could get pretty grouchy.

Ananias Cook, Clayton Isaiah, Jesse Jones, J. Y. Lott, Tony Lott, K. J. Oliver, Nathanial Youngblood

Fred Huvar, Sr.

The Sardine Wrapper

Fred Huvar was born in Colorado County. His father had come from Czechoslovakia and settled around Weimar, where he made his living as a farmer. His two sons, Fred and Henry, had a saloon in Garwood.

Daddy [Fred] came to Victoria in 1920 and opened up the Huvar Grocery Store on South Main Street. Later, he moved his business down the block. Until his death in 1972, he supplied most of the local farmers and ranchers with groceries, feed, grain, and some crop seeds.

Those were the days. Everybody had charge accounts and when he first started in business, food came in barrels, drums, and sacks. Flour, sugar, pickles, vinegar, and coffee were his principal wares. He sold bacon but no other meats. During cotton-picking season, the coffee grinder never stopped. Coffee was two pounds for twenty-five cents back then, and bulk sugar had to be put in two-, five-, and ten-pound bags. Sauerkraut came in forty-gallon drums; by the time we got to the bottom of the barrel, it was fermented. I used to scoop the kraut out of the bottom with a big metal fork. I got drunk off the fumes one time, and Daddy gave me a helluva whipping because he thought I was stealing his whiskey.

Daddy thought all the farmers and ranchers were fine people. Lots of them used to hang out there when they came to town. He was good friends with Joe Bianchi and Kite Tibiletti. He and Kite were aldermen together for years. They all used to call him the "Sardine Wrapper." That was a nickname for grocers in those days.

Fred Huvar, Jr.
Grocer
Victoria

THE COUNTRY DOCTORS

George E. Glover, Sr., M.D.

Dr. George Glover, 1917.

Dr. George E. Glover, Sr., graduated from medical school in Galveston in 1908. After his internship, he went to work in the British coal mines in Mexico as the company doctor. He had some very rigorous experiences there. The British were importing coolies at the beginning of the Madeira-Diaz Revolution. Frequently these laborers were treated roughly by the locals because they felt they were taking their jobs from them. My father had experience treating many very serious injuries on that job.

After leaving Mexico, he moved around for a while and then settled in Refugio. Later he set up his permanent office in Austwell and worked the whole county. Most of the time he operated in people's homes, but occasionally he worked at the hospital that Dr. William Dodson had established in Woodsboro. He was insistent on sterile surgical conditions, and that was probably why his surgery was so successful. My mother was his scrub nurse, and the local pharmacist gave the anesthesias. He mainly used chloroform and ether, but he also used a lot of local anesthesia. He had an ongoing professional war with a local *curandero* named Dr. Webb, and he finally won. He never let the people think he was afraid of Webb.

My father was gone a lot, often staying at the various ranches when he was called. He divided the obstetrical work equally between himself and the midwives. At one time, he was the county health officer, and he fought long and hard for sanitation, vaccinations, and a hospital. All these things were badly needed. He never refused to go to a patient, although he frequently was not paid for his services.

In those days a country doctor had full responsibility for the patient. He often had to stay with a surgical patient for days after the operation. He saw the introduction of sulfa, penicillin, intravenous solutions, and many radical changes in anesthesia. His recovery rate was very good, and due to his World War I experiences as a military doctor, he was particularly skilled at treating the many victims of oil-field accidents that occurred before the introduction of more rigid safety regulations.

Dr. Glover always said, "If you listen to a patient long enough, he will tell you what is wrong with him."

George E. Glover, Jr., M.D.
Victoria

William Milton Dodson, M.D.

My father grew up around Concho County, Texas. If you wanted an education back in those days, you had to figure out some way to get it. A Dr. Morse in San Angelo took him under his wing, and Daddy finally was able to study at John Sealy in Galveston and graduated from the University of Texas Medical School in 1913.

At that time, the ranches were hiring their own doctors. He wrote to the McFaddin Ranch and was accepted on a salary. The ranches were paying more money than the railroads, so he decided that this was the best thing to do. When he and mother arrived at Mariana, as McFaddin was then called, there were no supplies, not even bandages. Daddy would buy supplies as he collected fees. Often his patients would pay him with farm animals and produce.

The clinic was in a shed attached to the mercantile. He and mother stayed there several years and then decided to move to the Woodsboro area. Victoria already had a hospital and many doctors, and the Woodsboro-Refugio area was beginning to grow. His first office was located in the Risken Drugstore in Woodsboro.

Dr. George Glover and my father were close associates and good friends. When World War I broke out, Dr. Glover joined the army and Daddy stayed home to be the area doctor. He was also the surgeon for the Missouri-Pacific Railroad, which made it necessary for him to stay behind.

Dr. Dodson on Spider, at McFaddin Ranch, 1913.

Mother and I often went on calls with Daddy, packing a lunch and carrying his medicines. She always went with him to deliver babies even though she was not a trained nurse. They were out at all hours of the day and night, but my grandmother lived with us, so mother could go out with the doctor.

The doctor finally moved to his own office after several years and, at the time, it was considered very fancy and modern. The kitchen was in the center, the operating room faced west for good light, and the patients' rooms were upstairs to catch the cool breeze. The offices and x-ray rooms were downstairs. In those days nothing was disposable and medicines were not prepacked or premixed. Much time was spent boiling syringes and instruments and preparing the medicines. A doctor's basic medical supplies usually consisted of salves, ointments, morphine, barbiturates, aspirin, strychnine, ichthyol, some sulfas, as well as camphor and pine oil for disinfecting. Ether, chloroform, iodine, and alcohol usually completed the list.

The country doctors did not use folk medicines in their own practice, but they always had a lot of respect for people's belief in them. Religion also played an important role in doctoring. These doctors listened to the people and their beliefs, and treated their psyches much as psychiatrists do today. Listening and counseling were their major jobs.

The oil boom had an enormous effect on doctoring in the area. The local doctors were required to deal with new and very severe types of injuries. When Dr. Glover came back from World War I, he had acquired a tremendous amount of knowledge about treating wounds and had learned advanced techniques in surgery. He taught this to all the local doctors. Dr. Glover's knowledge of battlefield injuries was very helpful to Daddy and everyone at the time. In those days intravenous feedings were unheard of, and blood transfusions had to be given directly from one person to another. My father founded the Woodsboro Hospital in 1921, which we operated until the Refugio County Hospital opened in 1940.

Many doctors developed physical problems from the strain of their work. Daddy developed a heart condition but kept right on doing his job. He died delivering a baby. He loved children and his family practice, and remained firm in his belief that people heal themselves with enough time and their own built-in strength.

Pattie Dodson Gilliam, M.D.
Victoria

The High Sheriff

Ira Heard was tough, but he was a fine fella. He didn't bother nobody if you was from around here, but if you was stray, he'd lock you up. He wore two pearl-handled .45s. A lot of people didn't understand him, but durin' the oil boom we had everythin' comin' to Refugio. Rough people would camp everywhere, fights in town every day. He kept this town in control. He took care of the people who lived here and was always good to ranch hands. He would clothe and feed them at times and even built homes for some. Under Mr. Ira you didn't say "No"—everything was "Yes."

Seward Richardson
L. V. Terrell
Nathaniel Youngblood

"Ira Heard instilled in people a need for principles and toughness. He was one of the kindest and most intriguing persons I ever knew."

Pattie Dodson Gilliam, M.D.
Victoria

Ira Heard, Refugio Sheriff, Refugio County, 1895–1946.

THE SUPPORT SYSTEM: THE TOWNSPEOPLE

Bits, Branding Irons, and the World's Best Spurs

Joe Bianchi began blacksmithing in 1909 in Victoria, Texas, and continued to work at his trade until four months before his death. Born in Orrigio, Italy, he came to America with his family when he was fourteen years old. Many Italian families moved to this area at that time to work for the New Orleans, Texas, and Mexico Railway.

Young Joe learned his trade as a blacksmith's apprentice in Italy, and he would often tell stories about getting up early to prepare the shop for his employer. He came from a family of farmers, and when he first arrived in this country, he made his living by farming. Joe's brother, Paul, had already opened a blacksmith shop in Victoria, and in the late 1890s he persuaded Joe to join him in establishing the Bianchi Brothers Blacksmith Shop. At first they were across the river, then relocated the shop to the corner of Bridge and Juan Linn, and eventually moved to South William Street. In 1909 Joe opened his own shop.

As a young man, Joe did general blacksmithing and repair work, horse-shoeing, and some artistic fence work. He also made metal park benches that became one of his trademarks; they can be found in the park, at the convent, and other places around town. As he grew older, he began to concentrate on making spurs, bits, and brands.

Joe Bianchi's shop on William Street, ca. 1906.

Joe Bianchi was a warm, friendly man, a staunch Catholic, and an active member of the Victoria Fire Department. An artist with metal and an expert at tempering, he could even temper copper. He was meticulous, and a perfectionist about his work, and always wore a big, blue apron and smoked a pipe. His shop was a local hangout; although there were always people around, he was all business when he was working.

The back of his shop was like a rabbit warren. His office was tiny and contained an old safe where he kept his decorative coins and flat silver stock. He kept all of his accounts in his head.

Joe Bianchi
Spur and Bit Maker
1871–1949

Each pair of Bianchi spurs was made by hand and fashioned from a single piece of metal stock. They were never welded, and when he finished with them, there was not a mark on them. He threw away a lot of the spurs he made because he would never sell any that were not perfect. Inside every one of his catalogs appeared his terms and directions for ordering, brief and to the point: "All prices quoted in this catalog are net cash. Discounts will not be allowed anyone under any circumstances. I believe in treating everyone alike. Goods are generally sent by parcel post or express. Initials or brand or name stamps will be placed on bits and spurs without extra charge." And, to back up his work, he offered this guarantee: "All spurs and bits made by me are fully guaranteed and any that prove defective will be replaced or neatly repaired without charges, provided the defective parts are returned to me."

His handiwork on spurs was limited to one style, the Bianchi or Victoria spur, as it came to be known, with its distinctive bottle-opener shank, stationary buttons, Mexican-coin button and rowel-pin covers, unengraved silver mountings, and hand-stamped, serrated rowels. Over the years, many spur makers have attempted to copy his unique style, but few, if any, have succeeded.

Joe's branding irons were also considered the best by the ranchers and cattlemen who used them. He notched the irons so that they would not blot or burn the animals' hides. Every new iron he made had to be tested on his front door and approved by the purchaser before he would allow it to be taken out of his shop. His bits were lightweight and would never hurt a horse's mouth—a feature that was a source of great pride to him.

John Bianchi, Jr., Karnes City; Grace Fossati, Victoria; Xavier Fossati, Victoria

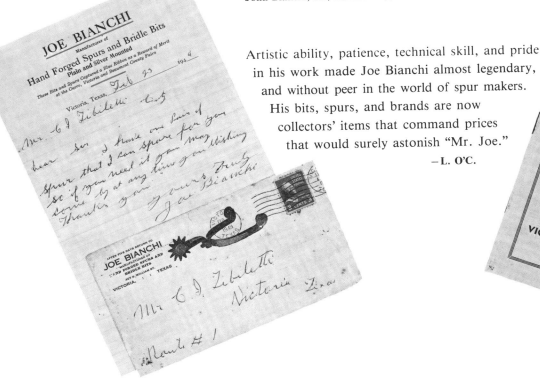

Artistic ability, patience, technical skill, and pride in his work made Joe Bianchi almost legendary, and without peer in the world of spur makers. His bits, spurs, and brands are now collectors' items that command prices that would surely astonish "Mr. Joe."

—L. O'C.

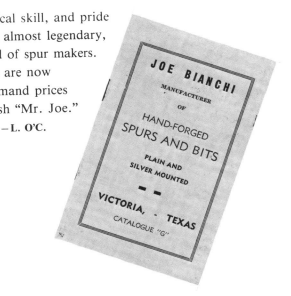

Joseph Lucchese
Boot Maker
1861-1943

They Wouldn't Wear Anything Else

The Luccheses, who came from Vicari, a suburb of Palermo, Sicily, have made boots and shoes for generations. Joseph and Sam Lucchese arrived in America around 1882 and landed in New Orleans; they left Italy for the same reasons that many others did—there was universal military conscription and many of the small businesses were unable to support the growing families. Like so many of the immigrants, they came looking for the "streets of gold."

The two brothers opened the Lucchese Boot Shop in New Orleans around 1883 and remained there for several years. It is not known exactly when they moved to San Antonio, but they found the area profitable. The army garrison at Fort Sam Houston was a major customer for their boots and Sam Brown belts.

Sometime around 1904, Joseph came to Victoria and opened his own boot shop, while Sam continued the business in San Antonio. Little more is known about Joseph's career in Victoria. He married Annie Bolsavo in 1892 and continued to make boots until 1911, when, according to family records, his eyesight went bad. He obviously had pleased his customers, because after Joe's sight failed, many Victorians traveled to San Antonio to get their Lucchese boots from Sam. They wouldn't wear anything else.

According to a family legend, there was a similar addiction to Lucchese boots in the old country. The story goes that during the time the Hapsburgs ruled Sicily, their boots and shoes were made by the Lucchese family. When they were deposed, they kidnapped one of the Luccheses and took him with them back to Austria, where he spent the rest of his life making their footwear.

Jacqueline Mercer Lucchese
San Antonio

One could fill a book with tales of Lucchese boots that rarely touched the ground and with stories of specially built and locked closets in ranchers' homes where they could safely house their Lucchese boots. They were removed the moment their owners dismounted, to protect and preserve them. A family of young, Italian immigrants created a legend out of leather. Their boots have been famous in Texas for generations and remain so to this day. —**L. O'C.**

THE SUPPORT SYSTEM: THE TOWNSPEOPLE

For Lawmen and Ranchers

Our family came from Sumirago, Italy, near the Swiss border. On the Castellioni side of our family, we go back to Pope Celestine IV. Joseph Tibiletti, my father, was a stonemason and bricklayer in Italy. After our parents were married, they immigrated to this country in 1889, looking for a better way of life as did most immigrants of that time.

My brother Kite and I were born in this country and grew up in Victoria and the surrounding area. Around 1906, our family moved to Illinois for a short time, but my mother hated the cold and so they returned to Victoria several years later. While Kite was in Illinois, he studied leather working with Hess and Hopkins in Rockford because he did not want to be a farmer.

He opened a shop in Victoria in 1908 on Juan Linn Street where Fred Huvar has his store now. Kite was a perfectionist about his work, and his leather tooling was easily recognizable. The shop was a hangout for boys and men; the kids from St. Joe's would come over and smoke and do whatever they weren't supposed to do. Most of the cattlemen hung out there,

Gaetano I. Tibiletti *(center)*
"Kite"
Saddle Maker
1890–1980

too, when they came in from the ranches. Tibiletti's Saddle Shop was right in the heart of town. They would often go next door to Fossati's for a beer.

If you think women were finicky about their shoes and purses, the men were a lot worse about their guns and holsters. Kite knew every lawman from here to the border. After word got out that he made good holsters, they all came in to have him make one for them. He made saddles for all the ranchers, and sometimes he got real mad at them because they were always in a hurry. He also made linemen's belts and sent them all the way to El Paso—wherever Central Power and Light went.

Many people came to Kite for specialty items. The ladies loved his sandals; he held a patent on them for twenty years. The big oil companies would have him make leather map cases for them. He even made a set of luggage for me.

Kite dabbled in a lot of things, but he was especially good at speculating in real estate. He was an artist at leather working.

I'm afraid this is a dying art.

Ann Tibiletti
Victoria

Kite Tibiletti at his shop.

G. I. ("Kite") Tibiletti was the third member of the Victoria triumvirate of Italian craftsmen. Also a leather artisan, his specialties were saddles, bridles, harnesses, and ladies' leather accessories. To this day, many of his saddles are still in use on area ranches, where they are considered prized possessions. — L. O'C.

Harry Thompson, cattle buyer.

So I'd Buy Some More

"I started buying cattle when I was seventeen years old. Bought fifteen hundred yearlings and kept them two years. I lost money on them and then I started shipping cattle to Fort Worth every week. Sometimes I'd make money and that would feel good. Sometimes I'd lose a thousand dollars and I'd feel terrible for about fifteen minutes, but that wasn't gonna do me no good—so I'd buy some more."

Harry Thompson
Cattle Buyer
From an interview
by Blan and T. F. Shephard, ca. 1959

"I've been in the cattle-buying business for forty-seven years and I'm still trying to get even from the first year. It's exciting, like gambling. Either you do or you don't on every deal."

Rhett Johnson
Cattle Buyer
Kenedy

Worlds of Cattle and Worlds of Work

My father and grandfather were in construction in Tennessee and Alabama, and then started moving west through Dallas and down to Corpus. Mr. James Welder designed, and they helped him build, a drainage ditch from Sharp's Lake to Copano Bay, and when that was completed, Dad went to work on the ranch.

As a kid, I worked cattle a lot. I moved the *remuda* and took care of the horses. Those were the tick-dipping and screwworm days, and by the time we finished with the cattle on one ranch, we just moved on to the next one. Wherever we stopped, the chuck wagon came out to us. We had more cattle back in those days than we do now. It was dangerous work, and we were only paid $1.50 a day. But there were some wonderful old guys working on the ranches in those days. Many of them worked in tennis shoes or bare-footed, wearing spurs. They were strong and courageous men.

We had worlds of cattle and worlds of work in those days, but life on these ranches was better than it is now. You didn't want and you didn't worry. The fellowship on these ranches was good. It was a community. The people in those days were living by God's laws. They were bound together, living the way they were taught by their fathers and grandfathers. They influenced my life, and they gave me a foundation to build on.

E. Phillips, D.V.M.
"Spec"
Victoria

Cedar Pencils and Coffee in Bed

I grew up in Victoria around the Mission Valley Road and, as a young girl, I decided that I wanted to teach. My father wouldn't let his girls work, but he would let me teach. I got my degree from Sul Ross State College, where I paid my own expenses by washing dishes, grading papers, and working in the registrar's office.

I don't know how I heard about the Power-Welder Ranch School, but Daddy took me down there to be interviewed by Mr. Jim Power. It took longer than half a day to get there on the dirt roads. There were no stops and no places to eat. Daddy and I visited with Mr. Jim and his wife, Jessie, and they hired me to start the following Monday morning. This was in 1925.

The first time I ever had coffee in bed was heaven to me—it was when I was interviewing for the job at the Power Ranch. Mrs. Jessie put me in the guest room, and early the next morning Aunt Phoebe, the Powers' maid, brought me my coffee.

As I remember it, all the cowhands on the Power Ranch were Mexican and all those on the Welder Ranch were black. I had kids from both ranches. The schoolhouse was very small, with a porch all the way around. Inside, we had four rows of benches with no backs and no place to put the books. I had just a table with a drawer and one chair. I taught the first through the sixth grades. There weren't any seventh-graders. We studied from a primer—this was after McGuffey's—and we had paper tablets and cedar pencils that we bought in bundles. I walked to school every day along the dirt road—it wasn't a highway then.

I made a lot of money teaching school there—one hundred dollars a month and free room and board. That was a lot back in those days. I had two rooms at the hotel in Vidauri. In one room there was an iron bedstead and two shelves. The other room was the kitchen and had an oil-burning stove. I bathed in a big wooden tub, and there was an outhouse. All this comes back to me clearly every once in a while. The schoolhouse was made of tin because of the prairie fires, and so was the hotel and the store.

I never could do math, so my uncle would teach me on the weekends. There were no bilingual classes, so I had the Mexican children speaking English in two months. I often taught them by telling stories. The black women taught me lots of great stories when I was a child, and I would repeat these stories to my kids—they loved them. I taught them a lot of history this way, too. Grammar was very hard for the kids and they didn't like geography either, but they loved learning the history of the rural areas, especially our local area, but not foreign history.

I learned a lot about people, teaching down there. The ranch schools were run the way the ranch owners wanted them run. They had full control, but they paid very, very well. This was a major difference between the ranch schools and the public schools in the towns.

I never had any discipline problems with the kids. I just didn't put up with any foolishness. I kept them busy and they had a good time. Every human being does things for a reason; if you can find out what those reasons are, then you know how to handle them.

Mostly, I taught the kids as a group. We would even go on roundups when the cattle were being shipped. We worked hard on our lessons so we would have the time to go out and watch the cowhands work. That was something! All those wild stories are the truth. They could do anything.

First you would see the dust and then you would hear the cattle bellowing. The cowhands would be slapping against their saddles with their ropes. Their boots and other equipment weren't much good. They were dressed in all kinds of things—but those big old hats! That's one thing—they almost all had good hats.

The cowhands had a lot of fun when they were loading cattle. There was competition among them, always trying to see who could do the hardest job. They were characters, and they had fun. Don't let anybody tell you they didn't. I know what I'm talking about.

Those cowhands could get drunk as lords, but they knew they had better be back out there on Monday morning—and they were. The ranch store was in Vidauri, and the hands got all their supplies there. They would come in early for their tobacco, usually Bull Durham, before they went out to work. There was always a cattle buyer around, usually a big drinker from New Orleans. There were big parties on the ranch whenever the buyers came down. It was an exciting time for all of us, but it was serious business, too. The cowhands didn't bring the cattle up on trucks—they herded them up with their horses and usually loaded the cattle on the trains early in the morning.

It looked kind of crazy, but it was organized. It took all day long. The cowhands enjoyed it. You could hear them whooping and singing at the cattle. There was a lot of joking and laughing when they got through. If there had been a saloon there, I'm sure they all would have gotten drunk. It wasn't very citified out there in my day—just the store, the hotel, and the ranch buildings. A road connected the Power and Welder ranches.

The ranchers were all darned good people, outstanding in all my dealings with them. But they were different. Their culture was not so much different from mine. It's just that their lives presented them with different opportunities.

They could have gone anywhere, but they didn't. They wanted to stay home. I guess their isolation made them different in some respects. They were happy with their lives and they had what they wanted. They didn't seem to want or need much outside contact. We all rode horseback and hunted and fished. The outdoors was our entertainment. I could really shoot a gun—I could kill a goose in flight as well as any man.

The women down here did what their husbands told them to do. They stayed at home and kept their kids and houses spotless. In the Mexican community, the women also stayed at home. They never left the ranch. The men even did all the shopping. The black women didn't seem to be as restricted; they had more fun and visited with each other a lot more.

To me, a good cowman was a good Stetson hat, good boots, a well-built body without an ounce of fat on it, neat, courteous, and a good conversationalist with a good sense of humor. You never saw a cowman in a pickup truck in my day. They were the politest people—such gentlemen. The cowhands were wonderful people, too. You know, the cowmen and the cowhands needed each other. They had a good relationship. They couldn't have gotten along without each other. The ranchers were good to their cowhands and their families, and Miss Lucille Welder often had us over for cards and ice cream. She was a wonderful person.

You know, there are people who love the land and people who don't. The strongest force in the whole world is our love for our heritage, and that means the land. It is the strongest attachment there is. It's almost unbelievable. It's a feeling, it's unexplainable. If you don't have the feeling, you don't understand. It's a deep, deep thing.

Isn't it great to see the land when it puts grass up to the cows' bellies? It's a sight that makes you feel good all the way through.

Abbie Walton Linam
Schoolteacher
Power-Welder School
Vidauri

CHAPTER NINE

THE SURVIVORS: THE NEW GENERATION

Armour Joe Keefe
Photo by Louise S. O'Connor.

THE SURVIVORS: THE NEW GENERATION

"Sometimes I feel like I belong
way back when people first
began ranchin' this country.
I would have fit back there."

Armour Joe Keefe
"Joe"
Straw Boss
O'Connor Ranches
Rancher

War and technology brought inevitable and deeply affecting change to the Coastal Bend ranchers, not much of it, as they see it, for the better. Such change, even to mankind's best planned and managed institutions, always causes upheaval—its effect is rarely benign. To a tradition-bound culture, it can prove fatal.

Pearl Harbor put an end to many of the old ways in the river bottoms and on the prairies, just as for the rest of America. The oil boom of the 1920s and 1930s had a significant, but somewhat less intense impact. The tremendous advancements in technology brought on by World War II were much more far-reaching.

Almost overnight, it seemed, the interdependence that made this corner of Texas unique was gone. With it went the once-strong, somewhat isolated communities of cowhands and ranch workers and their families. Gone too were the cow camps.

At one point during the war, helped only by a few aging ranch hands with deferments, some ranchers had to care for as many as 10,000 head of cattle. Several of those ranchers were responsible for supplying beef to a division of soldiers each year.

After World War II was over, technology and increasing Federal interference in ranch operations further influenced life in the Coastal Bend. The New Deal marked the beginning of United States government intrusion into all phases of agriculture, a presence that has become more and more visible and pervasive ever since.

Minimum wage rules, safety considerations, laws ending what the bureaucrats called child labor exploitation, restrictions on pesticides, herbicides, fertilizer, and mandatory brucellosis testing further complicated the ranchers' existence.

Everyone knows progress means change, but the changes wrought on Coastal Bend ranching were profound. A strong, well-entrenched, functioning social and economic system disappeared virtually overnight.

Today's cowhands drive pickups to work, then go home and watch television like everybody else. Their children no longer focus on horses and cow-work, because they are more a part of mainstream America than were their parents.

The faster-paced world of today does not nurture or even encourage the individuality and community spirit that supported the life-style the older cowhands, and ranchers grew up with. That world is gone forever, and the cowhand of the 1990s is a sharp contrast to his counterpart from 50 years ago. Working cattle is a life-long skill that must begin early to be learned well, and the apprenticeship of the old days has faded away.

Ranchers have been forced by these changing circumstances to become more involved in politics—and not only on the local level, which has always been their role. Going into the 1990s, they must be active on a national and even an international basis, a real challenge to them because when they grew up, it was merely ranchers against a rather gentle nature, not against a powerful Federal government or the global beef market.

So, World War II was the turning point between the old ways and the new. The technology that sprang from this war destroyed the essence of ranching as these men and women knew it. Electricity, jeeps, roads, and mobility changed the ranches the most. The old pride and interest, as well as the sense of community, are gone. More and more ranchers are having to become "camp counselors" in order to keep members of their families and nonresident owners, who have little or no interest in ranching, willing to continue their involvement and financial support.

Another change in modern ranching that has sprung from technology is the use of helicopters to work cattle. Helicopter pilots are unique in the world of ranching and cattle. Their perspective is different, in fact as well as in attitude. These men come from a technological background that is entirely different from that of the earthbound cowhand. They are doing the same work with the same animals; yet they have minimal contact with the land, the animals, and the people on that land. These differences influence their attitudes as naturally as the cowhands' attitudes are influenced by their exposure to animals and nature.

Roundup by helicopter on the Waggoner Ranch, early 1950's.

The flying cowboys are as skilled as the traditional cowhands, and have learned the habits and behavior of a cow as well as their counterparts on horseback. They are mounted men, but their horses are powerful, mindless machines that do their bidding far above the herd. They have no particular attachment to their mounts, as conventional cowhands do to their horses. Because they have no contact with the cattle, they naturally feel no attachment to them, either. Usually the most they know or care to know about a cow is how they like their steaks cooked.

Although they have tremendous respect for the cowmen and cowhands on

"These cowboys nowadays—they ride around in air-conditioned trucks—going to work at eight and coming in at five. Even the horses get more privileges now than we used to have."

K. J. Oliver
"K"
Itinerant Tophand

the ground, the men in the air have no desire to trade places. They, in turn, are respected and appreciated by the ranchers and cowhands whose jobs they make so much easier. Yet, even with their common purpose and mutuality of goals, the pilots are not really part of the cow crowd. With few exceptions, these men have no background in horsemanship, ranching, or cow-working. They come from varied backgrounds and have had traditional training in aviation. There is, however, no tradition of working cattle from the air.

The Waggoner Ranch is apparently the first place where someone thought of this technique. Evidently, there was a dearth of cowhands on the ranch during and after World War II. The ranch was covered in brush-choked pastures that were filled with maverick steers. The Waggoner had tried using slow-moving, fixed-wing planes to gather the cattle, but the experiment was unsuccessful. The ranchers then contacted Bell Helicopter Company, which had recently moved down to Texas from New York. Gil Eggleston was a helicopter pilot with Bell at the time, and ended up working for the Waggoner as their first pilot. Now retired, he claims that in three years he gathered 15,000 mavericks on the ranch using helicopters.

From here, the idea spread and soon more and more ranches began to use these new airborne horses. Some of these men were among the first post-World War II civilian helicopter pilots and each has his own story of how he literally tripped and fell into the ranching business. Because helicopters were so successful as ranch tools, their use caught on quickly. The demand from the ranches for machines and pilots grew rapidly. Most had been employed in some phase of the helicopter industry and were hired away to cowboy with their machines in the skies of South Texas.

Working cattle by helicopter in the Coastal Bend has been learned by trial and error. These are the men who tried it and made the mistakes, and are the only people capable of writing the book on how to do it. There were no fathers and grandfathers to teach them the business. These flying cowboys are true pioneers in their field.

In spite of the changes and the problems that now exist in the ranching industry, these people are still fighting for the preservation of their way of life and the survival of their ranches. Their struggle seems to be more for spiritual and emotional reasons than for economic ones, although they must endure financially if they are to save this land to which they are desperately and firmly attached.

It is more this attachment to the land than to the cattle business that keeps the younger generation coming back into the business. Their backgrounds are much the same as those in previous generations. Ranching or agricultural work has, with few exceptions, always been in their families in some form. Not all are able to do this work full time. Some must seek employment in other fields in order to be able to ranch. This is a way of life that they respect, enjoy, and need, and they are determined to save it and be a part of it even if it costs them financially. They have little tolerance for urban life and attitudes. They need the space and freedom that ranching provides.

THE SURVIVORS: THE NEW GENERATION

"My ambition was always to ranch—I really like it. I was fortunate to get to ride with the old guys. I learned how they did it back then."

James Robert McCan
"Bobby"
Rancher

There was an artistry that this work required, and it was fun. As technology killed off much of the need for this knowledge and skill, most of the fun was lost; it became just another job. The fun used to be in riding and roping and enjoying each other's superb abilities. These were the talents learned as the young people were trained before they were allowed to become full-fledged cowhands. Now anyone is permitted to do the work, regardless of training or experience. Today the fun usually consists of laughing at those who don't know what they're doing and, according to the older cowhands, this includes most of those trying to do the work.

The young ranchers are all open to the new way of doing things. They believe that experience in the field is still the best way to learn, but concede that the new technology learned in school is becoming more and more valuable. They understand that there is a place and a need for both methods. They will even consider farming where it is appropriate, whereas previous generations believed that plowing or doing anything other than raising cattle violated the land. To the young owners, having the land is more important than how they use it. They approach their jobs more from a standpoint of land usage and preservation than cattle raising. These young ranchers and cowhands consider themselves lucky and privileged to be a part of this life. Their idea of hell on earth is working in an industrial plant.

The new cowboys are not as proficient at cow-working skills as the older ones were, and they often trade speed for ability in this area. However, they are acquiring new knowledge and developing new skills—many of which were unknown to previous generations—that will better serve them in the world they must inhabit.

The Young Ranchers: Jacks of All Trades

We played cowboys and Indians a lot, but in the summer was when we did it for real. Those of us who got to be real cowhands didn't seem to play cowboy quite as much. Maybe the glamour has already worn off a little. When we were working out here in the summer, our main activity was to goof off—driving cars and shooting anything that moved.

Someone on the ranch, or even a neighboring rancher, taught us how to ride, fix windmills, clean troughs—just about everything we know. We usually were with this person every summer until we were old enough to work at the ranches. "Ranch Camp" we called it. It's amazing—truly amazing—that any of us are still alive when you think about the things we did. Even at that, when we moved over to the ranches to actually go to work, we still had to go through the same initiation rites as a cowhand off the road. That's because those tests were for everybody's safety—not just for fun. It's hard to remember when they quit testing us; maybe they still do. Sometimes the owner's kids got tested harder than anyone.

Ranching is not something you really choose. It's always there—it's part of you, it's a family thing, a way of life, and the land is ours.

We've all done other things, from working in banks to being mechanics—testing our wings, maybe—and we always wind up back here on the ranch.

It's a little different now—the relationships change and our roles on the ranches change. We are grown men now, and the changes were gradual. They happen over such a long period of time you hardly notice it. You don't wake up one morning and everything is different. Our relationships with the old hands have pretty much remained the same. They still try and teach us and still think of us as little kids, but they can also accept us as bosses. We can still be friendly with them and pal around, but not like we did when we were younger. We have to fall into the boss role with them now.

There is really nothing we would rather do. The responsibility isn't scary, or at least no scarier than any other one a grown man has.

This way of life has changed so much. The old way is gone. All we can do is hope we do the right thing when we make the changes. Every generation has to change to a certain degree. We are going to have to do things differently than our forefathers did. We will have to try new ways and hope they work.

It bothers us sometimes when we sit around talking, because it won't be the way we know it. When our ancestors first got here, they started the cattle industry and watched the evolution of the cowboy. That's all our families have ever done. Now it's phasing itself out and that's what scares us. We can see where it could all come to an end.

The way we have to look at it is that changing our way of life is better than losing the land.

"I always wanted to ranch. It's not something you think about; it's always been there. It's more what you are than what you do. It's a way of life—a family thing. The key to all of this is the land—it's mine. It's about being on the land more than being a cowman. It's security."

Ralph R. Gilster III
Rancher

Being able to go out on the land—the solitude, the space, the wildlife— that's what it's all about for us. Not being able to be out on that land would be the ultimate nightmare, right up there with working in a textile mill in New Jersey. We all admit to thinking about the ranches most of the time we are gone on a trip. You wonder what is going on out there, how it looks—it's always on your mind.

We've grown up out here and we know all the subtleties. People who come out from the city don't really get a full picture of it. It's a boy's dream, and we got to live it.

All the foremen who trained us did a lot to see that we were not treated special. They made us be a part of it. They all grew up on ranches, too, and knew what it would be like looking back on boyhood. They made us really get out there and work. It was good for us.

We learn from experience and from books. That's the way it will be from now on. We can't stay locked up down here and not learn the new technologies. We will have to know all this to survive. There isn't much room for mistakes now.

THE SURVIVORS: THE NEW GENERATION

Anything you own, owns you. When you own a piece of land, you have to spend time with it. It forms your opinions about everything. Being able to come out to these ranches seems to make us more intolerant of town people and urban life in general, but we were all born with more intolerance for urban life than most people, anyway.

We would all sacrifice a lot to keep this land. All this is about the land, not about being cowmen. It's our security and our lives. Hopefully our children can see what we've seen and have what we have.

John Welder Cliburn, Ralph Gilster III, James Robert "Bobby" McCan, Clay S. O'Connor, Thomas "Don" O'Connor [IV], Thomas Michael O'Connor, Jimmy Rathkamp, W. D. "Bill" Welder, John Welder V, Patrick H. Welder III, Robert H. Welder II, Roger Welder, William S. "Smithy" Welder

"I was not encouraged to ranch as a child, but I had to come down here and help after Uncle Billy [W. D. Welder] died. I knew construction, so that's what I did. I didn't like horses and cattle—that part of ranching never felt natural to me. I love the land; it's sacred to me. The destruction of that land by oil and technology drives me crazy. That's why I can't be involved any more."

William Smith Welder
"Smithy"
Agriculturalist
Marshall, North Carolina

"I want to ranch. I've done other things, but I always come back here. I consider myself privileged to have been born into a ranching family, to be able to go out on the land. That's what I like about it. Not being able to do that would be a real nightmare to me. It's a calm way of life."

Thomas Donald O'Connor [IV]
"Don"
Rancher

"Nowadays you have to be a psychiatrist, nursemaid, doctor, lawyer, engineer, accountant, politician, and ecologist, among other things. But there is still a freedom in this business to go out in nature, seeing things that can't be duplicated by man."

Thomas Michael O'Connor
Rancher

"I've spent all my life on the ranch. I started in the summers as a kid working with the old hands. That's what I was raised up to do; that's the nature of our family. I like to watch things grow."

John J. Welder V
"Little John"
Rancher

"It's tradition, but I choose to do it also. It's from the gut."

Clay S. O'Connor
Rancher

"I keep my eyes and ears open for what I can do to make it work, to make it continue. I'll change if I have to. I want to keep it going."

Patrick Hughes Welder III
"Pat"
Rancher

"It's history—it's heritage. I hold a lot of stock in that, passing down through the generations from 1833. That says a lot. You have to love something to stay with it over 150 years."

Robert Hughes Welder II
"Rob"
Rancher

"It's a combination of everything I want in life. There's a lot of reward in it."

Roger Welder
Rancher

Any Mistake Could Be Fatal

My father is a farmer and rancher, and I wanted to follow in his footsteps. I've pretty well been with it all my life. I look forward to working with live animals that have feelings. I couldn't sit in an office. I have to be outside, growing crops and working with cattle. You can't make a lot of money, but at least you can do what you enjoy. It's challenging to try to make it work. I'm out there to make a living. I have to know what I'm doing; any mistake could be fatal.

Jimmy Rathkamp
Rancher
Farmer

"It's in man's nature to want land and cattle. I was fortunate enough to have this; it's all I ever wanted to do."

John Welder Cliburn
Rancher

"I call myself a rancher, not a farmer. I like dealing with cattle a lot."

W. D. Welder
"Bill"
Rancher

THE YOUNG COWHANDS AND BOSSES:
You Don't Have to Live for the Weekends

Some of us wouldn't even know what to do without these ranches. I guess the real truth is that for some of us it's a habit that's hard to break and, for some, it's our lives and security. It's a special way of life—you have to love it. There is still a little romance and a little danger out here. As long as we can do some of what they did a hundred years ago, we're happy.

Out here, every day is good, it's real. The work isn't hard now—you just have to have the will to do it. There is satisfaction in this kind of work. The old guys are always telling us about long rides, camp wagons, and early hours. They say we don't know what tough is. Cowboy life is different today from what life was in years past, but there is still a lot more freedom than in other jobs. That is probably the main attraction now. It's a big privilege to be able to do this kind of work—not everybody can.

Mike Adames, Jr., Mark Barnes, Kai Buckert, Charley Christensen, Christine Marthiljohni Michael Perez, Rumaldo Perez, Rumaldo Perez, Jr., Ben Perkins, Eddie Rubio, Ed Steward, Jr. Ralph Tijerina, Rob Williams, Douglas Wolfshohl

"I follow the old guys—they know the trails. I take notes from them. If I got off this ranch, I don't know if I'd make it."

Mike Adames, Jr.
"Little Mike"
Cowhand
McFaddin Ranch

"Some days it's hot and some days it's rainin', but I like it anyway. I've been workin' off and on since I was seven years old. I learned from the old folks, especially my grandpa. I like this brush country, it's a challenge. I would like for my son to cowboy, too. It's not hard; you just have to have the will to do it."

Michael Perez
Cowhand
O'Connor Melon Creek Ranch

"I was here before I was old enough to be paid. I never played sports in school because I was always out here on the ranch. My grandpa knows I like it a lot, so he teaches me. I learn something from him every day. He's starting to believe in me a little now. I have it a whole lot easier than he did. I would have liked to do it the old way—at least for a while."

Rumaldo Perez, Jr.
Cowhand
O'Connor Melon Creek Ranch

"I always thought I was goin' to be a rodeo hand, but that didn't work out, so I fell into the next thing that I could do to make a living. I wanted to do something with animals. There is satisfaction in this kind of work."

Ben Perkins
Cowhand
McFaddin Ranch

"Cowboys have always been my heroes. I was raised up around the cowboy life. It's still a thrill for me to watch the old cowhands ride and rope. Cowboy life today is different from that life in years past. We have better transportation and easier working methods. The cowboy life is definitely for me."

Ed Steward, Jr.
"Junior"
Cowhand
O'Connor Melon Creek Ranch

"I enjoy being around this life. There's a lot of satisfaction in it. Freedom is the main attraction. There is no routine. I've worked in a plant, and I don't like that kind of life. It's a big privilege to be able to do this kind of work; not just anybody can."

Doug Wolfshohl
Itinerant Cowhand

"The old guys are always telling us about long rides, camp wagons, and early hours. They say we should have been here forty years ago if we think it's tough now. They're impatient with us, but they teach us a lot."

Eddie Rubio
Cowhand
O'Connor Ranches

"I always loved cowboying. I watched the old guys. My dad put me on a horse when I was six months old. I like the freedom—being on my own. I've done other work, but I just had to come back to the ranch."

Ralph Tijerina
Cowhand and Remuda Man
O'Connor Gaffney Ranch

"I've always thought about ranching. Nobody forced me to do it; it's what I like. That's the most important thing—the family tradition and the enjoyment. I guess I'm lucky. I grew up with it; it's me."

Robert V. Williams
"Rob"
Cowhand
O'Connor Ranches

THE SURVIVORS: THE NEW GENERATION

"There are a lot of pluses out here on a ranch. I could never work in industry. I like the ongoing traditions, as well as the freedom and the space. Every day is good. It's real—you don't have to live for the weekends. Out here, you can have an impact. I hope when I die, someone says, 'He was a helluva cowman'."

Charles March Christensen
"Charley"
Foreman
Welder Ranch
Vidauri

"You fall down and you keep on goin'—that's what cowboyin' is all about."

Rumaldo Perez
Cowhand
O'Connor Ranches

"Being a cowboy is special. It gives you a good feeling inside when people know what you do. You have to love it—with the terrible hours, the low pay, the hard work you have to do. But as long as you love it, it's like you make a million bucks a day."

Kai Buckert
Straw Boss
O'Connor Ranches

HELICOPTER RANCHING
Trial and Error

Cattle herding with helicopters began in 1949 as an experiment on the Waggoner Ranch in West Texas. I was sent there and simply told I was to herd cows. At the time, I had been selling airplanes and helicopters in Houston and knew absolutely nothing about cattle except that's where steaks come from. But off I went, and spent three weeks with the Waggoner boss trying to figure out how to herd cattle with this new machine. We ran the cattle through fences and everything else you could think of, trying to learn. After many wild experiences, I finally began to get a grip on how to do it. To my knowledge, I am the first man to work cattle from the air. We got nation-wide publicity when we started.

Some time later, I went to work for Mr. Dennis O'Connor [II]. They hadn't heard about working cattle with helicopters down there. One day, when he was talking about trapping cattle, I asked him if he would like me to do the job with a copter. I showed him, and from that day on,

Wayne Schlesinger at O'Connor Melon Creek Ranch.

helicopters have been used on many of these ranches in the Coastal Bend area as well as on the Waggoner Ranch.

For a long time I was the only copter pilot in Texas. Then Rufus [Rogers], Chuck [Norman], and several others took jobs on the other ranches. At the Waggoner, the foreman would tell me what he wanted and I would learn by trial and error. While we all really learned the basic principles there, it was on the O'Connor ranches that we refined these working techniques.

Cattle generally have some white on them and will invariably look up — this is how you spot them. In open pastures you make sounds through a loudspeaker similar to the noises cowhands use on the ground. Cattle follow their same herding instincts when being worked from the air as they do on the ground. The older the cows get, the easier it is to work them. They seem to know what they're supposed to do after a while, just as they do when the cowhands work them from horseback. Cattle will generally respond the same way every time you work them. They seem to know when you are working their pasture. Those in the next pasture will usually ignore you. Bulls work differently; they move slower than cows. If you hover between the last cow and the first bull, the bulls will eventually fall back. You can separate them this way. Bulls are more stubborn and gather more slowly into a herd.

Cowhands seem to appreciate us. We have a modern-day tool that has simplified their job. In a copter we can do in two hours what used to take two weeks, but we've never been a threat to the cowhands' jobs. They are not easily replaced. Many jobs still have to be done from horseback.

Cowhands are a breed of their own. They love to ride a horse, and the cold doesn't seem to bother them — only mosquitoes. Sometimes when I hover over them during the mosquito season, you can see both the cowhands and the horses look up and smile. You have to have something inside telling you to do that work. It's something in their blood. They're congenial people — good, solid human beings. They're a great bunch, and I respect their abilities on a horse. I don't mind working cattle from a copter, but I wouldn't want to be down there on a horse.

One of the funniest things that ever happened to me in a copter was when I took the Waggoner boss up with me to herd cattle soon after we had learned to work the herds fairly well. Every time I would go after strays, I would hear a terrible racket in the copter, usually when I accelerated. The copter, a 1948 model, had no bubble, only a windshield like a motorcycle. After hearing this noise several times, I landed to check it out. Then I discovered that the foreman had gotten into the copter still wearing his spurs. He had actually torn some holes in the side of the copter with his spurs in his enthusiasm to get the machine to move properly, just like he would his horse. I made him take off his spurs, we took off again, the noise quit, and we went on gathering cattle.

We learned day by day. It was hit-or-miss through years of learning. The ranchers learned to work cattle from a copter through experience — trial and error — just like we did. Use of helicopters was new and strange to them,

"I've been fascinated with machinery all my life. I like challenge and adventure, and this machine gives me both. I've worked cattle on the ground and from the air. At the end of a day on a horse, I'm tired. Flying this machine is more relaxing to me. It's fun. I like cowboying from the air."

Dennis O'Connor III
Helicopter Pilot
O'Connor Ranches

too. We basically learned this new way of cowboying side by side. In many ways, copters have revolutionized the cattle industry. They have given the owner more marketing abilities; he can now ship when he wants to, with less dependence on the weather. If you can ship cattle when the market is high, the machine pays for itself. Before copters, if the weather was wet, the cattle couldn't be gathered and the owners might miss a high market.

I don't think any of us have strong feelings about our machines. It's really just hours and hours of boredom interspersed with moments of sheer terror. We've had lots of wild experiences up in the skies over those ranches, but mercifully no one has ever been hurt. I very definitely feel that I'm a part of the ranches. I've developed a sense of responsibility about them. You become interested in what is going on, and you check many things out subconsciously as you fly along. Cattle are a different story, however. When you're herding cattle, you only look at one end. You don't develop much affection for them.

Wayne Schlesinger
Helicopter Pilot
O'Connor Ranches

Mechanized Pasture Riders

I grew up in San Antonio. Although we were horse raisers on my mother's side of the family, I always wanted to be a pilot. I flew some in the service during World War II, and flew fixed-wing planes for ten years after that before I ever got in a helicopter. They were such a curiosity. I probably met only four or five copter pilots while I was in the service. After the war, Bell came out with its Model 47, which was used mostly by the oil companies. I got interested and decided to learn to fly copters; I trained with Bell and then went to Petroleum Helicopters in Louisiana. Shortly after I left that job, I got a call to go to the Waggoner Ranch, where Wayne Schlesinger was already flying for them. I signed on around 1952.

As far as I know, we were the first in the world to use helicopters to work cattle. I learned at the Waggoner by going out with a foreman or a wagon boss, and after three years there I came to the O'Connor ranches. I sat there fairly stiff for a while when I was learning. The favorite way of working cattle with ranch people is downwind, and of course that's always a bugaboo with flying people. First thing I did was to take a copter out and do autorotations until I was sure I could come out of almost any situation.

I started helping out on the roundups, and when the roundups were over, I would go find the mavericks. We flew over the Wichita Mountains, pushing the mavericks to the cowhands down lower. That was rather exciting work. The cowhands would get bruised up, they would have some fine wrecks, but they were generally a pretty tough bunch. On the Waggoner, we would mostly run the cattle into a corner, and the cowhands worked them from there. Up there, they were mostly Anglos; I never saw a Mexican cowhand until I came here, and I think they generally make the best horsemen. But all the men love the work and really respect one another. There is very little friction in the cow crowd.

"I'll tell you one thing: that man has a helluva horse under him."

Ed Steward, Jr.
"Junior"
Cowhand
O'Connor Melon Creek Ranch

On the Waggoner, most of the work was done in the open. When I first came down here to the O'Connor River Ranch, they did a lot more of that than they do now. Most cowhands and ranchers seem to enjoy open work more than pen work.

I enjoy working cattle and find the work very exciting. I have always loved hunting, and, in a way, you are stalking your game when you work cattle from a copter. Each boss works differently. The owners down here in the Coastal Bend run their own ranches and are more personally involved in their operation. They are very helpful when you're working cattle; they know how to organize, and they have the timing down. They really know their business. Their personalities affect their ranches and how they work.

The country down here is different. It's greener than most ranching areas. Even the people are different—they're more outgoing than other cattle people I've seen. Working techniques on the O'Connor ranches are different from those at the Waggoner. Here, they mammy the calves with their mamas first before they cut them out of the herd. Up there, they just rope and drag the calves out, work on them, and turn them loose. I think the South Texas method is the best.

Rufus Rogers with the helicopter he learned to fly in.

My knowledge of cattle is very limited. You can't get to know cattle from the air as you do on the ground. But I know how they respond to my machine. I learned by my mistakes at first, and still do. Generally, I work with the lead cow, at the same time keeping the strays in the herd. My job is to keep the cattle moving ahead of the men on the ground most of the time. The more you train cattle, the better they work because they get to know what is expected of them. In brush country, cattle can get away from the cowhands and become harder and harder to work. After a while, they begin to realize that they can't get away from a copter and they become easier to control. You always have a few independent thinkers in the herd, but usually they're pretty trainable. Cattle are getting easier to work from the air. One of the main things you don't do is move them out of their herding area; that can really cause problems.

I enjoy being around the cow crowd. They are really independent, self-sufficient, conservative, unsophisticated, and straightforward. They all realize that copter pilots make their work easier. I guess that's why they put up with us. I'm accepted by them, but I'm not really a part of the cow crowd because I don't work on the ground. I'm a mechanized pasture rider, a general utility man.

We haven't made a lot of changes in our working techniques since we got started. The biggest changes have been in the machinery. Copters are versatile machines, and I know a lot about them—you have to for safety's sake.

It's hard to find good cowhands these days. That makes copters more and more useful all the time. A copter can do the work of twenty-five men, but there are still many things on a ranch that require horses and cowhands. We could never completely replace the men on the ground. I've watched a lot of ranch work. It all looks easy from up above, but I wouldn't trade places with them for anything. Working cattle on the ground is hard, hard work.

Rufus H. Rogers
Helicopter Pilot
O'Connor Ranches

They Scattered Like Ants

I like helicopters, but we have always used them differently from the other ranches. We don't use them unless we are in a big rush. We still gather cattle from horseback at McFaddin and seldom use a copter there. Down in the brush country on the Roche Ranch they are much more useful. When my father first got his copter in 1961, he gathered the ranch several times. One day he was busy and we had to work them horseback. The cattle went crazy and scattered like ants. We didn't use the copter much after that except to locate the cattle. I hate cattle you can't handle, and a helicopter can really make them wild.

Claude K. McCan, Jr.
Rancher

You Name It, We Can Do It

Back in the beginning, our helicopters were really bought as toys. It wasn't anytime after we got them, however, that it began to dawn on us just what you could do with them at the ranch. Now they've become absolutely indispensable to us. Our operation is built around them. Even though we could get by without them, it would mean we'd have to make some real major changes in our operations.

We gather cattle with them, check our water supplies, thrash pecan trees, find and put out fires, check the country in wet times, check fences, and check on cattle. You name it, we can do it with a copter. We can even create wind on a calm day so that a crew can check to see if they have properly repaired a windmill they've been working on.

One thing that is absolutely necessary is to have a cowhand-pilot. You can have the best pilot in the world, but if he doesn't know how to handle cattle, then you don't have a pilot who knows his business and he's useless. Take my grandson, Dennis. He learned to handle cattle as a child, and today I'd rather have him than the world's most experienced pilot who didn't know anything about cattle. Dennis picked up his knowledge of cattle on the ground, Rufus Rogers learned his in the air. But they both know cattle, and they never make them wild or cause problems for the men on the ground. That pilot is very important. When Rufus started working for me, he had already learned the basics at the Waggoner. I taught him my methods, and we've been working together very successfully for twenty-five years. He and I started working with copters long before there was any sophisticated equipment in them. We navigated with binoculars and by reading names on water towers back in those early days.

I can do anything with my helicopter that a man on horseback can do. Rufus and I can fly low over a pasture, and the cattle head for the roundup

"I was sittin' here thinkin' about how they work cattle up in the air now instead of on the ground like I used to. I had a mare named Old Gruilla— she was high enough for me."

Richard Harris
Foreman
Murphy Ranches
1891–1988

Photo by Louise S. O'Connor

grounds. We could even pen cattle if necessary, although this is really kind of a stunt. You work cattle from the air just like you do from horseback. You don't get as close as you do with a horse, but it's all basically the same thing.

There are a few places where copters don't replace the horse and rider, but very few. In the pens is one place. Using a copter is just not possible there. Pasture riding with a copter is too expensive, but otherwise they are the most versatile and useful ranch tool available today. Without them, we would need more horses, more men, and more vehicles. We have been able to nearly eliminate the very expensive, time-consuming job of brush control by using copters to flush the cattle out of the brush. This literally reduces working time from days or weeks to minutes, and also helps cut down on painful injuries to the cowhands.

That helicopter is no toy to me; it makes my life a helluva lot easier every day.

Tom O'Connor, Jr. [III]
Rancher

Almost as Good as a Gooseneck Trailer

Helicopters are real useful tools on a ranch. They're not 100 percent of the answer, but they do a real good job. A majority of the time they really help me, and they can be easier on the cattle than ground work if you have a good, experienced pilot with a little cow savvy. An inexperienced pilot can cause a lot of trouble, just like a green cowhand will. The men on the ground have to know how to do basic cow work and how to work with a copter as well.

You want to work with a copter exactly like you do with a horse. You have to move the cattle slowly. That's what I try to do—then you don't get craziness into the cattle. You will have some spoiled cattle no matter what, but basically if you work them like you do on the ground, it works well. Our cattle are trained to be worked with a copter. There's no reason to have outlaw cattle if you handle them easily with a horse or a copter.

I never saw them work at the Waggoner. They handle cattle differently up there. Here we have really refined the process and added to the machines' uses. After twenty-five years, we should have learned something.

The cowhands enjoy the aid of the copters. It doesn't spoil them—it just saves time for the ranch, them, and me.

One main thing about copter pilots—cattle will get confused if the pilot doesn't know how to handle them. The cattle don't know what you want them to do. The pilot's ability is very important, but having a team of a cowman and a pilot is the best situation. Having someone up there with the pilot to hold the reins tight or to let them out works well. A person who thinks more like a cow is a big help to any pilot. That person can pay more attention to the cattle and leave the pilot free to fly the aircraft.

Take young Dennis [O'Connor III]—he did it on horseback as a child, and he'll learn faster because of that experience. Now this morning he was a bit hard-mouthed, but he'll learn. You have to have experience both with the copters and with the cattle. It takes time, that's all, and our pilots have put in the time to learn to do it right.

The only time you will have trouble working with a copter is when you don't have teamwork between the air and the ground. That is absolutely necessary to make it all work out.

Sometimes now, when the copter is not available, we work the cattle the old way and we can still do it as well as ever. We haven't lost the ground ability, and we should always keep that. The pilots take a lot of teasing when we are able to brag that we can do it better without them. We have a lot of fun with the pilots and the machines—like one time when Mr. Tom (O'Connor, Jr. [III]) picked up the company radio microphone by mistake and cussed out a bull. We still laugh about that, but we don't have loudspeakers in the copters any more.

The pilots are not really part of the cow crowd. We can't risk getting them injured, especially if there is only one available to fly the machine. Because of this, they aren't really full-fledged members of the cow outfit. We fuss and argue a lot, but we all respect each other's abilities.

How do they help us? Well, this morning we checked five thousand acres and twenty water wells for a missing bull—all in two and one-half hours. That would have taken half a day in a pickup truck, or all day for two men on horseback, to do that same job. I remember one time back before we had the copters when the mosquitoes were real bad. The cattle were all in a mosquito herd—one big herd in the back end of the ranch. It took us hours to find the cattle. With a copter, we could have done it in minutes. Gooseneck trailers are the most valuable tools on the ranch, but copters run a close second.

> **Dennis Williams**
> **Foreman**
> **O'Connor Brothers Ranches**
> **Rancher**

It Used to Be Rough in That Brush

I don't know how we ever lived without helicopters in this country. It used to be rough in that brush. I've seen the time when my arms were ripped all the way to the elbows from brush riding. We used to leave here on Monday and get back two weeks later and we still wouldn't be through. Now we can do the work in hours instead of weeks. It would take a lot of reorganizing if we didn't have them. The first time we ever used a copter, we flew from headquarters to the Copano Creek camphouse. That took an hour and a half, and we had all the cattle gathered when we got there. That job would have taken four or five days if we had done it on horseback. That first trip sold me on copters.

Everything fell into place pretty easily when we first started. It took some training to change the cowhands' habits, but otherwise the changeover was easy. Helicopters have not made the cowhands obsolete—and never will. You still have to have them for lots of jobs. You also have to have a good pilot. They have to know cow-working to be effective and they also have to be safe. We've only had a couple of minor wrecks in all the years we've been using helicopters.

Is a helicopter a toy on a ranch? No way!

> **E. D. Coward**
> **"Rusty"**
> **Foreman**
> **O'Connor Melon Creek Ranch**

World War II: The Turning Point

The war was the big turning point. It brought many changes to these ranches. Everything was in confusion—all messed up. Many people left the ranches because things were so crazy.

World War II began the breakup of rural community life. Schools began scattering, Lewis's Bend broke up. Many people didn't know what to do or how to live this new life. People got accustomed to higher pay during the war as soldiers and industrial workers. Many stayed in town for the higher wages. The old experienced cowhands didn't come back. Lots who were soldiers stayed in California.

There were technological changes, too. Trailers, trucks, jeeps, roads, and attitudes were all different, to name a few changes.

These ranches had to start over after World War II.

Alex de la Garza, Jesse Jones, Coleman Joshlin, Quinn Love, Rufus Moore, K. J. Oliver, Seward Richardson, Victor Rodriguez, Elvin Scott, Leo Scott, L. V. Terrell, Julian Tijerina, Rev. Mack Williams, Nathaniel Youngblood

"The widespread changes we are seeing on these ranches now must be a lot like conditions here in the South after the Civil War."

Dennis Williams
Foreman
O'Connor Brothers Ranches
Rancher

"It is painful to me—watching our lifestyle change."

Herbert Bickford
"Buster"
Rancher

"You hear 'That's they way it used to be, that's the way it was.' It isn't that way any more. The fast lane has hit every aspect of ranching."

Armour Joe Keefe
Straw Boss
O'Connor Brothers Ranches
Rancher

Johnny Wayne Lott (J. Y. Lott).

Nathaniel Youngblood in Seattle during WWII.

Politics Now

Ranchers tend to be conservative. Conservative Democrats are the norm, but there are a lot of Republicans here, too. Whatever the party, the leanings were always conservative. It has to do with land ownership. Politics is very important to the ranches on a local and national level.

Government regulation can be very hard on the ranching industry. The government has the control, but we don't want the subsidies.

We have to be involved in politics to a certain extent, especially where you have lakes, rivers, and shorelines. We need to have our say, but we also have to get along with the politicians.

James Robert "Bobby" McCan
Claude K. "Kerry" McCan, Jr.
Leo Welder
Ranchers

We're Way Down the List of People to Please

Government regulation affects the ranches strongly. None of the new stuff helps us much. The big landowner is in the minority now. We are way down the list of people to please. The Feds have a bad approach to conservation. They go to extremes. They want to take our land and compensate us for its loss, thinking we don't know. They even send in cover organizations. There are some big fights coming over this. We all are happy to cooperate in saving wildlife, but taking our property away is not going to be taken lightly down here.

C. K. McCan, Jr.
"Kerry"
Rancher

I'd Rather Let the Cows Die of Old Age

David Wright, brucellosis testing.
Photo by Louise S. O'Connor.

Most cattlemen don't want any regulation and don't want the government subsidies, either. Once in a while, the government does something right, and the screwworm eradication program was one of them. It worked, and left no problems in its wake. It was good.

Now, brucellosis testing is another matter. It has been very destructive to the industry. The disease cannot be eradicated this way, and possibly not at all, simply because it is not carried only by domestic cattle. Many, many wild animals carry it, also. It is an impossible situation to control, and particularly absurd for us to try with beef herds. The numbers are far too vast. It cannot be stopped. Only milk, not beef, is affected by brucellosis. Again, there are lobbies stronger than ours who get the regulations passed. I let a lot of cows die of old age on the ranch rather than risk getting a pasture quarantined by selling them. The money it costs us, and the money spent fruitlessly by the government, is ridiculous. It is a perfect example of the damage done by mindless regulation. It is the worst thing to hit the cattle business — maybe ever.

There is a live-strain vaccine now in Europe, but the government will only let us have a half-strength dose. All this is just one example of the damaging effect of many government policies on the ranching industry.

Tom O'Connor, Jr. [III]
Rancher

The Oil Boom: The Up Side and the Down Side

Oil has helped us tremendously down here. There is no way we could say it has been bad. We bitch and raise hell about certain aspects of having oil on our land, but it enables many of us to make a living ranching that otherwise would be impossible. If nothing else, it has helped us to keep the family members who do not care about the land at bay. It keeps them from wanting to sell.

There really is more up side to oil than down side. It is a big thing with ranchers down here to have pride in making their ranches work without the infusion of oil revenues. Oil has complicated ranching from the business point of view. It hasn't really made the ranches any better, we just live better. It is better that oil money isn't used on these ranches. It would just confuse the issue. The oil won't last forever, and when it's gone. we will have to go on. It's unhealthy to manage a ranch under excessive income. Ends won't meet later if we do it that way.

It would be rough without oil, but we all hate what it does to the land. It really spoils it, and the people connected with it are none too nice either. They mess up the country. They have no respect for the land.

It did change the country a lot. It was rough in those early oil days. Sheriff Ira Heard held a tight rein on Refugio. Without him, no telling what would have happened down here. Ira was rough as a cob, but you didn't have to worry about your wife or daughter walking down the street. He kept trouble to a minimum, but Refugio was better before the oil boom.

Times were really hard down here during the Depression. When oil was discovered, it helped a lot. Oil is just another use of the land, but you do have to make the oil companies behave. You have to watch them. They have no sensitivity or morals.

Oil has saved these ranches. If we didn't have it, we would not have survived this long.

We will have to tighten our belts down here when the oil runs out.

Buster Bickford, Kai Buckert, Bevans Callan, Freddy Fagan, Armour Joe Keefe, Henry Clay Koontz [IV], James Robert "Bobby" McCan, C. K. McCan, Jr., Thomas Marion O'Connor [II], Alben Sommer, Leo Welder, Roger Welder

*Cattle and oil wells,
Tom O'Connor, Jr. [III],
at the River Ranch, 1970's.
Photo by Louise S. O'Connor.*

Slot Machines and New Roads

We were a little drag town before oil came in. Our pleasure was watchin' cattle come through town. Refugio was dead until Saturday and Sunday. It was a rural ranchin' community. When the boom came in, it changed everythin'.

Us cowhands didn't much feel the effect of the Depression; we always had jobs, but the oil boom really helped the economy down here for everyone. It changed the lives of quite a few people. People change a lot from acquirin' money. There was a lot of land and bankin' as always, but not too much loose money. After the oil came, many people quit farmin' and ranchin', and lived on their oil. Until then, it was work or die.

The boom brought in oil people that had no ties to the community. They didn't care about their behavior. Those rough characters caused a lot of disruption in the settled communities. Along with the oil came the gamblin' shacks, the bootleggers, and the revenuers. Down in Frisco, you could do whatever you wanted. Refugio was wide open during the boom. Slot machines were everywhere. Mr. Ira made us hide them when the Rangers came in. It was wild times in Refugio. There was heavy drinkin' and even some dope in those days.

The oil companies improved the roads, and the landowners made them hire local, so more jobs were available for everyone.

So, like everything else, there was some good and bad to the oil boom.

Henry Charleston, Richard Harris, Jesse Jones, Horace Joshlin, Rufus Moore, Seward Richardson, Elvin Scott, L. V. Terrell, Rev. Mack Williams, McKinley Williams, Nathaniel Youngblood

As I See It

Land prices went up drastically around here when oil was discovered. Ten-dollar-an-acre land went up to fifty dollars and higher.

There was no place for oil crews to stay when the boom first started. Many people took oil crews into their homes or gave them rooms in out-buildings. If they weren't nice people, they usually didn't stay around long.

Blowout, Refugio County, 1929.

They got run off. There were all kinds came in with the oil. There was good and bad, like there is with everything.

Ira Heard succeeded Old Man Charlie Fox as sheriff — he was one of the best we ever had. He very seldom ever packed a gun. He would tell anyone who got in trouble to be at the courthouse the next morning, and if they weren't, he went for them. There were usually two or three every morning from the brawls the night before.

The first oil activity in Refugio began in the twenties. It was rough. Ira started as Fox's deputy. He was good, but he tolerated no foolishness.

Refugio Field, early 1920's

He could almost be brutal if outsiders came in and messed around. He was kind of like the King Ranch. If he was for you, he'd kill for you. If you were against him, he would kill you.

Every kind of character in the world came in here with the oil. They drilled and drilled and drilled—all dry holes. Finally oil was found in Heard country.

As far as morality was concerned, there wasn't any. By drinking—men and women both—a lot of good people went to the bad.

Some of the landowners wanted oil to come in and some didn't. A lot felt that oil would ruin the land and the country. The only thing that broke oil loose here was the Depression. There just wasn't any money and times were tough. The landowners felt that they had to open up the country to oil before people starved to death. It brought lots of jobs and lots of money to people around here who needed it. There were many landowners, though, who hated the oil industry until the day they died. Many felt it violated the land. And to this day, this feeling still exists among many ranchers, even though they appreciate the good it does for them.

Clarence Preiss
Barber
Victoria

Drilling at Mitchell Pasture, Refugio County.

Root, Hog, or Die!

I was raised a damn Yankee in North Dakota, Minnesota, and Wyoming, even though I was born in Dallas. Daddy started out as a lumberjack. We moved to Cody, Wyoming, in 1906, where he went to cut lumber for the big dam they were building in Cody. We lived up in the mountains near Yellowstone. We lived in a tent, until the lumberjacks built us a thirty-by-thirty-foot log cabin. They cut those long pine trees and built us a house. I lost a sister to diphtheria and four others of us nearly died. I still have throat trouble from that. Daddy went to work in the oil fields in 1912.

Gas fired boilers used to operate the drills.

The 100-foot wooden derrick of Rooke No. 1, Refugio County, 1921.

I started working in the oil fields in 1917 when I was fifteeen years old, and I haven't signed a minor's release yet. Nobody in those days ever heard of such a thing or cared about them, and nobody cared whether you went to school, so I went to work for Empire Gas and Fuel. My first day working in the fields, I was driving mules hauling rig timbers to a wildcat well. It came in blowing fourteen thousand barrels a day. There were wells all around it. Nobody hit a thing—it must have been in a limestone crevice formation.

As a kid, I worked for forty-five cents an hour, nine hours a day, seven days a week. All the able-bodied men had gone to war and there wasn't anybody to work but kids or old men.

That work was too rough for older men. There was no such thing as a day off, and there wasn't no end to work in the oil fields. I worked twelve hours a day for many a year, seven days a week. Now, if these kids don't get off every four days, they can't stand it. You never got off until you completed the well. This was cable-tool days, before the rotary drill was ever invented. It took quite a little while to drill a well then. If you averaged fifty feet a day, you was really flying.

I never did learn to like the rotary drill, and I'll tell you why. With the old cable-tool rigs, there were only two men out there and you worked as a team. Now these rotary drillers, damn them, every one of them thinks he's God Almighty. Some of them wouldn't even get their hands greasy. On the cable-tool rigs, the driller and the roughneck were a team. The driller got a dollar a day more than the roughneck; now the rotary driller gets twice as much as the roughneck.

We worked on a standard derrick with bull wheels and cat wheels and a cable that went over the top of the derrick. You clamped on to the cable with the clamps. You let off on the cable ropes to get the drill down. Every time you made five or six feet of hole, you had to pull out and bail the mud out and dump it. Then you had to put water back in and run another screw and make some more hole. We had wrenches and a circle jack. We had a walking beam and a Samson post and the calf wheel. It was slow and cumbersome, but there was one thing about it, if you ran into a little formation, it would let you know. In 1925 I was working for the Magnolia Petroleum Company, working on the only cable-tool rig in the field. Our little cable rig found the formation and made a two-hundred-barrel-a-day well. The rotaries never did find that formation.

Cable tools were the original oil well machinery, and it's still the best in many ways, even though it's a lot like stomping a hole in the ground— it just battered. Now the electronic equipment makes rotaries accelerate, but not when they first came out.

You can't imagine how wild the early oil-field days were. You can't imagine how we lived and worked and operated. We used to pay more for a barrel of water than you can get for a barrel of oil now. We didn't waste much water in those days. We lived in tents and attics, and there was no safety-first in the fields. That was blowout days, and there were no precautions. It was wild and wooly and tough in those days. I don't know now how we survived it.

T. A. Jeffers with his dog, Rowdy.

I survived long enough to go to work for Humble Oil and Refining, and that's how we wound up down here. Humble transferred me to the O'Connor River Ranch April 1, 1934. I was working on a wildcat rig they shut down and they transferred me here to Victoria. It was muddy when I got here, but it was the best move I ever made.

When I first came here, we were still living by the skin of our teeth, and the foreman gave us a half-dead dogie calf. I raised him up and traded him to Albert Dick for groceries. There is no way I can tell you how much that helped us. I've never bought another mouthful of food on credit from that day to this. We lived a long time off that calf. He put us on the road to prosperity.

When I talked my way off the drilling rig and got to this ranch, I enjoyed it from the first day. I was put in production, tending the gauges. Our house was originally the Humble office. We had two rooms in the bunkhouse, and most of the buildings were trailers and pretty rough put-togethers. We did have modern conveniences—a bathroom and gaslights. There were three or four drilling rigs, the bunkhouse, a boarding house, roustabout quarters, and the office. When they moved, they left the office to us for a home.

My dog, Rowdy, he's buried by the pumphouse door. He was just a pup when I got him, and he followed me around as I checked my gauges. When I was pumping my oil away, the motor didn't have any governors on it, and the old pump was chain-driven. It would sound like it was going to explode when it got air in it. I used to run in there to shut it off and he would follow. One day, when Rowdy was eight months old, he ran in ahead of me and shut it off before I could get to it.

From that day until the day he died, he never missed a lick. That pumphouse was his. He'd grab anyone who went in there but me by the seat of the pants. I had a wheel valve on it, and he would paw until he got the wheel valve shut off. After he started that, I put a handle on it so he could jump up and shut it off. He'd come see what I was doing and why I hadn't done the job I was supposed to.

They said we would only be here a year, but we were here until 1952.

The big concrete stanchions you see on the way down to the river bottom are from the discovery well. It made six to eight hundred barrels of oil a day, and they shut it down to build some storage tanks for it. It never flowed again; no one knows why. If you got a well, leave it alone. All kinds of crazy things like that happened in the early days. I had seven producing wells when I moved here. They were steam rigs then. There were three big gas-fired boilers sitting around each one.

A gas line ran right under our kitchen, and the house had to be moved after we left. We lived over that line for eighteen years. If I had known that, I'd have never slept a wink. Back then, we burned the excess gas— you couldn't sell enough to scorch your whiskers. The one here, burned a million and a half feet a day for eighteen years. Just think—if you had that all in one sack now, this would be worth $29.5 million at 1982 prices.

There were all kinds of oil produced by these wells I baby-sat. Every hole produced something different.

The oil companies have changed, times have changed, and people have changed and, say what you will, it's not for the better. World War II was the beginning of it. During the war, the ranches couldn't get any help, and my job didn't require any exertion so I often helped them bale hay. They tried to pay me for it and I said, "Absolutely no." I was making a living here with the oil companies. By that time, Tom O'Connor, Jr. [III] had taken over and always saw that I had hay in my barn. He also allowed me to hunt on the ranches when no one else could. It was such a good relationship.

It was a different time with different people when we first got here. Even the foreman, Lester Long, was a real frontiersman. He believed in getting up early and working late. Rustling still went on out there in those days. We carried guns and we were ready. There was a beautiful old wooden barn at headquarters. You could climb up in that cupola and see the whole world in front of you.

We lived by the side of the road for many years and I have put gasoline in everything, including an airplane. There was an old couple camped in the river bottom one time, and the woman came up one noon break and asked for gasoline. I gave it to her, and she asked what she owed. I said forty cents, so she gave me fifteen cents and said, "I pay for what I can and trust the Lord for the rest," and picked it up and left. I wouldn't take a caution for that.

Rotary drilling rig.
"Everything was rotary
in this country."

We often sat around the Manhattan Cafe for coffee. All those ranchers loved to have me tell them how oil was drilled and produced. There was lots of laughing and joking—it was fun. There were lots of characters on the ranches in those days: Lonze Edwards, Parson Weathers, Lester Long, Alfonso Soliz, Emmet Fagan, and the old maids. I'm telling you, Parson Weathers was one of the most interesting people I ever knew.

Times have changed so drastically; today is the time of mechanization on the ranch. I used to get on a horse and ride him to the Middle Well; that used to take time, lots of time. I went out a few times with Rafael [de la Garza] when they were still driving a chuck wagon. I remember one time they had an old black horse they wanted to give to Parson Weathers. I rode out there to The Hollow, and it was sundown when we got there. I rode the old horse in. I just knew we were going to get lost, but he knew what he was doing and we made it. There wasn't a marker anywhere—no lights, no nothin'. It was dark out there in those days.

I started working for Humble for sixty cents an hour roughnecking. Then they needed a foreman, and I got the job and was raised to eighty cents an hour. You know, I ran a little test on the Quintana discovery well.

I grew up firing boilers, and the O'Connor Ranch was the first real home we had. Our relationship was always the best in the West—always. I was here before they brought in the Tomoconnor No. 1. These people became our friends, and they are still a part of our lives. They made us welcome there. It will always feel like home. There was a sense of community in the oil fields because the townspeople wouldn't accept us. We helped one another, kind of like everyone did on these ranches.

When I came here, they were already drilling around the river on the ranch. Mud was neck deep, you couldn't get anything done. I made $137 a month. It was rough. I was a pumper and a gauger. No overtime.

I remember Milam Thompson. He was the first man ever fed me mountain oyster stew. Our food in the oil fields was good solid food. We never ate sandwiches. Had what we called a forty-horse dinner pail. It had three compartments—one for coffee, one for jars of food, and in the top was half a pie.

The oil out of that field was hard. It was a mess. I finally talked them into putting a boiler out there and kept it at 186 degrees to keep the oil movable. That particular sand finally played out, thank God. It's the only oil I ever saw you couldn't treat. It was 22 gravity. The Greta stuff is 40 gravity. Contrarily, there was condensate so pure out here that people could fill their cars right out of the barrel. I was working at Greta helping set up a tank battery when they moved the first rig into the big Tomoconnor field down there. Mud was neck deep to a tall Indian. They had bulldozers pulling the wagons in. Everybody laughed at them, saying they were going to drill a dry hole. Well, they didn't and the rest is history.

White Point is down near Corpus at Gregory. That blowout was in the crater. You could see it blowing and burning for a thousand miles.

There were more rotary men boogered up with these chains breaking—it was pathetic. I had some awfully close calls. There were absolutely no safety measures in the early days at all. It was root, hog, or die. Jump and grab it and run. Get an armload of it and get after it. That's what the early oil days were like.

We used to make coffee with the boilers and the firemen would wash our clothes with the steam. We used to carry 325 pounds of steam pressure. The old steam rigs were dismantled and moved with mules. The derricks were wooden. The rig builders were the first group to come out. They used sixteen-by-sixteen-inch timbers, the derrick was eighty-four feet high. The only part of the oil business I never worked on was building the rig.

We used to shoot those cable tool holes with nitroglycerin. I poured many a gallon of nitro. I've known several that got blown up. An old fella named Charlie Price walked with two five-gallon cans full. He was drunk as a skunk and fell, but the cans didn't explode. That was another close call for me. The shooter's job was a high-paying job. I poured a many a gallon of that stuff, but I never drew the wage. People didn't realize how dangerous having an oil field around was. It was wild and dangerous. A wildcat well was anything over a mile away from a proven field.

Women's lives were very monotonous in the oil fields. They were tied down. It was very unusual if they went to town twice in a year. They stayed home and raised kids. It was work, work, work.

All the cowhands I was ever around at the River Ranch, I considered my friends. They helped us, and we helped them. All of them would come over and listen to our radio. Sophie and Betty and I would read their mail to them. It was a very friendly and happy situation. They were good, honest, family people. We never locked our doors. We knew the ranch people would watch it for us.

I asked to be moved to Fortran instead of going to the Great Camp. I went to Corpus to the head man, and they let me go there. We sure hated leaving the River Ranch in the worst way, but I had so much seniority and retirement with Humble; I had to go.

Those ranches have provided me a lot of recreation, too. I have always been allowed to hunt—even after I left—and my grandson and I have had many a fine day out there together. It was our first real home. It always will be.

T. A. Jeffers
Oil Gauger
O'Connor Brothers River Ranch
1901–1988

Survival of the Smartest: A Look at the Future

There was a simplicity to life back then—not run-of-the-mill, but routine. You did what the routine was. You always worked cattle the same way in the old days. Now they change all the time. In the old days, we just raised cattle. Ranches are more business now. It was a lot different in those days—more hospitable. The feeling of a ranch has changed. Modernization has been rapid here. We have to be mobile and work fast. Everyone is in too big a hurry now. Trucks, trailers, and helicopters started that attitude. We now depend on computers and other machinery rather than the human eye for cattle breeding.

Technology has ruined this way of life. The ranches are in such economic trouble that money has to be put above quality of life. We have to be absolutely efficient now. Everything has to produce. An animal has to earn her keep.

In the old days, we worked on a horse. Everything was slower and quieter.

There is a whole generation of young people in ranching now who never saw hard times until recently. In the old days, we could ride out hard times and live off the land. Now, with income taxes, you can't do that.

The oil may run out here, and we will have to go back to making the land pay off.

Better education is necessary now. You can't just grow up learning about cattle. There are too many changes in every area of ranching. It's all very technical now.

Everyone used to roam the ranches freely in the old days. No one gave you any trouble. People destroy things now. You have to be careful.

One hundred years ago, when this was prairie, the river bottoms were more important than they are now. The bottoms provided fuel, building materials, and water. Game lived mostly in those bottoms, and most ranch headquarters were near water.

Economics and government regulation have also destroyed the cattle industry. You could see everywhere down here forty or fifty years ago. The land looks real different now. It's mostly brush, and it has become a real problem. The brush seems to have begun when cattle began to be shipped from the brush country to the prairies rather than being driven

Dennis Williams and
Earl Ward at daybreak.
Photo by Louise S. O'Connor.

overland on foot. The cattle emptied out when they were being moved by slower methods. But now they move so fast that the seeds get spread to the open prairie land.

There has been an enormous cutdown in the amount of usable pasture land for cattle in this area, and brush is one of the main reasons, along with the land lost to roads, highways, and oil fields. Because of this land loss, herd sizes have had to be reduced.

There are lots of weather changes, too. It's just plain hotter than it used to be, and there seem to be more floods and short-term droughts now.

Weather is becoming more severe here. There have been totally different weather patterns in the last few years.

We used to get up early and work until dark. There was none of this "hours" stuff. Everything since World War II has been speeding up. All the old cowboys are gone. Everything had its place and you belonged somewhere. Now, nobody cares. Everyone is transient and moving around.

It's real disconcerting to see these ranches being cut up and families dividing. You used to be able to get away from the man-made world out on these ranches, but not now. That's tough to watch.

In this industry now, it's survival of the smartest. We can't keep going the same old way. There will have to be changes. It's going to be very, very difficult. We will have to own the land outright to even think about survival.

There are lots of problems down here now. Oil is ready wealth, but when it plays out, economics will toughen up. We are in danger of becoming stagnant in an uneconomic system. We must maintain in certain areas and progress in others. The public attitude about red meat is bad now. Water and wildlife and growing wildflower seeds will become extremely valuable at some point, too.

We will have to open our minds and our eyes and really deal with land-use management here.

We have to look to new ways and try new ideas or we just won't make it.

Buster Bickford, Kai Buckert, Bevans Callan, John Cliburn, Freddy Fagan, Richard Harris, Charlie Hernandez, Henry Clay Koontz [IV], Quinn Love, James Robert "Bobby" McCan, Thomas Marion O'Connor [II], Thomas Michael O'Connor, Leo Scott, Wallace Shay, L. V. Terrell, W. D. "Bill" Welder, Dennis Williams, Rev. Mack Williams, Lawrence Wood

Epilogue

These people are nurtured by the land. They would die—emotionally
if not physically—without their space around them. These ranches are
not assets they would sell. It would be like selling their children. The struggle is not about making money—it is about space and home. It is not an
illusion or a dream to them—it is their reality. They live every day with
their space and their freedom, and never for one minute do they fail to
appreciate it. Even when this business is at its worst, with bad weather,
low cattle prices, and hard unromantic hours, they never stop feeling
privileged and grateful to be a part of it. The old cowhands and ranchers
do not like retirement, and most would go right back out there and work
today if they could. Others are still working long past the age when men
in other jobs would have quit. They just cannot seem to give up this work;
this life is too much a part of their existence to let it go. Those who cannot
work any longer sit on their porches and remember the old times, or relive
their cow-working days in their dreams. They lived as cowmen and cowhands and they will die the same. The people who lived and worked in this
culture grew up in a world where the natural order of the universe was
more intact, in a world they understood. Now, they do not understand
or particularly like the world around them, and yet they still face each
day with a tremendous amount of courage and hope.

It was, and in many ways still is, a magical occupation.

*"When I was a cowhand, I thought I had the world in a jug. If I could get
well enough to get out of this chair, I'd work for you all for free. I'd crawl
on my hands and knees to work cattle one more time—to ride just one more
bad horse with the T-C brand on him."*

Clayton Isaiah
Tophand
O'Connor Ranches
1927–1983

Clayton Isaiah spent his last years in a nursing home. He never rode
again.—L. O'C.

*"This life is drifting away from us. It's changed immensely. I don't know
how you stop it, or if it can be stopped. Not many people do this work
any more and others don't have the same feelings I do. Unless I'm talking
to someone in ranching, I'm by myself. It's a lonesome business now."*

Dennis Williams
Foreman
O'Connor Brothers Ranches
Rancher

Photo by Louise S. O'Connor.

Glossary

Angelita Ranch	A ranch belonging to the Angelita Cattle Company, owned by Martin O'Connor, John J. Welder, and James F. Welder, Jr. In 1916, James bought out the other two partners. Now owned by the J. F. Welder Heirs, the property is located on the Nueces River five miles south of Odem in San Patricio County.
Arroz	Rice, a staple of the cowhands' diet
Boll weevil	A greenhorn; an outsider; someone unable to do cow work properly
Buy ground	The ground hit by a cowhand when thrown by a horse or bull
Big Prairie	Area of the O'Connor ranches that was unfenced in the early days, it comprised what is now the Lake Pasture, the Beef Pasture, and part of the north end of the Melon Creek Ranch.
Bite a horse's ear	Method of quieting down a frisky horse
Black Jacks	A small black community located about two miles east of Lewis's Bend; now defunct
Booger	To scare, also proper name, slang
Breaking a mill, making a sweep	Techniques for working a herd of cattle
Caballito	Little horse, rocking horse
Can't to can't	From early morning to late at night (i.e., from when you can't see until you can't see)
Caporal	Foreman
Carne	Meat, a staple of the cowhands' diet
Carreta	Cart
Chause	To run or handle an animal roughly
Chickadee	Sap of a gum tree used for chewing gum
Chick Sale	An outhouse
Come on with the come on	Literally, "put up or shut up"
Compadre	Companion, close friend
Coon Can	Card game
Cotch	Card game
Curandero	Faith or spiritual healer, herbalist
Dirt men	Anyone who did not ride a horse (fence workers, road builders, etc.)
Dudlow Joe	Bed
"El Coyote Prieto"	The very dark coyote
Empresario	Colonizer, land agent
Father Hidalgo	A Franciscan priest in Texas, who in 1810 led a revolt against the Spanish crown to declare independence for Mexico. The revolt was short-lived, and he was captured and executed in 1811.

The Presidio of La Bahia was declared a town in |

1829 by the Congress of Coahuila and Texas, and its name was changed to Goliad, an anagram of Hidalgo.

Frijoles	Beans, a staple of the cowhands' diet
Frisco	Black section of Refugio
Fresnos	Earth-moving equipment
Greta	A former railroad shipping point for cattle, located between the San Antonio River and Refugio on U. S. Highway 77; around the turn of the century the largest cattle herds in the world were assembled here for shipping.
Gruilla	Dark grey horse
Guero	Blonde, fair
Halfsies	Tenant farming; sharecropping; the income from a crop was divided in half between the landowner and the tenant farmer.
Headright	Tract of land that an individual, married or single, would be eligible to receive according to law during colonial times
Highlife a horse	To put carbon tetrachloride under a horse's tail to make it pitch and run
The Hollow	Camphouse and working pens in the middle of the Beef Pasture, O'Connor Brothers River Ranch.
Hooraw, hoorawing	To tease or make fun of
Inari	An old settlement, now defunct, at the juncture of U. S. Highway 77 and U. S. Highway 239
Itinerant	A worker on several ranches in this three-county area
Javelina	A peccary; an animal similar to a small hog.
Jesus	Spanish proper name meaning Jesse
Kineno	Cowhand from the King Ranch
Labore	A 177-acre unit of land for farming and grazing, in addition to 4,428 acres of open land, given to early colonizing families in return for $60 in fees paid to the state and its officials
Lapo	Lash or blow (as with a cane or whip)
League	A 4,428-acre unit of land given to the colonists together with *labores*
Leggins	Leggings, or chaps, worn by horsemen to protect their legs when riding through brush and thorns
Lewis's Bend	A now-defunct black community that grew up after emanicipation about fifteen miles east of Goliad along the San Antonio River. The land was donated by the Terrell family, and many of the freed slaves in the area located here. Active until about 1941, the community was the location of Mt. Zion Baptist Church, Simms Ferry, and Simms Store.
Lobo	Timber wolf

Mammy the calves	The practice of keeping a calf with its mother temporarily after "working" it and before turning it loose on the ranch
Mexican Water Hole	A campsite on the O'Connor Melon Creek Ranch consisting of two camphouses and some working pens; it was used when the cow crowd was working that area of the ranch for extended periods and when pasture riders needed a stop-off place to eat or sleep.
Moss cattle	To feed cattle with moss cut from trees on the ranches, usually during winter or feed shortages
Mother wit	Common sense and/or intelligence; a sixth sense; psychic power
Mott	Clump or cluster of trees on the open prairie
The Motts	A grove of trees located about two miles south of the Perkins Ranch off Ranch Road 2441
Mug a calf	To grab an animal by its head and twist it to the ground
1907 Division	The first partition of the O'Connor ranches; land was divided among Thomas O'Connor [II], Martin O'Connor, Joe O'Connor, Mary O'Connor Hallinan, and their mother, Mary Virginia Drake O'Connor (Mrs. Dennis O'Connor [I])
Old One Hundreds	Church hymns from slavery times, sung a cappella
Papas	Potatoes, a staple of the cowhands' diet
Redlew	Country store on the Welder Vidauri Ranch
Remuda	Herd of working horses
Rough	Very good
Rowel	Spiked, revolving disc at end of spur
Running iron	Branding iron consisting of a single rod used to draw the desired marks on an animal
St. Mary's	Former community near present-day Bayside that flourished from the 1850s to the 1870s as one of several small ports serving the Gulf Coast; devastated by hurricanes in 1876 and 1886
Santone	The San Antonio River
Sarco	A small community with a mercantile, barber shop, and post office located between Goliad and Refugio off present-day Ranch Road 2441; Sarco Creek and Little Sarco Creek were nearby.
Seeny bean	Pods of the sienna bean plant, a tall, slender prairie shrub
7-up	Card game
Shamefaced	Disgraced by being too bold with the boys (i.e., becoming pregnant out of wedlock)
Sop	Combination of lime and water, or axle grease or

	other substances used after branding to make fresh burns heal quickly and peel cleanly; each ranch had its own recipe
Spriggs' Bend	A small black community located about seven miles west of Tivoli on Texas Highway 239; now defunct
Stove up	Injured; stiff
Straw boss	Assistant to a foreman
Tasso	Beef jerky, from *tassajo*
Thick	Close
Tophand	A better than average cowhand
Twin Mott	A lake centrally located on the original O'Connor Ranch; now located where the Peach Mott, Melon Creek, River, and Salt Creek ranches intersect
The Valley	The region of South Texas along the American bank of the Rio Grande River. It is composed of four counties: Cameron, Hidalgo, Starr, and Willacy. It is one of the most productive garden spots in the United States, and produces large quantities of fruits and vegetables. Due to the ideal conditions of climate and soil, production and harvesting is a year-round business.
Vaquero	Mounted cowboy, herdsman
Vidauri	A Mexican land agent and member of the Power-Hewetson colony. Originally spelled Vidaurri, one *r* was later dropped in the spelling of the town and the ranch of that name.
Yaupon	Type of holly found in the southern United States; its smooth elliptical leaves were used in medicinal teas